RHS

GOOD FRUIT & VEG GUIDE

LONDON, NEW YORK, MUNICH, MELBOURNE, DELHI

Project Editor Becky Shackleton
Project Art Editor Rebecca Tennant
Senior Editor Helen Fewster
Senior Art Editor Joanne Doran
Managing Editor Esther Ripley
Managing Art Editor Alison Donovan
Jacket Designer Mark Cavanagh
Picture Researcher Sarah Hopper
DK Images Claire Bowers
Database Manager David Roberts
Production Editor Joanna Byrne
Production Controller Mandy Inness
Associate Publisher Liz Wheeler
Publisher Jonathan Metcalf
Art Director Peter Luff

Writers Ann Baggaley, Guy Barter, Helena Caldon,
R.L. Rosenfeld, Pamela Ruch, Diana Vowles, Rosemary Ward

RHS Consultants Jim Arbury, Guy Barter
RHS Editors Rae Spencer-Jones, Simon Maughan

First published in Great Britain in 2011 by
Dorling Kindersley Limited, 80 Strand, London, WC2R ORL
Penguin Group (UK)

Copyright © 2011 Dorling Kindersley Limited, London

2 4 6 8 10 9 7 5 3 1
001—179521—Mar/2011

ISBN 978 1 4053 6180 4

Printed and bound by Star Standard, Singapore
To find out more about RHS membership, visit our website
www.rhs.org.uk or call 0845 062 1111

Discover more at
www.dk.com

RHS

GOOD FRUIT & VEG GUIDE

CONTENTS

HOW TO USE THIS GUIDE

This guide showcases over 1,000 of the best available fruit and vegetable cultivars, chosen for their flavour, reliability, and ease of cultivation. More than 100 different crops are covered, and each has a guide to successful growing. Every entry includes a description of the cultivar's important features and qualities, and many are also pictured.

ICON KEY

Each fruit or vegetable entry is accompanied by a set of icons that offer information on essentials such as when to plant and harvest, hardiness, and disease resistance. These help you see at a glance which plants are the right choice for your garden.

- The pot icon indicates whether the cultivar can or cannot be container grown.
- The trowel icon indicates the best season to sow or plant.
- The bug icon is accompanied by the level of resistance to common pests and diseases.
- The snowflake icon denotes hardiness information: hardy, fairly hardy, or not hardy.
- Used only in the fruit section, the tree icons give pollination information. A single tree indicates the cultivar is self-fertile; two trees mean that another plant is needed for fertilization to occur. The flowering season is included where applicable.
- The basket icon shows when the crop is ready to harvest.

THE RHS AWARD OF GARDEN MERIT ♥

The AGM is intended to be of practical use to the home gardener. It is therefore only awarded to a plant that meets the following criteria:

- It must be available.
- It must be of good constitution.
- It must not require specialist growing conditions or care.
- It must not be particularly susceptible to any pest or disease.
- It must be reliable, and not prone to reversion.

WHY GROW YOUR OWN

There is nothing quite like pulling your own carrots from the ground or eating juicy plums straight from the tree. More and more people are discovering the satisfaction of growing their own, and it's easy to see why – it's not only rewarding, it can be cost-effective, eco-friendly, and organic too. Whatever your plot size, whether you own a large allotment or a windowbox, you will be able to grow crops – your options are only limited by your imagination.

HOW TO CHOOSE

Nurturing healthy and happy crops is hugely enjoyable but it will also take time and effort, so you need to make sure that you grow the tastiest, most productive crops possible. That's what this book is all about: we've researched the best crop varieties and identified their key features and advantages, from flavour through to disease resistance. You can hand-pick the crops you really want to grow, and make the best of your time and space.

Most importantly, this book showcases superior, and sometimes unusual, fruits and vegetables that you'll never find in the one-or-two-types-fits-all greengrocers section of your local supermarket. Some plants have also been given the Royal Horticultural Society's Award of Garden Merit, which recognises crops that are readily available, particularly disease-resistant, and easy to grow. Don't limit your choices – there is a huge range of fruits and vegetables out there, and this book will help you to discover them for yourself.

WHERE TO SHOP

All the plants and seeds featured in this book should be readily available. When buying plants, ensuring that they are healthy is of the utmost importance. Be cautious if you are buying plants over the Internet – if possible, try to buy from reputable companies so that you can guarantee the quality. If you are buying from a garden centre or specialist nursery, check for signs of pests and diseases, and be vigilant with pest control and garden hygiene after planting (see growing guides for advice).

PLANNING YOUR PLOT

If you have the luxury of an allotment or large garden, make the most of it by ensuring that you plan your plot carefully. Bear in mind that some crops require differing soil types, locations, and micro-climates, and that some will spread and become quite large (see individual growing guides for details). Keep a record of what you grow year-on-year and consider rotating crops to get the best from your soil and ensure high yields.

DESIGN YOUR LAYOUT

Sketch out the dimensions and boundaries of your plot and decide which crops you want to grow. Start by inserting the features that will be permanent, such as compost bins, sheds, paths, and fruit trees. Think next about the micro-climates that exist in your garden, such as frost pockets, where plants are less likely to thrive, or a south-facing wall that could act as a shelter for cordons of delicate fruit. When planning your plot, make sure that you create an environment that will be easy for you to work in. Leave pathways between rows so that you can reach crops easily for watering and weeding. Make beds an accessible size to avoid damaging surrounding plants; the ideal width is about 1.2m (4ft).

PLANT YOUR CROPS

Some crops require specific planting schemes, sweetcorn for example is best planted in a fairly dense grid formation to increase its chances of pollination, while crops such as potatoes are traditionally grown in rows – consider which crops you want to grow and how their specific needs might affect your planning. Think also about the way that light hits your plot during the day – you don't want to plant smaller crops, such as lettuce, in the shade of taller plants, such as runner beans.

INTEGRATE YOUR GARDEN

Even if you have a smaller space there is a design to suit, whatever your taste – from formal potagers or kitchen-garden layouts, to more flexible cottage-garden or mixed planting systems. If you are growing crops in your garden and are sharing the space with,

A carefully planned plot makes full use of available space and can look attractive.

perhaps, a dining area or children's play space, consider this when you decide your plan. If you don't fancy a fence, a row of bean poles or fruit trees might protect your other crops from an errant football, while growing salad leaves close to a dining area might serve as an easy-access outdoor salad bowl. Consider mixing crops into flowerbeds for a more naturalized look – plants such as marigolds, nasturtiums, or basil act as companion plants, and can help to divert insect predators. Bear in mind that you might need to plan ahead to prevent gaps in your flowerbed after harvesting.

RAISE YOUR BEDS

Creating raised beds for your crops not only provides them with deeper, better-draining soil that will warm up quicker in spring, but also adds architectural interest to your garden. Use old railway sleepers, bricks, slates, or even wooden boards for the sides, and then build up the level of the soil with good quality compost.

GROWING IN SMALL SPACES

A plant pot on a windowsill is all the space you need to grow a shallow-rooted plant such as a lettuce, so don't despair if you don't have much room to play with. Make the most of whatever space you have; create a raised bed in a compact garden, or plant up pots and containers for a patio, decking, or even a balcony. Be creative; grow crops such as tomatoes in hanging baskets, or grow fruit trees in tubs.

Plant a basket of decorative tomatoes.

VERTICAL GARDENING

Don't feel limited to growing at ground level. If you have an unused vertical surface, a garden wall or sturdy fence for example, consider fastening pots and baskets to it, and grow tiers of crops while using no floor space at all. Hanging baskets are an attractive and resourceful use of space, although be careful that they are mounted firmly enough to support their eventual weight. Not all plants will tolerate this relative lack of soil, but some, such as strawberries and salad leaves will thrive quite happily.

Grow a bowl of blackberries on your patio.

Consider planting your crops in with other trailing plants; a mixture of tumbling tomatoes

Fill a raised bed with salad leaves.

and upright colourful flowers can look incredibly attractive. If you decide to attach pots to a wall, ensure that you leave enough space for the crops to grow, and try to ensure that the lowest aren't cast into permanent shade. Fasten securely, bearing in mind the eventual weight.

CLIMATE

Examine your space, however small, and work out the best situations for your crops. Many prefer full sun but others, such as raspberries and blackberries, will flourish in shade. If you are growing crops in pots or baskets you have the flexibility to move them about, which in some cases can be highly beneficial – citrus

trees, for example, enjoy a sunny position outside in summertime, and can then be moved inside or under cover in colder months.

STYLISH RECYCLING

We all know that recycling is important, so think creatively when acquiring pots and containers for your garden. Create stylish and unique growing locations by re-using anything from tin cans, for shallow-rooted plants such as radishes or chillies, to buckets, bins, and Wellington boots. You'll need to create drainage holes, and bear in mind that you'll need to water your crops frequently, as the soil will dry out much quicker than in a regular bed.

TIP   VALUE FOR MONEY

We all want to feel that we're getting the most for our money, so why not try these tasty, high value options:

- Raspberries – plant three canes to a pot and support with trellis.
- Blueberries – ensure that plants have acidic, well-drained conditions.
- Sweetcorn – grow dwarfing types in a warm, sunny position.
- Salad leaves – harvest as cut-and-come-again crops for a large yield.

Raspberries taste delicious, are easy to grow, and are expensive to buy in shops.

WATERING

All your crops will need frequent watering, especially during critical stages in their growth (see individual growing guides for details). The most effective way to water a large plot is with a seep hose, which dribbles water where it is needed at the base of the plant above its roots. A watering can may be all you need for a small plot or patio, but bear in mind that crops in cultivation dry out more quickly than in the ground. Consider a micro-irrigation system, which allows you to tailor a precise network of pipes or sprays to your containers or beds, and can be automated using a timer.

Water in the cool of the morning or evening to reduce evaporation. Direct the water at the soil and avoid spraying the leaves – this is not only ineffectual, but water on a hot day and you also risk scorching them. Remember also that a good soak twice a week is better than a light spray every day, and will encourage stronger, deeper roots.

Keep young, leafy crops well supplied with water.

IMPROVING THE SOIL

To produce healthy crops, fruit and vegetable plants remove a lot of the nutrients from the soil. It's vital to replenish these by digging in an organic material, such as compost or manure, and applying fertilizer during growth.

COMPOST AND MANURE

Fill a compost bin with plant matter and kitchen waste, ensuring that you provide it with air, warmth, and moisture, and over the following months microorganisms will break down the waste into crumbly, sweet-smelling compost.

Making leaf mould is a slower process, taking up to a year. Pile decaying leaves into wire cages or punctured plastic bags containing a small amount of garden soil, and leave to rot down.

Farmyard and stable manures are packed with nutrients and are highly beneficial to the soil but need to rot for at least six months so that the ammonia doesn't "scorch" young plants.

Apply your compost or manure by either spreading a 4in (10cm) layer on the surface of the soil as a mulch, or by digging it into the soil the autumn before planting.

Turn your kitchen waste into compost.

Mulch plants with nutrient-rich leaf mould.

Apply well-rotted farmyard manure.

WEEDING

Weeds make your garden look untidy and can be hard to control. But as well as being unsightly they compete with your crops for water, nutrients, light, and space, often harbouring pests and diseases. It's vitally important to keep them under control.

THE NEED TO WEED

Annual weeds, such as speedwell and chickweed, can be controlled by hoeing. Slice weed stems just below the soil surface. Be careful to do this before they flower or they will create a fresh generation of seed. Preferably, weed on a dry day so that the sun will dry out and kill any upturned roots.

Perennial weeds, such as bindweed and brambles, are much harder to destroy. To remove them completely you will need to dig out every trace of root or rhizome from the soil, or they will regenerate. Do this diligently as soon as you see weeds reshooting and you will win the battle eventually, but on a very overgrown patch you may want to use a weedkiller. Wear protective clothing and a mask, and spray carefully to prevent it reaching nearby crops.

MULCHING

A mulch is a layer of material spread around the base of a plant that can serve a number of useful purposes in the fruit or vegetable garden. Black plastic sheeting or old carpet can be used to warm the ground, trap moisture, or suppress weeds by depriving them of light. Mulching with compost and manure improves soil structure and boosts it with vital nutrients. Using a straw mulch helps by raising crops such as strawberries or courgettes off the soil surface, allowing air to circulate beneath them, and keeping them out of the path of pests, such as slugs. See individual growing guides for details on mulching specific crops.

Protect strawberries with a straw mulch.

FROST PROTECTION

If you are planning year-round crops or just want to get ahead in spring, some kind of frost protection is essential. Not everyone has access to a greenhouse, but there are plenty of other solutions.

CONTROL YOUR CLIMATE

Cold frames and cloches (see right) are ideal for when your seedlings are young and at their most vulnerable. They help to maintain a constant temperature for your crops, and at the same time provide protection from pests such as birds, mice, and insects. If you are sowing into modules indoors before planting out, keep crops in a cold frame to harden them off before transferring into the ground. Ensure your cold frame is well-insulated, and can be partially opened to provide good ventilation. Before sowing seed into the ground, cover the soil with a cloche to warm it beforehand, then place a cloche over the seed to help to maintain a constant temperature while it germinates.

You can improvise a cheap and easy cloche by cutting a plastic bottle in half and using the top part to cover seed or a young plant. Unscrew the lid to ventilate. For larger areas of crops, create your own polytunnel by stretching plastic film or horticultural fleece over wire or plastic hoops, and pin it down securely.

Protect your plants with a cold frame.

Recycle to create your own cloches.

A HEALTHY GARDEN

The varieties of fruits and vegetables in this book have been chosen for taste and reliability, but also in many cases, for their resistance to pests and diseases. However, no plant can be completely resistant and all will benefit from good growing conditions, vigilance, and fast action at the first sign of damage.

PESTS

The pests in your garden range from slugs and snails that love to feed on young seedlings, to aphids that secrete honeydew on plants on which sooty mould can develop. Methods of control can be biological, organic, or chemical.

Slugs target vulnerable new plants.

PREVENTION

Try to pest-proof your plot with a few of these methods:
• Cover seeds or young plants with a protective enclosure, such as a cloche or polytunnel, to prevent attack from insects, birds, and small mammals.
• Interplant your crops with companion plants, such as marigolds, to divert insect pests.
• Encourage insect predators, such as ladybirds, by providing them with a wildlife habitat.
• Set up traps or other deterrents to thwart slugs and snails.
• Hang old CDs, or place upturned plastic bottles on sticks – as the wind catches them, the noise and movement will help to discourage unwanted visitors.
• Use fine netting to deter birds.
• Place grease bands around the trunks of susceptible fruit trees.

TREATMENT

• Use a chemical pesticide. Be aware though that these often kill more than just your pests, and might have a knock-on effect in your garden's food chain.
• Use parasitic nematodes, which enter the bodies of slugs and snails and trigger a fatal infection.

DISEASES

Plant diseases are caused by
viruses, fungi, or bacteria.
They are often more difficult to
prevent and contain than pests;
they can be spread by spores in
the air, rainwater splash, animals
and insects, and also by poor
garden hygiene. Diseases vary
in severity – some are fairly
superficial and can be treated,
while others are severe enough
to cause the plant to die (see
growing guides for specific
information and advice).

PREVENTION

• Rotate your crops to prevent
a build up of diseases in the soil.
• Seedlings and young plants
are especially vulnerable to
the microorganisms that are
sometimes present in stored
water. Instead, use mains tap
water while plants are young.
• Give crops plenty of space
so that air can circulate freely
around and between them.
• Destroy any diseased plant
matter that you remove – do
not compost it as this risks
further contamination.
• Keep your plants strong and
healthy with regular feeding,
watering, and weeding.
• When pruning fruit trees,

Grey mould coats and damages crops.

remove diseased or dead material
immediately. Be careful not to
tear the wood as this creates
an open wound through which
diseases might enter.
• Make sure that you clean and
sterilize your tools and equipment
regularly. If you use a greenhouse
or potting shed, keep it clean and
well ventilated – diseases will
reproduce rapidly in warm, wet,
stagnant conditions.

TREATMENT

• Some fungal diseases are
preventable with fungicides, but
these may not be effective if the
disease has already taken hold.
Plants with bacterial infections
may survive if diseased plant
parts are removed quickly, but a
plant with a viral disease should
be removed and destroyed.

Fruit

Tree Fruits

- Apples
- Pears
- Plums, Damsons, and Gages
- Cherries
- Peaches and Nectarines
- Apricots
- Figs
- Medlars and Quinces
- Citrus
- Nuts

APPLES *Malus domestica*

The quintessential tree fruit, apples offer an astounding array of varieties, wide-ranging fruit flavours, and a large choice of training forms, from freestanding trees and wall-trained cordons, to compact stepovers and standards. Choose a cooking apple, such as 'Bramley's Seedling', for a classic apple crumble, or choose a dessert variety, such as 'Jonagold' or 'Cox's Orange Pippin', for a tasty snack straight from the tree.

	SPRING	SUMMER	AUTUMN	WINTER
PLANT				
HARVEST				

PLANTING

If you are buying a container-grown tree, ensure that it is healthy and has not become pot-bound. Although container-grown trees can be planted at any time of year, it is preferable to plant in autumn. Bare-root trees should be planted between autumn and early spring, as long as the soil is not frozen.

Apple tree cultivars vary in fertility – some are self-fertile, some are diploid, requiring another pollinator, and some are triploid, requiring two other pollinators (see individual cultivar entries for specific information), so ensure that you plan carefully, and if in doubt seek specialist advice when buying your trees.

Select certified disease-free trees.

Although they are not as frost-sensitive as other fruit trees, apples like a warm, sheltered site, with full sun for dessert varieties. Give trees a fertile, well-drained soil with a pH of about 6.5, and ensure that they have enough space to develop comfortably: dwarfing trees may need as little as 1.2m (4ft) space between each

other, while vigorous trees will become very large and may require as much as 8m (25ft).

Dig in well-rotted manure or compost before planting. Trees will need staking for the first three or four years, so ensure that the stake is sturdy before you plant your tree. Attach any horizontal training wires before planting cordons or espaliers.

Beautiful apple blossom in springtime.

CROP CARE

Young apple trees need to be kept well watered while their fruits are developing, especially those that are trained into fans and cordons, or growing in pots.

Feed trees in early spring with a general fertilizer, and consider applying extra nitrogenous fertilizer to culinary apple trees.

Mulch after feeding with a layer of well-rotted manure or compost. If the soil is particularly poor, you may want to apply a mulch bi-annually; if the soil is rich, bark chippings may suffice.

Although apples generally blossom later in the season than trees such as pears or cherries, and are therefore less vulnerable

TIP GROW IN CONTAINERS

If grown on a dwarfing or non-vigorous rootstock, apples will thrive in containers and in limited space. Feed with fertilizer in early spring, and ensure that you keep your tree well-watered as containers will dry out faster than the open ground. Pot on every few years. Growing trees in containers enables you to cover them with netting against pests, or protect against frost with fleece.

Dwarfing apples will happily produce a crop in a confined growing space.

to frosts, you may want to cover container-grown or wall-trained trees with horticultural fleece.

HARVESTING

Depending on the variety you grow you may have apples ready to harvest as early as midsummer, but the timing of the harvest is crucial. If you harvest fruits too soon you may prevent them developing their full flavour; too late and they may not store well. Ripe apples should pull away from the tree easily, do not rip them away or you risk damaging the spur. Be careful not to bruise the fruits as you remove and store them. Fruits will not all ripen at exactly the same time; if you have varieties with different harvesting seasons you may be able to pick for many months.

STORING

Generally, the later the season, the longer the apple will store. When apples are ripe remove them gently from the tree and, spacing them so that they are not touching, lay them out on trays, or wrap them in tissue paper and hang in plastic bags. Store them in a cool, dark, place and check the fruits regularly for signs of decay.

PESTS AND DISEASES

Apples are prone to a range of diseases, most commonly canker, scab, powdery mildew, and brown rot. If any of these occur, increase the air flow through the tree's branches by pruning out the diseased wood. Spray with an appropriate fungicide.

Apples are prone to pests such as wasps, birds, winter moth caterpillars, aphids, and capsid bugs. Net to deter birds; set up a jam-trap to attract wasps and use grease bands on the tree and its stake to prevent winter moth caterpillars climbing the trunk and laying eggs in the tree. If aphids or apple sawfly are detected, remove damaged fruits and spray trees with an appropriate insecticide. Resistance to pests and diseases can vary between cultivars, so check the apple catalogue.

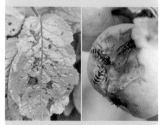

Capsid bugs target young leaves, creating spots and ragged holes (left). Wasps (right) will target damaged fruits and feast on the sweet, ripe flesh.

'Cox's Orange Pippin'

Championed by many as the finest English eating apple, the orangey-yellow skin is tinged with red and covers a crisp, juicy, and superb-flavoured flesh. The blossom is sensitive to frost however, and the trees have poor resistance to diseases.

🪣	on a dwarfing rootstock
🌱	autumn to early spring
❄	some resistance
❆	hardy
♂	self-fertile (mid)
🔒	mid-autumn

'Golden Delicious' ♀

This trouble-free variety is best grown in a warm, sheltered site for the most flavoursome crop. The large, yellow-green apples have a light, crisp flesh and sweet flavour; they are best eaten fresh. They store for up to eight months.

🪣	on a dwarfing rootstock
🌱	autumn to early spring
❄	excellent resistance
❆	hardy
♂	needs 1 pollinator (mid)
🔒	mid-autumn

'Jonagold' ♀

A widely grown tree, it produces heavy yields but has some susceptibility to scab and canker. The large, yellow-green, red-flushed fruits are crisp and juicy, and their creamy flesh has a sweet, honeyed flavour. The fruit will store until the New Year.

- on a dwarfing rootstock
- autumn to early spring
- some resistance
- hardy
- needs 2 pollinators (mid)
- late autumn

'Elstar' ♀

This variety produces heavy crops of yellow- and red-marbled apples that have an intense, very sweet flavour, and a crunchy yet slightly soft texture. The fruits are excellent for keeping and can be stored until early winter.

- on a dwarfing rootstock
- autumn to early spring
- good resistance
- hardy
- needs 1 pollinator (mid)
- early autumn

'Laxton's Fortune' ♀

An old British variety, the yellowish-green apples are flushed with red stripes. Fruits have a firm, aromatic flesh that has a good blend of sweetness and acidity. The apples will keep until well into the New Year.

- on a dwarfing rootstock
- autumn to early spring
- good resistance
- hardy
- partially self-fertile (mid)
- early autumn

'Gala'

One of the most widely grown dessert apples, these shiny orange-red fruits have a sweet flavour and crisp, juicy flesh. The trees crop heavily, producing apples that keep well once picked, although this variety is susceptible to scab and canker.

🥃	on a dwarfing rootstock
✂️	autumn to early spring
❋	some resistance
❄️	hardy
🌼	needs 1 pollinator (mid)
🔒	mid-autumn

'Pixie' ♀

This easy-to-grow variety bears very high yields of yellow-green apples with red stripes and flushes. The diminutive fruits are crisp, aromatic, and juicy – perfect for children – and will store into the New Year.

🥃	on a dwarfing rootstock
✂️	autumn to early spring
❋	excellent resistance
❄️	hardy
🌼	needs 1 pollinator (mid)
🔒	mid-autumn

'Egremont Russet' ♀

Considered the best russet apple, the tree produces heavy crops of small, golden fruits with patches of russetted skin. Its crisp flesh has a flavour of nuts and honey. Apples are best eaten fresh but will keep until the New Year.

🥃	on a dwarfing rootstock
✂️	autumn to early spring
❋	good resistance
❄️	hardy
🌼	partially self-fertile (early)
🔒	late summer

'Mother' ♀

This old American variety, also known as 'American Mother', bears slightly conical, yellow-green fruits with red stripes and a soft, yellow, juicy, sweet flesh. It is a slow-growing tree with good scab resistance. The early fruits will store well until the New Year.

- on a dwarfing rootstock
- autumn to early spring
- good resistance
- hardy
- partially self-fertile (late)
- early autumn

'Herefordshire Russet'

A relatively new, heavy-cropping variety of exceptional quality, the tree produces golden-brown fruits, which are small, but rich and aromatic. Although they are best eaten fresh, they will store well until the New Year.

- on a dwarfing rootstock
- autumn to early spring
- good resistance
- hardy
- partially self-fertile (mid)
- early autumn

'Sunset' ♀

This heavy-cropping descendant of 'Cox's Orange Pippin' produces red and gold apples with a similar flavour. However, this tree is easier to grow; it is hardy, compact, and has excellent disease resistance.

- on a dwarfing rootstock
- autumn to early spring
- excellent resistance
- hardy
- self-fertile (mid)
- early autumn

'Adam's Pearmain'

This trouble-free, old variety produces conical-shaped fruits with yellow-green, red-striped skin. The aromatic yellow flesh is crisp and firm with a nutty flavour. Stored correctly, the fruit will keep well into the New Year.

🪣 on a dwarfing rootstock
🌿 autumn to early spring
✹ excellent resistance
❄ hardy
👬 needs 1 pollinator (early)
🔒 mid-autumn

'Helena'

A clone of the classic 'Braeburn', this excellent crisp and juicy apple crops about ten days earlier. The red and green apples are ready for picking from mid-autumn and can be stored for up to four months.

🪣 on a dwarfing rootstock
🌿 autumn to early spring
✹ good resistance
❄ hardy
👬 needs 1 pollinator (mid)
🔒 mid-autumn

'Ribston Pippin' ♀

A classic English apple, and one of the parents of 'Cox's Orange Pippin', its fruits have a firm, crisp flesh and a strong aromatic flavour. Trees produce heavy yields of red-flushed, yellow-green fruits with some russeting. Fruits store well until the New Year.

- on a dwarfing rootstock
- autumn to early spring
- good resistance
- hardy
- needs 2 pollinators (early)
- early autumn

'Worcester Pearmain' ♀

This old favourite produces medium-sized, bright red-flushed apples whose sweet, aromatic flavour is enhanced if left on the tree until fully ripe. Although hardy and resistant to mildew, it is susceptible to scab and canker.

- on a dwarfing rootstock
- autumn to early spring
- good resistance
- hardy
- partially self-fertile (mid)
- early autumn

'Lord Lambourne' ♀

This early-fruiting, compact tree is good for small gardens. The round fruits are a gold-green colour with a touch of russet, and their aromatic flesh is crisp and juicy and pleasantly acidic. The apples keep well until Christmas.

- on a dwarfing rootstock
- autumn to early spring
- good resistance
- hardy
- partially self-fertile (early)
- late summer

'Ashmead's Kernel' ♀

A classic old variety, this apple is still one of the best late dessert varieties. The pretty blossom makes way for aromatic-tasting fruit with crisp yellow flesh and russet colouring. It is relatively low-yielding but has good scab resistance. Fruits store well.

- 🪣 on a dwarfing rootstock
- 🍂 autumn to early spring
- ✳️ excellent resistance
- ❄️ hardy
- 👥 needs 1 pollinator (mid)
- 🔒 mid-autumn

'Falstaff' ♀

This modern variety is an easy-to-grow, compact tree that has excellent disease and frost resistance. It produces heavy crops of attractive, red-flushed, golden apples with a crisp, juicy texture and good flavour.

- 🪣 on a dwarfing rootstock
- 🍂 autumn to early spring
- ✳️ good resistance
- ❄️ hardy
- 👥 partially self-fertile (mid)
- 🔒 late summer

'Scrumptious' ♀

This modern variety is excellent for all gardens, but is particularly good in frosty sites. The crisp, juicy flesh of this bright red apple has a honey-like sweetness, with a hint of strawberry, and a touch of acidity.

- 🪣 on a dwarfing rootstock
- 🍂 autumn to early spring
- ✳️ good resistance
- ❄️ hardy
- 👤 self-fertile (mid)
- 🔒 late summer

'Greensleeves' ♀

This pretty tree for the garden produces heavy yields of greeny-yellow fruits early in the season. The apples have a sharp flavour that mellows as they ripen, but they will only store for a few weeks. These very hardy trees are ideal for colder regions.

- 🪣 on a dwarfing rootstock
- 🍂 autumn to early spring
- 🐛 excellent resistance
- ❄️ hardy
- 🤝 partially self-fertile (mid)
- 🔒 early autumn

'Ellison's Orange' ♀

These red-striped, yellow-green fruits have a distinctive aromatic flavour tinged with aniseed. The tree produces early crops of apples, occasionally biennially, which are best eaten fresh but will store for several weeks.

- 🪣 on a dwarfing rootstock
- 🍂 autumn to early spring
- 🐛 good resistance
- ❄️ hardy
- 🤝 partially self-fertile (mid)
- 🔒 late summer

'Tydeman's Late Orange'

A reliable, easy-to-grow, and late-cropping variety, this tree produces small, orange-red fruits with touches of russet. Their rich and aromatic flavour is similar to a cox variety, but sharper. Apples will keep until early spring.

- 🪣 on a dwarfing rootstock
- 🍂 autumn to early spring
- 🐛 good resistance
- ❄️ hardy
- 🤝 needs 1 pollinator (mid)
- 🔒 mid-autumn

'Kidd's Orange Red' ♀

A rival to 'Cox's Orange Pippin', this green, red-flushed dessert apple is similar, but its yellow-cream, juicy flesh has a sweeter, aromatic taste. It produces good, regular yields that will keep until Christmas. It is generally untroubled by scab and mildew.

- 🪴 on a dwarfing rootstock
- 🍂 autumn to early spring
- 🕷 good resistance
- ❄ hardy
- 🌼 needs 1 pollinator (mid)
- 🔒 late autumn

'Court Pendu Plat'

One of the oldest dessert varieties still in cultivation, it produces green-flushed, red apples with an aromatic, sweet flavour. A hardy and late-flowering tree, it is ideal for frost-prone areas. Picked fruits will store until late spring.

- 🪴 on a dwarfing rootstock
- 🍂 autumn to early spring
- 🕷 excellent resistance
- ❄ hardy
- 🌼 needs 1 pollinator (late)
- 🔒 mid autumn

'Charles Ross' ♀

An old dual-purpose variety, this tree produces large, showy, yellow-green apples, flushed orange-red. The flesh is sweet and juicy when first harvested, but becomes dry and loses flavour with storage.

- 🪴 on a dwarfing rootstock
- 🍂 autumn to early spring
- 🕷 good resistance
- ❄ hardy
- 🌼 partially self-fertile (mid)
- 🔒 early autumn

'Blenheim Orange' ♉

This excellent dual-purpose tree produces heavy yields of red- and russet-striped, golden fruits, with white flesh and a nutty flavour. It is vigorous, so is best on a dwarfing rootstock. It has good mildew resistance, although scab can be a problem.

- on a dwarfing rootstock
- autumn to early spring
- good resistance
- hardy
- needs 2 pollinators (mid)
- late autumn

'James Grieve' ♉

One of the finest early-fruiters, this popular dual-purpose variety produces heavy crops of yellow- and red-speckled apples. The juicy fruits are acidic on picking, but after a few weeks the flavour will sweeten and become milder.

- on a dwarfing rootstock
- autumn to early spring
- some resistance
- hardy
- partially self-fertile (mid)
- early autumn

'Bountiful'

This compact, dual-purpose variety has good disease resistance, and bears heavy crops of large, sweet apples that are pale green with a red blush. The fruits are best eaten fresh as their flavour mellows in storage.

- on a dwarfing rootstock
- autumn to early spring
- good resistance
- hardy
- needs 1 pollinator (mid)
- early autumn

'Bramley's Seedling' ♀

The most popular cooker, it bears heavy crops of extra-large yellow-green fruits in mid-autumn, although it tends to crop biennially. Apples have creamy, juicy, and full-flavoured flesh. It is a vigorous variety but has poor scab resistance.

- 🪣 on a dwarfing rootstock
- 🔪 autumn to early spring
- ✳ some resistance
- ❄ hardy
- 🌼 needs 2 pollinators (mid)
- 🔒 mid-autumn

'Arthur Turner' ♀

Beautiful blossom makes way for heavy yields of yellow-green apples, flushed orange-brown. This outstanding baking apple has a good sweet flavour. A particularly hardy tree, it does well in colder regions.

- 🪣 on a dwarfing rootstock
- 🔪 autumn to early spring
- ✳ some resistance
- ❄ hardy
- 🌼 partially self-fertile (mid)
- 🔒 mid-autumn

'Edward VII' ♀

This compact, hardy variety is ideal for small gardens or colder regions. The moderate crops of medium-sized, shiny, green, mild-flavoured apples will store until mid-spring. It has good resistance to scab.

- 🪣 on a dwarfing rootstock
- 🔪 autumn to early spring
- ✳ good resistance
- ❄ hardy
- 🌼 self-fertile (late)
- 🔒 mid-autumn

'Golden Noble' ♛

The juicy flesh of this large yellow-green apple cooks to a golden purée and has a sharp flavour and creamy texture. A reliable cropper, this tree is fairly vigorous and does well in cooler areas. The fruit keeps well, too.

- 🪣 on a dwarfing rootstock
- 🗓 autumn to early spring
- 🕷 excellent resistance
- ❄ hardy
- 🌳 needs 1 pollinator (mid)
- 🍎 mid-autumn

'Howgate Wonder'

This spreading tree is excellent in frost-prone areas, bearing heavy crops of red-striped, golden apples. It produces the largest cooking apples of any variety; they have a good flavour and store for over two months.

- 🪣 on a dwarfing rootstock
- 🗓 autumn to early spring
- 🕷 good resistance
- ❄ hardy
- 🌳 partially self-fertile (mid)
- 🍎 mid-autumn

'Newton Wonder' ♛

This vigorous tree produces heavy crops of large, red-tinged green apples. The fine flavour of the fruits is less sharp than a 'Bramley' and the juicy flesh cooks down to a golden fluff. Stored fruit can be eaten raw.

- 🪣 on a dwarfing rootstock
- 🗓 autumn to early spring
- 🕷 good resistance
- ❄ hardy
- 🌳 self-fertile (late)
- 🍎 late autumn

PEARS *Pyris communis* and *P. pyrifolia*

When harvested at their sweet and juicy best, pears are simply unbeatable. They are delicious eaten fresh, used in cooking, or bottled in alcohol and stored for later use. Although less widely-grown than apples, they can be just as easy, are vulnerable to fewer pests and diseases, and arguably much tastier – just give them a sheltered site and provide them with some frost protection in winter.

	SPRING	SUMMER	AUTUMN	WINTER
PLANT				
HARVEST				

PLANTING

Choose your trees carefully: if you have only a small space, pears can be grown on a semi-dwarfing rootstock. These will need around 3m (10ft) of space between trees, whereas more vigorous types need about 5m (15ft). They can be grown as free-standing trees or trained; fans, cordons, or espaliers are ideal for a south-facing wall, as pears require more heat and sunshine than apples.

Although some pear cultivars are classified as partially self-fertile, all will benefit from pollination from another tree, so choose carefully, selecting trees that will flower within the same period. Bear in mind that pear pollination can be

Allow trees plenty of space to develop.

complicated; there are some trees that produce very poor pollen and make unsatisfactory pollinators (although they are not suggested in the pear catalogue of this book). Some combinations of trees will simply not pollinate each other, such as 'Doyenné du Comice' and 'Onward', while others are triploid – meaning that they need at least two other pollinators to produce fruit.

Seek specialist advice at the time of purchase.

Container-grown trees can be planted at any time of year, although autumn is preferable; ensure that they have not become pot-bound when you choose your tree. Plant bare-root trees between autumn and early spring. Pears need a warm, sheltered, sunny site with well-draining, fertile soil, and a pH of around 6.5. Dig in plenty of well-rotted manure or compost before planting – a thin, acidic, or chalky soil can encourage lime-induced chlorosis.

Thin out fruits to encourage large pears.

CROP CARE

Pear trees will require careful watering, especially while young or during their growing season – do not allow them to dry out. Pears need feeding with a general or nitrogenous fertilizer in late winter, then weeding, and mulching with well-rotted manure or compost in spring.

If your tree produces lots of fruits, thin them out to encourage the tree to channel its energy into the remaining fruits,

TIP PRUNING

Pear trees should be pruned in winter while the tree is dormant to reduce the risk of infection. Cut back any diseased wood and aim to improve ventilation through the branches. If training the tree, prune so as to direct its growth, and tie in where necessary (see right). Do not over-prune as too much pruning can encourage an excess of leafy growth and fewer fruits.

Tie in branches with twine or garden string to guide growth for training.

producing the largest possible. Thin them to leave about 10–15cm (4–6in) between fruits (see left).

Pear trees are more susceptible to frost damage than apple trees because they produce their blossom earlier in the season – if possible, protect trees with horticultural fleece.

HARVESTING

It is crucial to time the harvesting of your pears carefully; if you harvest early or mid-season pears too soon and leave them indoors for too long, or harvest them too late, they may become grainy and unpalatable, or rot prematurely. Test fruits to check that they are sweet, and then pick them while they are still slightly underripe. When late-season pears pull easily away from the tree, they can be brought inside and stored.

STORING

Pears store for varying times – some varieties will keep until the following spring, so see individual cultivar entries for more specific information. Pears need to be kept in a cool, dark place. Ensure that fruits are not touching each other, and check regularly for signs of decay.

PESTS AND DISEASES

Comparisons are often made between apples and pears, and when it comes to fighting off pests and diseases, pears are the clear winners. Although they are not completely invincible, they face far fewer problems.

If aphids are spotted or pear leaf midge suspected, use a plant oil wash in winter and, if necessary, spray trees with an insecticide after blossom has dropped. Place grease bands around the trunks to prevent winter moth caterpillars climbing up and laying eggs.

Trees may be vulnerable to diseases such as scab and brown rot - pick off any infected fruits and remove diseased parts. Destroy infected plant material, do not compost it. Using sterilized tools when pruning will help reduce the risk and spread of disease.

Wasps will target existing holes in fruits to feast on the sweet flesh (left). Pear leaf midge cause leaves to roll and turn to red then black in colour (right).

'Gorham' ♀

Bearing a dual-purpose pear with a sweet, musky flavour and smooth-textured, juicy flesh, this is a moderate to good cropper, with upright growth. It is a good pollinator for other varieties, especially 'Doyenne du Comice', and is partially self-fertile.

- unsuitable for containers
- late autumn to late winter
- good resistance
- hardy
- partially self-fertile (late)
- early autumn

'Packham's Triumph'

A tree of relatively weak growth, it crops so heavily that fruits may need thinning. They have pale yellow-green, smooth, juicy flesh; for the best flavour, leave on the tree as long as possible. Plant in a warm, sheltered location.

- unsuitable for containers
- late autumn to late winter
- some resistance
- hardy
- needs 1 pollinator (early)
- mid- to late autumn

'Conference' ♔

This reliable and heavy cropper is partially self-fertile. The long, greenish-russet fruits have creamy-white, very crisp flesh for dessert or culinary use. It is good for cordon and espalier training, but is susceptible to canker, mildew, and scab.

- unsuitable for containers
- late autumn to late winter
- poor resistance
- hardy
- partially self-fertile (mid)
- late autumn

'Glou Morceau'

Given a warm, sheltered spot, this variety is a reliably heavy cropper. The fruits are medium-sized to large, with greenish-yellow skin and smooth, juicy white flesh. Leave to ripen on the tree for as long as possible.

- unsuitable for containers
- late autumn to late winter
- good resistance
- hardy
- needs 1 pollinator (late)
- mid-autumn

'Onward' ♔

With fruits rather like those of 'Doyenne du Comice' with soft, juicy, sweet flesh that has a slightly acid note, 'Onward' also offers hardiness, blossom that can withstand late frosts, heavy crops, and some resistance to scab.

- unsuitable for containers
- late autumn to late winter
- good resistance
- hardy
- needs 1 pollinator (late)
- early to mid-autumn

'Concorde' ♀

This new, partially self-fertile variety bears a very heavy crop on a compact tree, with pale green fruits turning pale yellow-green with russet patches. The flesh is juicy and sweet with a very good flavour, and fruits can be stored until midwinter.

- 🪣 unsuitable for containers
- 🌿 late autumn to late winter
- 🕷 good resistance
- ❄ hardy
- 🌼 partially self-fertile (mid)
- 🔒 mid-autumn

'Williams' Bon Chrétien' ♀

The fruits of this vigorous, hardy tree have bright yellow-green skin and white, very smooth, juicy flesh with a musky flavour. They are borne in profusion and are dual-purpose. Pick promptly when ripe or they may rot.

- 🪣 unsuitable for containers
- 🌿 late autumn to late winter
- 🕷 excellent resistance
- ❄ hardy
- 🌼 partially self-fertile (mid)
- 🔒 late summer to early autumn

'Beurré Hardy' ♀

This variety may be slow to
bear its first crops, but from
then on produces an abundance
of medium to large fruits with
green, bronze-russeted skin
and aromatic, juicy flesh. Pick
while hard and ripen in storage.

- 🪣 unsuitable for containers
- 🌱 late autumn to late winter
- 🦠 good resistance
- ❄ hardy
- 🌼 needs 1 pollinator (mid)
- 🔒 early autumn

'Merton Pride'

While it is not a heavy cropper,
this vigorous upright tree
produces fruits of excellent
flavour, with brown-russeted,
yellow-green skin, and smooth,
soft, very juicy flesh. Eat them
soon after picking.

- 🪣 unsuitable for containers
- 🌱 late autumn to late winter
- 🦠 good resistance
- ❄ hardy
- 🌼 needs 2 pollinators (mid)
- 🔒 early autumn

'Invincible'

This variety bears two sets of
blossom, so if frost affects the
first it will still fruit; without
frost, it has a long cropping
season. The gold-tinted green
fruits are sweet, succulent, and
tender, and store until winter.

- 🪣 unsuitable for containers
- 🌱 late autumn to late winter
- 🦠 good resistance
- ❄ hardy
- 🌼 self-fertile (mid)
- 🔒 mid-autumn

'Clapp's Favorite'

A hardy variety with upright growth, this tree crops prolifically, producing an early yield of scarlet-flushed, yellow-green fruits with crisp, sweet, juicy flesh that is good for both cooking and eating. Pick as soon as the fruit is ripe.

- unsuitable for containers
- late autumn to late winter
- excellent resistance
- hardy
- needs 1 pollinator (late)
- late summer to early autumn

'Moonglow'

This vigorous upright tree bears yellow-green, pink-flushed, very juicy pears, with a sweet, musky flavour and smooth texture, good for both dessert and culinary use; pick before fruits are ripe. This hardy variety is resistant to scab.

- unsuitable for containers
- late autumn to late winter
- excellent resistance
- hardy
- needs 1 pollinator (late)
- late summer

'Catillac' ♀

An old French variety with spreading growth and attractive blossom, 'Catillac' is one of the best culinary pears, bearing heavy crops of large, greenish-yellow fruits, ready for use from late winter to mid-spring.

- unsuitable for containers
- late autumn to late winter
- excellent resistance
- hardy
- needs 2 pollinators (late)
- mid- to late autumn

'Doyenne du Comice' ♀

The large, gold-green fruits of this variety have a fine flavour and juicy, smooth flesh; they are best picked early and ripened indoors. It has some resistance to mildew but is susceptible to scab. Grow in a warm location for the best crop.

- unsuitable for containers
- late autumn to late winter
- some resistance
- hardy
- needs 1 pollinator (late)
- mid-autumn

'Beth' ♀

A fast-growing, heavy-cropping, and reliable variety, it produces small- to medium-sized fruits with pale yellow-green skin and creamy-white, juicy, sweet flesh, with a soft texture and excellent flavour. It is compact and hardy.

- unsuitable for containers
- late autumn to late winter
- good resistance
- hardy
- needs 1 pollinator (late)
- late summer to early autumn

'Nijisseiki'

An Asian "apple-pear" from Japan, 'Nijisseiki' has fruits that resemble an apple in shape and crispness but have the juiciness and sweet flavour of a pear. They will store in the fridge for several months with no loss of quality.

- unsuitable for containers
- late autumn to late winter
- good resistance
- hardy
- needs 1 pollinator (mid)
- late summer to early autumn

PLUMS, DAMSONS, AND GAGES

Prunus domestica, Prunus salicina, and *Prunus insititia*

With their beautiful blossom and their sweet, juicy fruits that are excellent for use in jams, puddings, pies, and crumbles, there is every reason to want to grow your own plum tree. Their close relatives, the gages, are even richer in flavour and are wonderful eaten fresh from the tree. Damsons are too sharp to eat raw but are delicious cooked.

	SPRING	SUMMER	AUTUMN	WINTER
PLANT				
HARVEST				

PLANTING

Plums, damsons, and gages all need a well-drained soil with a pH of about 6.5, and a warm, sunny position. A south-facing wall is ideal; frost pockets should be avoided. You need to select the right variety and rootstock for your garden as not all plum varieties are self-fertile. If you opt for trees that aren't, ensure that they flower at the same time in the season and that the combination you choose are compatible, as some trees will simply not pollinate each other. If in doubt, seek specialist advice when you buy your trees.

Choose a rootstock that works for your space. Plum trees can grow quite large, so if you don't have a large plot choose a

Protect blossom from early frosts

semi-dwarfing rootstock. If you choose a semi-vigorous type, ensure that trees have enough room to spread as they get older. Leave about 7m (22ft) between freestanding trees, but less if you are training the tree into a fan or cordon shape, as it will require less space.

Container-grown trees can be planted at any time of year, provided that the weather is

not too hot, but ensure that trees have not become pot-bound. Bare-root trees should be planted between late autumn and early spring, unless the soil is frozen.

Dig in plenty of well-rotted manure or compost before planting as plums, damsons, and gages all prefer a fertile soil. Water in well, and apply an organic mulch around the base. Young trees need staking for their first few years.

Thin out fruits to encourage strong growth.

CROP CARE

Keep trees well-watered to help prevent fruits splitting (see box, right). Feed trees with a general fertilizer in late winter and a nitrogenous fertilizer in early spring. Mulch around the base of trunks with well-rotted

manure, compost, or bark chippings after feeding.

Plums, damsons, and gages flower relatively early in the season, and may need protection with fleece if frosts occur. This may not be feasible with larger trees, but will be much easier for container-grown or wall-trained specimens. Plums, damsons, and

TIP PRUNING

Whether you are training your tree or simply pruning it, only do so between late spring and early autumn to reduce the risk of infection from silver leaf or bacterial canker. Use sterilized tools, and prune out diseased wood first to promote an open, well-ventilated branch structure. Plums fruit on two- or three-year-old wood, so the aim of pruning is to tidy the tree rather then remove too much of the old wood.

Like other stone fruit, prune plums in summer while in active growth.

gages need far less pruning than apples or pears (see tip box, left). Freestanding trees may not require pruning at all.

Fruits may need thinning out if the crop is heavy (see left), as this encourages larger fruits to form. Some fruits will fall in early summer in the "June drop". Thin out any remaining fruits to leave around 5–10cm (2–5in) between them.

HARVESTING

Plums and gages should be ready to harvest in midsummer; damsons in mid-autumn. Leave plums that you plan to eat to ripen on the tree. Squeeze them gently to test – when they are soft to the touch they are ready to pick. Plums to be used for cooking can be harvested earlier and will keep a little longer in the fridge. Pick plums with a short amount of stalk attached to prevent the fruit skins tearing. Fruits ripen in succession, so keep checking the tree for those that are ripe.

STORING

Plums, damsons, and gages will keep for a short time in the fridge, but try to use them as soon as possible after harvesting to prevent them from spoiling.

PESTS AND DISEASES

Wasps, flies, and birds are drawn to sweet, ripening fruits, so do all you can to discourage them. Try to ensure that trees receive a constant level of moisture as irregular watering can cause the fruit skins to split, leaving them open to attack from both pests and diseases, notably brown rot, which will shrivel fruits, covering the skins in spores. Net container-grown or wall-trained trees to deter birds.

Winter moths can be a real problem, and will munch their way through leaves – attach sticky grease bands around the trunks of trees and pick off any caterpillars you find. If aphids are a problem, spray with insecticidal soap. Be wary of diseases such as bacterial canker, plum sawfly, plum fruit moth, and pocket plum as well.

Wasps will feast on sweet, ripe fruits (left), so set up a jam-trap to distract them. Bacterial canker (right) causes holes in, and then withers, leaves.

'Victoria' ♀

Probably the best-known and most widely grown dual-purpose English plum, this tree reliably bears heavy yields. The pale purple-red, medium-sized fruits have a yellow-green, juicy flesh that is sweet but has a much better flavour when cooked.

🪣	unsuitable for containers
🌱	autumn to early spring
🐛	some resistance
❄️	fairly hardy
🌼	self-fertile (mid)
🔒	late summer

'Seneca'

This hardy, upright, and vigorous tree reliably bears good crops of very large, purple-red fruits late in the season. The plums have bright yellow-orange flesh and are delicious eaten fresh from the tree.

🪣	unsuitable for containers
🌱	autumn to early spring
🐛	good resistance
❄️	hardy
🌼	partially self-fertile (mid)
🔒	late summer

'Early Laxton' ♔

One of the earliest cropping plum varieties, this compact tree produces regular crops of round, medium-sized, yellow fruits, whose skins are flushed with pink. Plums have juicy golden flesh and are good eaten straight from the tree or cooked.

- unsuitable for containers
- autumn to early spring
- good resistance
- fairly hardy
- partially self-fertile (mid)
- early summer

'Avalon'

This new variety bears some of the finest dessert plums. The large, oval, red fruits have a juicy flesh and sweet flavour. The strong-growing trees have good disease resistance but may crop lightly until well-established.

- unsuitable for containers
- autumn to early spring
- good resistance
- hardy
- needs 1 pollinator (early)
- midsummer

'Edda'

A new, very hardy, early variety, this is an excellent dual-purpose plum. The yellow flesh of these large, oval, blue-black fruits has a rich flavour when eaten fresh, but the taste is superior when cooked.

- unsuitable for containers
- autumn to early spring
- good resistance
- hardy
- needs 1 pollinator (early)
- late summer

'Stanley'

This variety is widely grown because of its excellent, reliable cropping nature, and its tendency to produce heavy yields. The large, purple-blue plums have a sweet and juicy greenish-yellow flesh that is delicious eaten fresh or when dried.

- unsuitable for containers
- autumn to early spring
- good resistance
- hardy
- self-fertile (late)
- late summer

'Methley'

One of the best Japanese plums available, this variety is a very heavy cropper; its fruits often need thinning out early in the season. The tree bears medium-sized, reddish-purple fruits with juicy, mild-flavoured, red flesh.

- unsuitable for containers
- autumn to early spring
- good resistance
- hardy
- self-fertile (mid)
- midsummer

'Warwickshire Drooper'

As the name suggests, this tree has an attractive drooping habit. It bears heavy crops of large, yellow plums late in the season; fruits are good for cooking, or if picked later, their juicy, yellow flesh can be eaten fresh.

- unsuitable for containers
- autumn to early spring
- good resistance
- fairly hardy
- self-fertile (early)
- early autumn

'Opal' ♀

A very hardy, vigorous, upright variety, which bears heavy crops of dessert plums that mature early in the season. Inside the small, bite-sized, purplish-green fruits the pale yellow flesh has a distinctly greengage-like flavour.

- unsuitable for containers
- autumn to early spring
- good resistance
- fairly hardy
- self-fertile (mid)
- early to midsummer

'Jubilaeum'

Also known as 'Laxton's Jubilee', this very hardy, very reliable, dual-purpose plum is considered to be an improved 'Victoria'. The high yields of large, flavourful fruits have a light-red skin and sweet, juicy, yellow flesh.

- unsuitable for containers
- autumn to early spring
- excellent resistance
- fairly hardy
- self-fertile (mid)
- midsummer

'Blue Tit' ♀

These reliable, very hardy trees produce heavy crops on compact plants, which makes them ideal for small gardens. The medium-sized, blue-black fruits have a juicy, yellow flesh with a good flavour – eat fresh or cooked.

- unsuitable for containers
- autumn to early spring
- good resistance
- hardy
- self-fertile (late)
- midsummer

'Giant Prune'

A reliable and prolific cropper also known as 'Burbank', this tree bears large, oval, purple-red fruits that keep well. The purple flesh is excellent both for cooking and for eating fresh. This variety also has good frost tolerance and disease resistance.

- 🪣 unsuitable for containers
- 🌱 autumn to early spring
- 🌸 excellent resistance
- ❄️ fairly hardy
- 🔓 self-fertile (late)
- 🔒 late summer

'Shiro'

This Japanese variety is a vigorous, reliable, easy-to-grow tree, bearing extra sweet, medium-sized, yellow fruits early in the season. The crisp, yellow flesh of these plums is excellent eaten fresh, cooked, or preserved.

- 🪣 unsuitable for containers
- 🌱 autumn to early spring
- 🌸 good resistance
- ❄️ fairly hardy
- 🔓 needs 1 pollinator (mid)
- 🔒 early to midsummer

'Satsuma'

Medium to large oval-shaped fruits, with distinctive dark skin and juicy red flesh, have a sweet rather than tart flavour, and are excellent for eating fresh and for preserves. However, this variety is susceptible to brown rot.

- 🪣 unsuitable for containers
- 🌱 early spring
- 🌸 poor resistance
- ❄️ hardy
- 🔓 needs 1 pollinator (early)
- 🔒 late summer

'Marjorie's Seedling' ♀

This variety is popular for the quality of its fruit and its good disease and frost resistance. The large, oval, purple plums are produced late in the season; the sweet, sharp, yellow flesh is best cooked, but can be eaten fresh.

	unsuitable for containers
	autumn to early spring
	excellent resistance
	fairly hardy
	self-fertile (late)
	early autumn

'Castleton'

This US-only variety bears heavy crops of blue-purple fruits that are excellent for eating fresh as well as drying. Although self-fertile, it bears better fruits when planted near another European plum, such as 'Stanley'.

	unsuitable for containers
	early spring
	some resistance
	hardy
	self-fertile (mid)
	midsummer

'AU Producer'

This US-only, disease-resistant cultivar best suits warmer climates. It bears small, round, firm fruits that are red inside and out. Fruit flavour is excellent and trees have good resistance to a variety of diseases.

	unsuitable for containers
	early spring
	good resistance
	hardy
	self-fertile (early)
	midsummer

'Old Green Gage'

Often considered the finest of all the dessert plums, the medium-sized, yellow-green fruits produced by this variety have a superb, sweet, luscious flavour. Although not always a reliable cropper, the yields are usually of a decent size.

- unsuitable for containers
- autumn to early spring
- good resistance
- fairly hardy
- partially self-fertile (late)
- midsummer

'Oullins Gage' ♀

This gage-like plum is a reliable, heavy-cropping variety. The large, round, light green fruits have a sweet flavour. The plums can be picked early for cooking or left to ripen for eating fresh, but are also excellent for bottling.

- unsuitable for containers
- autumn to early spring
- good resistance
- fairly hardy
- self-fertile (late)
- midsummer

'Imperial Gage' ♀

Also known as 'Denniston's Superb', this is the most reliable gage, regularly producing heavy crops. It is very hardy, so is ideal for colder locations. The medium-sized, round, green-yellow fruits have a firm, yellow, juicy flesh.

- unsuitable for containers
- autumn to early spring
- good resistance
- hardy
- self-fertile (mid)
- late summer

'Cambridge Gage' ♛

One of the most popular and reliable dual-purpose greengages, the compact trees produce decent yields in all but the coldest areas. The small, yellow-green, juicy fruits have an excellent flavour, and can be eaten raw or cooked.

- unsuitable for containers
- autumn to early spring
- good resistance
- fairly hardy
- partially self-fertile (late)
- late summer

'Merryweather Damson'

This very popular, heavy-cropping tree bears the largest of the damsons. The blue-black fruits look like small plums but their sharp, acidic, yellow flesh has the distinctive damson flavour. Use in jams and pickles.

- unsuitable for containers
- autumn to early spring
- good resistance
- fairly hardy
- self-fertile (mid)
- midsummer

'Prune Damson' ♛

Also known as 'Shropshire Damson', this compact variety is easy to grow even in colder areas. Heavy yields of small, deep purple fruits have a sharp flavour that mellows with cooking. They are excellent for jams and for drying.

- unsuitable for containers
- autumn to early spring
- good resistance
- fairly hardy
- self-fertile (late)
- early autumn

SWEET AND ACID CHERRIES

Prunus avium and *P. cerasus*

Not only are sweet cherries a delicious treat picked and eaten fresh, but the trees are also renowned for their breathtaking displays of spring blossom. Although they are too sour to eat fresh, acid varieties are also worth growing – they are hardier than their sweet relatives, and the fruits are wonderful cooked and used in jams, puddings, and pies.

	SPRING	SUMMER	AUTUMN	WINTER
PLANT				
HARVEST				

PLANTING

Select your cherry tree carefully – most are self-fertile, so if you only have space for one ensure that you invest in this type. If you are growing more than one tree, make sure that their seasons of flowering are the same – but bear in mind that there are a few varieties of sweet cherries that will not cross-pollinate each other, even if they both flower at the same time. Seek specialist advice at the time of purchase.

Cherry trees grow fast and can become large, so if you only have a small space, choose a tree grown on a dwarfing rootstock. Trees may be bare-root or container-grown; if you are buying the latter, ensure that it has not become pot-bound.

Protect blossom from frost and rain.

Sweet cherries need a warm, sheltered site, and a well-drained, moist soil with a pH of around 6.5. They need protection against frost, so growing them against a south-facing wall is ideal since they can then be easily covered over with fleece or netting, or plastic sheeting, to protect the trees from rain. Acid types are less fussy, and although they need the same soil conditions

as sweet varieties, they will happily grow in cooler locations – even trained against a north-facing wall or fence.

Dig in some well-rotted manure or compost shortly before planting. Your trees will need support, so insert stakes for freestanding trees before planting, and stake and fix horizontal wires in place for trees to be trained. Some compact varieties of cherry can be grown in containers; ensure that your pot is at least 45cm (18in) deep, and that the soil is well-drained.

Protect your precious crops with netting.

CROP CARE

Cherry trees should be kept well-watered while they are young and need an application of general-purpose fertilizer in early spring. Mulch around the base of trees with well-rotted manure or compost after feeding. Acid cherries will also benefit from a late winter feeding with a nitrogen-rich fertilizer.

Bear in mind that due to their restricted conditions, container-grown trees will need more water than those planted in the soil.

TIP PRUNING

- When the tree is young, prune to encourage strong growth. Once the tree is established, prune in early spring to encourage growth, and again in summer after fruiting.
- Use sterilized tools. Prune out any diseased or damaged wood first.
- Prune strategically so that branches are not crossing or rubbing – the tree is vulnerable to infection if the bark has been rubbed away.

Prune in spring when blossom and new leaves are present on the tree.

They will also need feeding with a high-potash fertilizer in spring.

To discourage the spread of diseases, such as silver leaf, always prune in early spring and summer. Cherries, like other stone-fruit trees, produce their crop on year-old wood, so prune to remove old, fruited wood, and to train the tree into shape. Cherries are commonly grown as fans or pyramids (see pruning tip box, left).

Cover both sweet and acid cherries with fleece while the delicate flowers are blossoming. Trees will also need netting to deter birds, as these will happily strip the tree of all of its fruits.

HARVESTING

When they are ripe, cut the cherries from the tree with their stalks attached using scissors or secateurs. Hold the fruits by the stalks while you cut them to prevent the fruit from dropping and damaging. You may need to go over the tree several times to collect the entire harvest.

STORING

Cherries do not store well after harvesting, so eat them fresh as soon as possible, use them for cooking or making preserves, or freeze them for later use.

PESTS AND DISEASES

Sudden changes to moisture levels can cause the cherry skins to split, leaving them vulnerable to wasps and flies. To discourage this, ensure that you water the tree regularly and do not let it dry out. Net the trees to deter birds, and be wary of other pests such as aphids and fruit flies. If you spot signs of these, spray the affected trees with an appropriate insecticide.

Cherry trees are prone to diseases such as bacterial canker, silver leaf, and brown rot (see below). To discourage the emergence or spread of disease, practise good garden hygiene: ensure that the trees have sufficient ventilation and space, always prune with sterilized equipment, and remove and destroy any affected fruits, foliage, or branches promptly.

Cherries affected by brown rot shrivel and develop creamy-white spots.

'Emperor Francis'

A reliable and hardy tree that produces heavy crops of medium-sized, yellow fruit with a light red blush, that darken as they ripen. The juicy cherries have an excellent sweet flavour and are delicious eaten straight from the tree.

- unsuitable for containers
- autumn to early spring
- good resistance
- hardy
- needs 1 pollinator (late)
- midsummer

'Stella' ♀

One of the oldest, more compact, and easy-to-grow varieties, this has long been the preferred choice for gardens. It reliably produces an abundant crop of large, dark red, almost black, juicy fruits with a sweet flavour.

- unsuitable for containers
- autumn to early spring
- good resistance
- hardy
- self-fertile (mid)
- midsummer

'Summit'

This relatively new American variety produces good crops of cherries in the middle of the cherry season. The large, slightly heart-shaped fruits are a light red colour and their strong, sweet taste is delicious straight from the tree.

- unsuitable for containers
- autumn to early spring
- good resistance
- hardy
- needs 1 pollinator (late)
- midsummer

'Kordia'

This heavy-cropping tree has a compact shape, which makes it a good choice for smaller gardens. It bears dark red, glossy, heart-shaped fruits with sweet, juicy flesh in midsummer, which are delicious straight from the tree.

- unsuitable for containers
- autumn to early spring
- good resistance
- hardy
- needs 1 pollinator (mid)
- midsummer

'Merchant' ♀

A relatively new, early season variety, this tree produces very heavy crops of large, black fruits with an excellent flavour. A regular, reliable cropper, it also has some resistance to bacterial canker.

- unsuitable for containers
- autumn to early spring
- some resistance
- hardy
- needs 1 pollinator (mid)
- early summer

'Summer Sun' ♀

A good all rounder, this late-flowering variety is relatively compact with good frost tolerance and some resistance to bacterial canker. It bears heavy and reliable yields of dark red, plump, sweet fruits at the end of the summer.

- unsuitable for containers
- autumn to early spring
- good resistance
- hardy
- self-fertile (mid)
- late summer

'Sweetheart'

A relatively new variety, this tree produces fruits that do not ripen all at once, making the harvesting period longer than for many other types. The heavy crops of cherries ripen to a dark red colour, with an excellent sweet flavour.

- unsuitable for containers
- autumn to early spring
- good resistance
- hardy
- self-fertile (late)
- late summer

'Hertford' ♀

This upright tree produces very heavy crops of large, black fruits in mid- to late season. The cherries have pinkish-red flesh and an excellent, sweet flavour. This variety has some resistance to bacterial canker.

- unsuitable for containers
- autumn to early spring
- good resistance
- hardy
- needs 1 pollinator (mid)
- late summer

'Merton Glory'

These compact, upright trees are perfect for small gardens and produce good yields of large, golden-yellow cherries flushed with red. The heart-shaped fruits have firm, white, sweet flesh and are ready early in the season.

- unsuitable for containers
- autumn to early spring
- good resistance
- hardy
- needs 1 pollinator (mid)
- early summer

'Sweetheart'

'Lapins'

This upright tree bears heavy crops of large, good-quality fruits. The cherries are a dark red, almost black colour when they are fully ripe, and have an exquisite, sweet flavour, both straight from the tree and when cooked.

- 🪣 unsuitable for containers
- 🍂 autumn to early spring
- 🕷 good resistance
- ❄ hardy
- 🌼 self-fertile (mid)
- 🔒 midsummer

'Penny'

A modern, late-season variety that reliably bears regular crops of very large, firm fruits. As they ripen, the cherries develop in colour from dark red to black. These well-flavoured fruits are delicious straight from the tree.

- 🪣 unsuitable for containers
- 🍂 autumn to early spring
- 🕷 good resistance
- ❄ hardy
- 🌼 needs 1 pollinator (mid)
- 🔒 late summer

'Colney' ♀

This heavy-cropping variety is a relatively new one, and much of its appeal lies in its excellent canker resistance. The very late, large, black cherries are sweet and very juicy – they are delicious raw or used in cooking.

- 🪣 unsuitable for containers
- 🍂 autumn to early spring
- 🕷 excellent resistance
- ❄ hardy
- 🌼 needs 1 pollinator (late)
- 🔒 late summer

'Morello' ♀

Probably the most popular acid cherry, this relatively small tree produces huge crops of large red fruits, even in slightly shaded or north-facing gardens. The cherries are sour when eaten straight from the tree and so are best cooked.

- 🪣 unsuitable for containers
- 🍂 autumn to early spring
- 🌸 good resistance
- ❄️ hardy
- 🌼 self-fertile (late)
- 🔒 late summer

'Nabella'

An improved version of the 'Morello' cherry, this compact tree produces heavier crops of larger, dark red, almost black, cherries than its relative. The fruits have a good flavour but are acidic and are best eaten cooked.

- 🪣 unsuitable for containers
- 🍂 autumn to early spring
- 🌸 good resistance
- ❄️ hardy
- 🌼 self-fertile (mid)
- 🔒 midsummer

'Meteor'

This naturally dwarf, US-only variety bears large, oblong, bright red fruits. The acidic, juicy yellow flesh is excellent for pies. Bred for winter-hardiness, it is leaf-spot resistant, and an easy choice for a small garden.

- 🪣 unsuitable for containers
- 🍂 early spring
- 🌸 good resistance
- ❄️ hardy
- 🌼 self-fertile (late)
- 🔒 midsummer

PEACHES AND NECTARINES

Prunus persica and *Prunus persica* var. *nectarina*

Sweet, juicy, and delicious, fuzzy peaches and smooth nectarines are delicious eaten fresh or used for making jams or puddings. Requiring cold weather over winter, protection from frost in spring, and sun in summer, peaches and nectarines are fussy trees. Try growing them in movable containers so that you can guarantee them the conditions they'll need.

	SPRING	SUMMER	AUTUMN	WINTER
PLANT				
HARVEST				

PLANTING

Peaches and nectarines need a warm, sheltered site. A south-facing wall is ideal if you are growing them outside, as they can then be easily protected against frost, predators, and rain with fleece, netting, or plastic sheeting. They will grow happily under cover in a greenhouse, and some types are suitable for containers, so can be moved indoors or out as the weather dictates.

Peaches and nectarines prefer a deep, slightly acidic soil, a pH of between 6.5 and 7 is ideal, that does not become water-logged. Prepare your plot by digging in well-rotted manure or compost a few months before planting. Trees can be purchased either

Plant in a sheltered site to protect blossom.

bare-root or growing in containers. If you buy container-grown trees ensure that they have not become pot-bound. Plant both types between autumn and early spring, to the same depth as the soil mark on their stems.

If you are training your tree against a wall, fix horizontal wires before planting. Freestanding trees need staking for a few years; insert a stake before planting.

CROP CARE

Peaches and nectarines are self-fertile, so technically you do not need more than one tree in your garden to produce a crop. That said, the trees may benefit from a little help as they flower in early spring, when few insect pollinators are around. To ensure a crop, gently transfer pollen from one flower to another using a small paintbrush.

Both fruits will need protection against frost, which may kill off their early blossom. If your tree is compact, or is growing against a wall, it will be relatively easy to protect with horticultural fleece. Alternatively, cover your trees with plastic sheeting over winter to keep them dry; this will help protect them from peach leaf

Thin out fruitlets when they are young.

curl, which may be transferred between trees by rain. Birds may also be a problem as fruit develops, so cover trees with netting to deter them. This may be problematic for freestanding trees, but attempt where possible.

Both peach and nectarine trees will benefit from a feed with a general fertilizer in late

TIP PRUNING AND TRAINING

If you don't want a freestanding tree, peaches and nectarines can be trained into fans on walls, or grown as bushes or pyramid forms – start from scratch with a feathered maiden or buy a two- or three-year-old pre-trained tree.

Prune peaches and nectarines (along with other stone-fruits) in summer. The trees fruit on year-old wood, so prune to remove old wood that bore fruit the previous year.

Train your tree along wires to allow good ventilation and easy picking access.

winter, and then a general-purpose liquid feed while fruits are developing. Keep the trees weeded and well-watered.

THINNING

It is essential to thin out peaches and nectarines while the fruits are young. This will force the tree to focus its energy on forming larger, higher-quality peaches or nectarines. When the fruits are very small, thin to leave one fruit per cluster, removing all the others. When fruits have grown larger, thin them out again so that there is about 20–25cm (8–10in) between peaches and 15cm (6in) between nectarines; the space they need to grow to their full size.

HARVESTING

Peaches and nectarines are ready to harvest once they become soft – take care not to drop them as they bruise and spoil easily. They are ready to pick when they pull easily away from the tree.

STORING

Once picked and fully ripened, peaches and nectarines will only last for a few days before they go bad and begin to spoil. Freeze or use for jam-making if you cannot eat the fruits fast enough.

PESTS AND DISEASES

Peaches and nectarines can be affected by a range of problems. Creating a barrier will guard against some of them: covering with plastic sheeting reduces the risk of peach leaf curl, netting can help deter birds, and if it is very fine, wasps too. Other problems are harder to combat:

- Aphids stunt growth and cause leaves to curl. Spray affected leaves with an appropriate insecticide or soap.
- Red spider mite cause leaves to appear "bronzed". Treat as for aphids.
- Silver leaf disease causes leaves to appear silvery. Remove the damaged plant material and destroy it. Sterilize your tools afterwards.
- Bacterial canker causes round holes to form in leaves, and gum to ooze from the bark. Treat as for silver leaf.

Aphids (left) cause leaves to curl; they may become sticky with honeydew. Peach leaf curl (right) causes leaves to distort and become bright red in colour.

'Peregrine' ♀

This white-fleshed variety is popular for its reliability, ease of cultivation, and large, superbly flavoured fruits. It is more productive in cool summers than most varieties but, unless grown in a warm area, does need a warm wall or a greenhouse.

- unsuitable for containers
- late autumn to early winter
- some resistance
- fairly hardy
- self-fertile (early)
- mid- to late summer

'Red Haven'

Dark pink flowers in spring are succeeded in late summer by heavy crops of peaches with firm yellow flesh, reddening towards the centre; the skins are yellow with a red flush. It is a hardy tree, and resistant to peach leaf curl.

- unsuitable for containers
- late autumn to early winter
- good resistance
- hardy
- self-fertile (early)
- late summer

'Duke of York' ♀

White-fleshed, sweet, very juicy peaches with a red-flushed skin, borne early in the season, and in abundance, make this variety one of the best. It is most productive against a south-facing wall or in a greenhouse.

- unsuitable for containers
- late autumn to early winter
- some resistance
- hardy
- self-fertile (early)
- midsummer

'Garden Lady'

This slow-growing, dwarf variety produces attractive pink flowers in spring, followed by yellow-fleshed fruits with sweet and juicy flesh. Grow it in a container in a warm spot, and move it indoors for the winter.

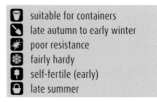

- suitable for containers
- late autumn to early winter
- poor resistance
- fairly hardy
- self-fertile (early)
- late summer

'Red Haven'

'Saturn'

This new variety has unusual flattened peaches, resembling a doughnut in shape. The white flesh is firm, very sweet, and has an excellent flavour, while the skin is white, flushed with dusky pink and red. It is susceptible to peach leaf curl.

- unsuitable for containers
- late autumn to early winter
- poor resistance
- hardy
- self-fertile (early)
- mid- to late summer

'Rochester' ♛

As it flowers after the worst frosts, this is a reliable and generous cropper. It produces large, juicy peaches with soft yellow flesh and red-flushed orange skin. It is vigorous and hardy, with some resistance to peach leaf curl.

- unsuitable for containers
- late autumn to early winter
- some resistance
- hardy
- self-fertile (early)
- late summer

'Hale's Early'

This heavy-cropping, early variety bears large pink flowers, followed by medium-sized, rounded peaches with good-flavoured, yellow flesh, and attractive pale skin, flushed crimson and dark red.

- unsuitable for containers
- late autumn to early winter
- poor resistance
- hardy
- self-fertile (early)
- midsummer

'Fantasia'

This easy-to-grow, vigorous, frost-resistant variety bears large, yellow-fleshed nectarines with orange-red skin. Harvested early, they have a slightly acidic, tangy flavour; later, a rich, sweet juiciness. It is resistant to bacterial canker and some pests.

- unsuitable for containers
- late autumn to early winter
- good resistance
- hardy
- self-fertile (early)
- late summer

'Early Rivers' ♛

One of the earliest nectarines to ripen, the prolifically borne fruits of 'Early Rivers' have pale yellow skin, blushed with red, and very sweet, translucent white flesh with a rich flavour. It can be grown in a large container.

- suitable for containers
- late autumn to early winter
- some resistance
- hardy
- self-fertile (early)
- midsummer

'Lord Napier' ♛

Early-ripening, large, aromatic nectarines make this a popular variety. The flesh is white and the skin yellow, flushed dark red. It needs a warm site, such as a south-facing wall, to bear the heavy crops of which it is capable.

- unsuitable for containers
- late autumn to early winter
- some resistance
- hardy
- self-fertile (early)
- late summer

APRICOTS *Prunus armeniaca*

Home-grown apricots are a delicious treat, perfect for eating fresh or for cooking or jam-making. Because they flower very early, apricots will need adequate frost protection during colder months, and may need help with pollination. Since they are self-fertile you will only need one tree to produce a crop, and if you choose a dwarfing variety, you can harvest fresh, flavourful fruit from even a tiny space.

	SPRING	SUMMER	AUTUMN	WINTER
PLANT				
HARVEST				

PLANTING

Apricot trees prefer a warm, sheltered site – a south-facing wall is ideal, although they will also grow happily in a greenhouse or in a large container that can be moved under cover in colder months. As with all fruit trees, if you are buying them container-grown, ensure that they have not become pot-bound.

Plant trees in autumn to early winter. Dig in plenty of well-rotted manure or compost a few months before planting. Apricots will grow well in most fertile, well-drained soils, but prefer a pH of between 6.7–7.5. Attach some supports if growing your apricot against a wall. Stake young trees, and ensure that they are kept well-watered.

Colourful buds break in early spring.

CROP CARE

Apricot trees are fully hardy, but since they produce blossom very early in the year – even as early as late winter – they may still need protection against frost. Move container-grown plants indoors, and cover wall-trained trees with fleece (see right). If you are growing your apricots indoors, or where they will receive few insect pollinators,

you may need to pollinate trees by hand. Use a small paintbrush, and gently transfer the pollen between flowers. Only prune trees in spring or summer, as this helps to reduce the risk of infection and dieback.

HARVESTING AND STORING

Harvest fruits when they are soft and ripe. Picked apricots will not store well for long, so eat them when they are as fresh as possible.

PESTS AND DISEASES

Ensuring that trees have enough space and are well-pruned will help to avoid common problems.

TIP PROTECTION

Training your apricot tree against a south-facing wall will make it easier for you to protect it. In colder months, cover it with a layer of horticultural fleece or protect against strong winds and weather with waterproof sheeting.

Protect vulnerable wall-trained trees.

'Alfred'

A hardy, early-flowering variety, 'Alfred' has medium to small fruits, with pink-flushed, orange skin and juicy, orange flesh, with an excellent flavour. It is less susceptible to die-back than other apricot varieties and is reliably productive.

- suitable for containers
- late autumn to midwinter
- good resistance
- hardy
- self-fertile (early)
- mid- to late summer

'Moorpark'

Bearing large, crimson-flushed fruits with sweet, juicy, orange flesh, this 18th-century variety is reliable and crops generously. It does best against a wall, but will crop freestanding in a frost-free position. It is prone to die-back.

- suitable for containers
- late autumn to midwinter
- some resistance
- hardy
- self-fertile (early)
- late summer

'Tomcot'

This is an early and heavy-cropping variety that produces very large, red-blushed, golden-orange fruits, particularly noteworthy for their flavour. It bears abundant blossom. It is reliable, but for best results grow it against a south-facing wall.

- suitable for containers
- late autumn to midwinter
- some resistance
- hardy
- self-fertile (early)
- midsummer

'Flavorcot'

Large, juicy, red-blushed apricots with an intense flavour are abundantly borne on a medium-sized tree ideal for a small garden. It is reliable and crops well in warm regions; elsewhere, it will need a sheltered spot.

- suitable for containers
- late autumn to midwinter
- some resistance
- hardy
- self-fertile (early)
- late summer

'New Large Early'

In spite of its name, this variety was raised in the 19th century. It is one of the earliest apricots, producing its large, pale-skinned fruits in midsummer. The flesh is rich and sweet, with a very good flavour.

- suitable for containers
- late autumn to midwinter
- some resistance
- hardy
- self-fertile (early)
- midsummer

FIGS *Ficus carica*

Although they look and taste exotic, figs are relatively easy to grow, and will provide you with a good yearly crop as long as you contain their roots, give them plenty of sun and warmth, and keep them well-watered. Figs are available year-round and can be planted any time from early autumn. Try building yourself a fig pit and training your tree into an attractive fan shape against a south-facing wall.

	SPRING	SUMMER	AUTUMN	WINTER
PLANT				
HARVEST				

PLANTING

Figs need a warm, sheltered site and should be located carefully, away from strong winds and frost pockets. Preferably, grow them against a south-facing wall, or under cover in a greenhouse. Figs will grow happily in a fig pit (see right) or in containers, and as long as the pot is not too heavy, you may be able to move your fig as the seasons change.

Figs prefer alkaline conditions, although they will grow happily in most well-drained soils. Avoid planting in rich soil, as figs may grow too rapidly, producing plenty of foliage but few fruits.

If growing against a wall you will need to provide supports for your fig tree – fix horizontal wires every 30cm (12in).

New leaves will burst forth in spring.

CROP CARE

Fig trees need to be watered regularly, especially if they are growing in a pot, because allowing them to dry out causes them to drop their fruits. Pot- and pit-grown trees will need feeding with general fertilizer every year, and all figs benefit from a compost mulch in early spring. Pot-grown fig trees will need re-potting every few years.

In colder regions, protect trees against frost in winter using horticultural fleece.

HARVESTING

Harvest fruits when they are soft and fully ripe. The fruits will hang downwards, and their skin will split slightly near the stem. Break them from the tree and eat as soon as possible.

PESTS AND DISEASES

Figs are a relatively trouble-free crop; the biggest problems are likely to be birds and wasps, which will be attracted to the ripened fruits. Protect with netting.

TIP BUILD A FIG PIT

Fig trees thrive if their roots are kept in check, so dig a 60 x 60cm (24 x 24in) pit, line with paving slabs, and lay old brick and rubble as a base. This will encourage the tree to use its energy to produce fruits rather than foliage.

Contain fig roots and the tree will reward you with larger crops.

'White Marseilles'

This slow-growing, hardy tree, produces medium to large, rounded fruits with yellowish-green, slightly ribbed skin, and whitish, almost translucent flesh, with a very sweet flavour. If grown in a greenhouse, it will bear two crops each year.

- suitable for containers
- late autumn to late winter
- poor resistance
- hardy
- self-fertile
- early autumn

'Brown Turkey' ♀

With glossy, palmate leaves and a spreading habit, this variety is ornamental as well as productive. The most reliable UK variety, it bears an abundance of sweet, juicy, pear-shaped fruits, with purplish-brown skin and red flesh.

- suitable for containers
- late autumn to late winter
- some resistance
- hardy
- self-fertile
- late summer to early autumn

'Brunswick'

This old English variety produces heavy crops of large, pear-shaped fruits, with greenish-yellow skins and yellow flesh, red in the centre. It has very large, deeply divided leaves, and is more tolerant of cold, wet conditions than most figs.

- suitable for containers
- late autumn to late winter
- poor resistance
- hardy
- self-fertile
- late summer to early autumn

'Alma'

This variety is productive from an early age, bearing heavy crops of small to medium-sized, pear-shaped fruits with golden skin and flesh, and a sweet, delicate flavour. It is fairly vigorous and does best in a greenhouse.

- suitable for containers
- late autumn to late winter
- good resistance
- hardy
- self-fertile
- late summer

'Celeste'

The small to medium, purplish-brown, red-fleshed fruits borne by this cold-hardy, US-only variety have tightly closed eyes that inhibit insect entry. 'Celeste' will grow well in a container or in the ground.

- suitable for containers
- very early spring
- some resistance
- hardy
- self-fertile
- midsummer to autumn

MEDLARS AND QUINCES

Mespilus germanica and *Cydonia oblonga*

These unusual tree fruits look highly ornamental, and are an acquired taste, but are well worth growing if you have the space. Rose hip-like medlars (below) should be left to "blet" until sweet and almost rotten before eating. Quinces (right) are rarely soft enough to eat raw when grown in a cool climate, but are delicious cooked or used in jams or jellies.

	SPRING	SUMMER	AUTUMN	WINTER
PLANT				
HARVEST				

PLANTING

As with all trees, ensure that container-grown medlars and quinces have not become pot-bound. You can plant container-grown trees any time, but autumn is best. Plant bare-root trees between late winter and early spring.

Medlars and quinces are best planted in a warm, sheltered site and well-drained soil. Both are self-fertile, so will not need another tree to produce fruit. Dig well-rotted manure or compost into the soil a few months before planting.

CROP CARE

Young trees will need staking for the first few years. Quinces appreciate regular feeding and

Leave medlars to "blet" before picking.

watering, especially during spring and summer if the weather is dry. Medlars need feeding and watering while young, but after a few years will cope without any extra watering. Mulch well around young trees with compost, manure or bark chips. Quinces and medlars will be largely untroubled by frost, provided they have been sited correctly.

HARVESTING AND STORING

Ripe medlars will pick easily from the tree in mid-autumn. Dip the stems in a concentrated salt solution to preserve them, and then leave for several weeks in a cool, dark place, with the "eyes" facing downwards, to decompose, or "blet". They will then be ready to eat – "bletting" gives the flesh an almost sickly-sweet flavour.

Quinces can be harvested when fruits are golden-yellow in colour, and provided conditions are frost-free, they improve the longer they are left on the tree. Store in a cool, dark place, leaving space between the fruits.

PESTS AND DISEASES

Quinces are sometimes affected by leaf blight and brown rot. To discourage disease, prune in winter, and allow good airflow. Water regularly to prevent fruits splitting (below, left). Medlars are usually trouble-free.

Blight (right) discolours quince leaves.

'Royal'

More compact than other medlars, with an upright habit, this variety is ideal for smaller spaces. The medium-sized golden brown fruits have a better flavour than most and can be eaten fresh, without the need for bletting.

- unsuitable for containers
- autumn to early spring
- some resistance
- hardy
- self-fertile (mid)
- mid-autumn

'Breda Giant'

An ornamental and productive tree, this Dutch variety reliably bears large, tasty fruits early in the season. Medlars have a particularly good flavour and the soft, brown flesh is excellent for jelly, or for eating after bletting.

- unsuitable for containers
- autumn to early spring
- some resistance
- hardy
- self-fertile (mid)
- mid-autumn

'Nottingham'

This attractive, ornamental tree produces the best flavoured fruits. It has a semi-weeping, compact habit with thick, downy foliage and white flowers. It bears heavy crops of medium-sized, caramel-flavoured medlars.

- unsuitable for containers
- autumn to early spring
- good resistance
- hardy
- self-fertile (mid)
- late autumn

'Vranja'

A popular quince, these attractive, medium-sized trees bear an abundance of large, pale green, pear-shaped fruits that become golden as they ripen. Leave the fruits on the tree as long as possible to develop their exceptional perfume and flavour.

- unsuitable for containers
- autumn to early spring
- good resistance
- hardy
- self-fertile (mid)
- late autumn

'Pineapple'

With a flavour that resembles its namesake, this US-only variety bears heavy yields of large, pear-shaped, golden-yellow quinces that are best cooked or used in jellies. The attractive trees bear rose-pink blooms in spring.

- unsuitable for containers
- early spring
- some resistance
- hardy
- self-fertile
- early autumn

'Smyrna'

This US-only variety bears large, highly fragrant quinces with lemony-yellow skin. The fruits are rich in flavourful tannin, and pectin, which makes them good for jellies and preserves. The fruits store exceptionally well.

- unsuitable for containers
- early spring
- some resistance
- hardy
- self-fertile
- early autumn

CITRUS *various*

Although most citrus fruits will only grow well outdoors in very warm, sunny climates, it is possible to grow them in the UK if you can provide them with the heat and protection they need in winter. For most people this will probably mean growing them in containers under glass. There is a wide range of citrus fruits to choose from: lemons, limes, and oranges (see image, right) are the most obvious choices.

	SPRING	SUMMER	AUTUMN	WINTER
PLANT				
HARVEST				

PLANTING

Citrus trees should be bought as young specimens and grown on. Trees can be grown from seed but it's a difficult and lengthy process. Since most citrus take a relatively long time to develop fruits, buying a young tree will ensure that you get a crop as soon as possible. Most citrus trees are self-fertile, so even if you only have space for one, you will still be rewarded with fruits.

Citrus trees prefer a fertile, well-drained, and slightly acidic soil, and should be repotted in spring. If you are growing your tree outside in summer, ensure that it has a warm, sunny site, as the amount of heat the plant receives will affect the flavour of the fruits. When growing under

Grow lemons in a container in a hot spot.

glass in winter, ensure that your tree has a sunny position, which is well-ventilated. Your tree will grow well in a container, allowing you to move it in and out of doors as the weather dictates.

CROP CARE

Wherever you have sited your tree, do not allow it to dry out. Trees grown in containers may need more frequent watering in

summer, and when bearing fruits. Apply a nitrogen fertilizer every month while fruits are developing. If your tree is outside it will need a minimum temperature of 15°C (59°F). Overall try to keep the temperature as stable as possible.

HARVESTING AND STORING

When fruits have reached a good size and their rich colour has fully developed, taste them to check whether they are ripe enough to harvest. Use them as soon as possible after picking; they will not keep for more than a few weeks in the fridge, but will keep for longer on the tree.

PESTS AND DISEASES

If you are growing under glass, citrus fruits are most likely to be affected by pests such as red spider mite and mealy bugs. Pick off bugs and spray trees with insecticide. Practise good garden hygiene and keep trees well ventilated to stop diseases spreading.

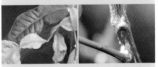

Red spider mite (left) and mealybugs (right) attacking leaves and stems.

Mexican lime

Also known as Tahiti or key lime, this medium-sized, bushy plant produces fragrant fruits, popular with bartenders. The limes are produced year round, but more abundantly in summer, and have a thin, smooth skin that is yellow-green when ripe.

- suitable for containers
- spring or autumn
- some resistance
- not hardy
- self-fertile
- year round

Persian lime

This compact tree is ideal for growing in containers, producing limes with thicker skins than Mexican types, and with a greater degree of hardiness. The fruits are ideal for culinary use, but are not as flavourful as some.

- suitable for containers
- spring or autumn
- some resistance
- not hardy
- self-fertile
- year round

Makrut

Although the unusual-looking, bumpy-skinned, mid-green fruits produced by this tree are largely inedible, it is worth growing for its wonderfully fragrant leaves, which are widely used in Thai cuisine.

- suitable for containers
- spring or autumn
- some resistance
- not hardy
- self-fertile
- year round

Citron

These unusual-looking, fragrant, ornamental fruits are believed in some cultures to grant good luck. What is certain is that their rind is excellent in cooking. 'Buddha's Hand' (pictured) requires higher temperatures than other citrus.

 suitable for containers
spring or autumn
some resistance
not hardy
self-fertile
year round

Lemon

The quintessential citrus fruit, lemons are fast-growing, bearing acidic fruits useful for flavouring a variety of dishes. Try 'Meyer', whose compact plants produce orange-hued fruits that are sweeter than other varieties.

suitable for containers
spring or autumn
some resistance
not hardy
self-fertile
mid- to late summer

Limequat

Hardier than a Mexican lime, but less so than a kumquat, this intergeneric hybrid will grow in a container in a warm, sheltered site, if it is brought indoors in winter. Its small yellow fruits are juicy with an excellent lime taste.

suitable for containers
spring or autumn
some resistance
not hardy
self-fertile
early winter to summer

Kumquat

In winter, semi-dormancy makes this subtropical tree fairly hardy. In temperate climates, kumquats such as 'Nagami' (pictured) can be grown in pots, and their decorative form and fragrant flowers enjoyed indoors in winter. Eat the fruits skin and all.

- suitable for containers
- spring or autumn
- some resistance
- not hardy
- self-fertile
- winter to spring

Grapefruit

With their sharp, acidic taste, grapefruits are refreshing, but not to everyone's taste. Available in red, white, and pink types, they tolerate cold temperatures but not frost, and need to be brought inside in winter.

- suitable for containers
- spring or autumn
- some resistance
- not hardy
- self-fertile
- midsummer to early winter

New Zealand grapefruit

Also known as "poor man's orange", it produces medium to large, yellow-skinned, yellow-fleshed fruits, that are less acidic than other grapefruit types. The fruits are excellent for juicing or for making marmalade.

- suitable for containers
- spring or autumn
- some resistance
- not hardy
- self-fertile
- year round

Orange

Packed with vitamin C, oranges look wonderful and have a wide range of culinary uses. Try 'Valencia' (pictured), which produces sweet, medium-sized oranges that are ideal for juicing. Or, try sour 'Seville' oranges, which are excellent for marmalade.

- suitable for containers
- spring or autumn
- some resistance
- not hardy
- self-fertile
- late winter to early spring

Calamondin

This easy-to-grow citrus needs warmer outdoor temperatures to thrive or can be kept indoors year round. The shrubby, compact, evergreen tree bears fragrant white flowers, followed by good crops of sour oranges.

- suitable for containers
- spring or autumn
- some resistance
- not hardy
- self-fertile
- mid- to late summer

Mandarin

The mandarin family is a sprawling group that includes clementines, tangerines, and satsumas. They have thinner skins and are therefore easier to peel than oranges, and are good in fruit salads or as a snack.

- suitable for containers
- spring or autumn
- some resistance
- not hardy
- self-fertile
- year round

NUTS *various*

With some trees providing architectural garden value, and others beautiful spring blossom, nuts are not as commonly grown as they ought to be. In the UK a range of nuts can be home-grown – walnuts, cobnuts (see image, right), almonds, and sweet chestnuts. Don't worry if you don't have a large amount of space, as some, such as almonds or cobnuts, will grow as bushes in containers.

	SPRING	SUMMER	AUTUMN	WINTER
PLANT				
HARVEST				

PLANTING

If you buy a container-grown tree, ensure that it is healthy and has not become pot-bound. Some nut trees, such as walnuts, will eventually establish very long roots. Nut trees are generally very tolerant and will grow in a range of conditions. They prefer well-drained soil, and a pH of around 6.5.

It is important to ensure that you give trees enough space to grow – walnuts for example will need planting at least 12–18m (40–60ft) away from other trees, as their roots inhibit the growth of other plants. Sweet chestnut trees will also grow large if permitted, and will need a space of at least 8m (25ft). Cobnuts and almonds can

Almond nuts (left) and blossom (right).

be trained as fans, but will still need space; give cobnuts 4.5m (15ft), and almonds 4.5–6m (15–20ft). They are suitable for growing in containers as bushes. Stake young trees for the first few years of growth.

CROP CARE

Keep trees well-watered, especially if the weather is dry, and feed with a general fertilizer

in early spring. Mulch around the base of trees for the first few years with well-rotted manure, compost, or bark to suppress weeds and keep the soil moist.

HARVESTING AND STORING

Most nuts will be ready for harvesting in autumn. If you leave them on the tree too long you risk them being stolen by squirrels or, in the case of walnuts, birds. Clean and dry the harvested nuts thoroughly. Store them in a cool, dark place, ensuring that no rats or mice can get to them. A net bag is ideal as it will provide airy conditions.

PESTS AND DISEASES

Walnuts are generally problem-free, but may come under attack from walnut leaf blight and walnut blotch, which cause black and brown spots on leaves and fruits. Remove and destroy any diseased plant material.

Cobnuts may become infected with powdery mildew – remove and destroy leaves and spray the tree with a suitable fungicide. Treat almonds as for peaches and nectarines.

The biggest threat to other nut trees will probably be squirrels, so net where possible, and if space allows, create a wire mesh fruit cage around trees.

'Broadview'

This slow-growing and relatively compact variety becomes productive earlier than most walnut trees, usually three to four years after planting. It is very hardy and flowers after the frosts, reliably producing heavy crops of well-flavoured nuts.

- unsuitable for containers
- late autumn to late winter
- good resistance
- hardy
- self-fertile
- late autumn

'Franquette'

This large, slow-growing tree produces the finest flavoured walnuts. The kernels have a high oil content which makes them sweet and moist. The trees will crop within three to four years of planting, producing good crops late in the season.

- unsuitable for containers
- late autumn to late winter
- good resistance
- hardy
- self-fertile
- mid-autumn

'Lara'

A modern introduction that bears early, heavy crops of walnuts. This spur-bearing tree is more dwarf than other varieties. The good-quality nuts are delicious eaten dried or fresh, with a distinctive creamy flavour.

- unsuitable for containers
- late autumn to early winter
- good resistance
- hardy
- self-fertile
- early autumn

'Lake English'

This US-only variety originated in an area extending from the Balkans to the Himalayas. It is hardy, productive, and somewhat self-pollinating, though it sets heavier quantities of nuts if another walnut variety is nearby.

- unsuitable for containers
- early spring to autumn
- some resistance
- hardy
- partially self-fertile
- early to mid-autumn

'Franquette'

'Mandaline'

This sweet almond grows well in colder climates, flowering in late spring after most frosts, and is a good pollinator for other trees. The soft-shelled nuts fall when ripe, are easy to crack, and contain delicious sweet kernels.

- unsuitable for containers
- late autumn to late winter
- good resistance
- hardy
- self-fertile
- mid-autumn

'Robijn'

This attractive tree is a reliable cropper. The light pink, spring blossom may need protection from frost in order to produce heavy crops of soft-shelled, sweet almonds. Avoid planting near peaches, to prevent hybridization and bitter-tasting nuts.

- unsuitable for containers
- late autumn to early winter
- good resistance
- hardy
- self-fertile
- early autumn

'Kentish Cob'

Also known as 'Lambert's Filbert', this is a popular commercial variety due to its heavy crops of long, flat nuts with shaggy husks. The nuts ripen early and are delicious eaten fresh.

- unsuitable for containers
- late autumn to early winter
- good resistance
- hardy
- needs 2 pollinators
- late summer to early autumn

'Webb's Prize Cob'

A new, strong-growing variety that produces heavy crops of long, large nuts. The cobnuts have a sweet flavour, whether eaten green or allowed to ripen. The trees are most productive when grown in groups.

- unsuitable for containers
- late autumn to late winter
- good resistance
- hardy
- needs 2 pollinators
- mid-autumn

'Regal'

A relatively compact sweet chestnut tree that is ideal for large gardens. The fragrant mid-season blossom gives way to clusters of spiky nuts that fall to the ground when ripe. Nuts are produced within two or three years of planting.

- unsuitable for containers
- late autumn to late winter
- good resistance
- hardy
- needs 2 pollinators
- mid-autumn

'Maraval'

This new French hybrid crops earlier in its life than most other sweet chestnut varieties, just two years after planting. Clusters of spiky shells are borne mid-season that encase large, shiny, dark mahogany-red nuts, with an excellent flavour.

- unsuitable for containers
- late autumn to late winter
- good resistance
- hardy
- partially self-fertile
- mid-autumn

'Marigoule'

An early to mid-season, vigorous variety that produces heavy yields of large, dark brown sweet chestnuts that fall when ripe. The tree bears fruits within two to four years, and is the best variety to grow without other pollinators.

- unsuitable for containers
- late autumn to late winter
- good resistance
- hardy
- partially self-fertile
- early to mid-autumn

'Marron de Lyon'

A reliable French sweet chestnut that bears crops from an early age, often two or three years after planting. A compact tree, it bears single, large kernels, rather than clusters of two or four, each with a delicious, sweet flavour.

- unsuitable for containers
- late autumn to late winter
- good resistance
- hardy
- self-fertile
- mid-autumn

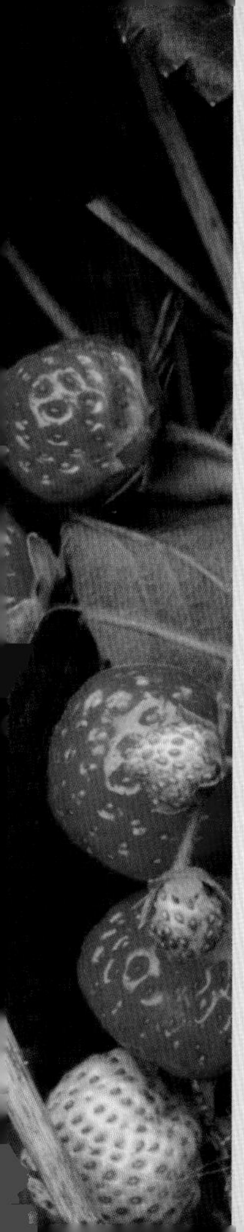

Soft Fruits

- Grapevines
- Strawberries
- Raspberries
- Blackberries and hybrid berries
- Gooseberries
- Blackcurrants, Whitecurrants, and Redcurrants
- Blueberries
- Cranberries
- Melons

GRAPEVINES *Vitis vinifera*

Scrambling grapevines are highly ornamental as well as productive, and look wonderful trained over an arch or used to create a screen. Grapes can be grown for wine-making or for eating fresh – some grape varieties are suitable for both – although sweet dessert grapes will need to be grown under cover in the UK. If you don't have much space, grow a vine in a container and train it into a standard.

	SPRING	SUMMER	AUTUMN	WINTER
PLANT				
HARVEST				

PLANTING INDOORS

Vines can be planted under cover in a greenhouse, or planted just outside and trained through a hole in the wall or vent. Planting outside and training in will mean that you do not need to water the vine as often, as its roots will run deep outside. However, the soil will warm up more slowly.

If you plant vines inside you will need to ensure that you give the plant the water, nutrients, and soil conditions that it needs. Grow indoor grapevines as cordons, and allow them about 1–1.2m (3–4ft) space. Some varieties suit containers.

PLANTING OUTDOORS

Grapevines tolerate most soil types, and ideally like a neutral

Buy only certified disease-free plants.

pH. Plant vines out in early spring, at a depth of about 30cm (12in).

Grapes are vigorous plants both above and below ground. The amount of space you need to allow your vine depends on how you train it. Cordons will need 1–1.2m (3–4ft), guyots 1m (3ft), and double guyots 1.5–2m (5–6ft) (see tip box on p.110 for details).

CARE OF INDOOR VINES

Ensure your vines receive enough water, especially while fruits are developing, but do not allow them to become waterlogged. Dessert grapes will need thinning to encourage larger fruits – using scissors, reduce each bunch by about a third.

Thin bunches to encourage larger fruits.

Although most grapevines are self-fertile, those grown undercover need help because they are not exposed to the wind – their usual method of pollination. Shake the vine gently to help it transfer its pollen. Move container-grown plants outside for a month in winter – the cold induces flowering.

In winter, feed the vines with a high-nitrogen fertilizer, and mulch around them with well-rotted manure or garden compost. Do not allow the mulch to touch the vine stems.

Ensure that vines are kept well-ventilated by opening greenhouse vents over winter to allow air to circulate. It is important not to allow the air to become stagnant, as diseases will thrive in these conditions.

TIP   PRUNING AND TRAINING

All grapevines will require annual pruning in winter, while the plant is dormant. Vines can be trained into cordons, which are the most common greenhouse form, with the fruiting stems branching from a vertical main stem. For guyot shapes, the fruiting stems branch upwards from the main horizontal branches. Ensure that you provide your plant with adequate supports, and tie in stems securely.

For cordons, remove the weakest side-shoots, and train along wires.

Do not allow the temperature to drop below 5°C (41°F).

Scrape away any old bark, where pests such as red spider mite may be hiding. Remove any bugs by hand and use an appropriate insecticide.

Plants will become heavy over time and will need pruning and training (see tip box left).

CARE OF OUTDOOR VINES

Feed and mulch outdoor vines as for indoor-grown types, and water newly planted vines in dry spells; once established they will not require further watering.

Thin foliage in late summer to allow sunlight to reach the fruits; trim back with sterile secateurs, taking care not to touch the delicate fruits. Prune and train as for indoor vines (see tip box).

HARVESTING AND STORING

As fruits ripen, their skins become slightly translucent and develop a bloom. Sample the fruits to check whether they are fully ripe, and use scissors or secateurs to cut a whole bunch free at a time. This helps to prevent damage to the fruits. Once picked, grapes will not keep fresh for more than a few days, so eat them or use them as soon as possible after harvesting.

PESTS AND DISEASES

Due to the higher temperatures, grapes grown in greenhouses are more at risk from pests and diseases than those grown outside, although outside vines may need to be netted to prevent birds stealing the fruits.

Common diseases include grey mould, and downy and powdery mildew. Common pests include mealy bug and red spider mite. Be vigilant, and inspect for early signs of damage. It is especially important to maintain good garden hygiene in the warm climate of the greenhouse.

Ensure that plants have sufficient space and ventilation, and that they are neither over- or under-watered. Also be aware that vines are easily damaged by weedkillers, and can be prone to magnesium deficiency.

Vine leaf blister mite (left) create yellow-brown blisters on leaves. Powdery mildew (right) coats the fruits, causing them to split.

'New York Muscat' ♀

This black grape grows well outdoors on a sunny wall, producing good yields of high-quality fruits that can be eaten fresh, or used to make sweet white wine. The oval, reddish-blue grapes have a blackcurrant flavour and few seeds.

- unsuitable for containers
- early spring
- excellent resistance
- hardy
- self-fertile
- early autumn

'Bacchus'

An excellent dual-purpose vine that is suitable for growing outdoors as well as indoors. The seeded, green grapes have a good flavour, and are reliably borne in heavy yields early in the harvesting season.

- unsuitable for containers
- early spring
- good resistance
- hardy
- self-fertile
- late summer

'Phönix'

A popular hybrid, this white outdoor variety bears generous bunches of large, green grapes that yellow as they ripen. They have a light muscat aroma and excellent flavour, making them ideal for eating or wine-making.

- unsuitable for containers
- early spring
- good resistance
- hardy
- self-fertile
- mid-autumn

'Regent'

A fairly vigorous hybrid vine that bears good yields of very large, blue-black grapes with a sweet, refreshing flavour. In hot summers the fruit ripens to true black. The autumn foliage takes on fiery orange and red colours.

- unsuitable for containers
- early spring
- excellent resistance
- hardy
- self-fertile
- early to mid-autumn

'Himrod'

This American variety bears loose clusters of small- to medium-sized, yellow fruits of outstanding flavour. It is one of the best white, seedless table grapes for colder areas; fruits can also be used for juice or raisins.

- unsuitable for containers
- early spring
- some resistance
- hardy
- self-fertile
- late summer to early autumn

'Muscat Bleu'

This mildew-resistant, vigorous variety bears reliable, early crops of blue-black, juicy grapes that are good for eating fresh or wine-making. An attractive ornamental vine, the leaves take on a red flush in autumn.

- unsuitable for containers
- late winter to early spring
- good resistance
- hardy
- self-fertile
- early autumn

'Interlaken'

This sister to 'Himrod' is a good choice for locations with short growing seasons. The compact, medium size clusters of seedless, green to golden grapes ripen very early, and are excellent for eating fresh and drying. Vines are moderately mildew-resistant.

- unsuitable for containers
- early spring
- some resistance
- hardy
- self-fertile
- late summer

'Siegerrebe'

A hybrid variety's parentage includes the spicy 'Gewürztraminer' grape. The medium-sized, golden-brown grapes mature early with a sweet, aromatic taste. The fruits can be left to ripen on the vine for a more intense flavour.

- unsuitable for containers
- early spring
- good resistance
- hardy
- self-fertile
- early autumn

'Palatina'

A new German variety that is perfect for home cultivation, reliably bearing good crops early in the season. The vines produce large bunches of green, very juicy fruits that are delicious eaten fresh or used to make wine.

- unsuitable for containers
- late winter to early spring
- good resistance
- hardy
- self-fertile
- early autumn

'Boskoop Glory' ♀

This spectacular-looking, reliable, variety bears heavy yields of blue-black grapes in large bunches, followed by dramatic purple foliage. Fruits have a good flavour, and can be eaten fresh or used in wine-making.

- unsuitable for containers
- early spring
- good resistance
- hardy
- self-fertile
- mid-autumn

'Siegerrebe'

STRAWBERRIES *Fragaria* x *ananassa* and *F. fresca*

Picked and eaten fresh from the garden, served up with cream and meringue, or used for jams and puddings, strawberries are the quintessential summer treat. They are classified according to their fruiting habits. Summer-bearing do just that, perpetual varieties fruit sporadically from summer to autumn, while day-neutral strawberries fruit indoors or out, wherever the weather is warm enough.

	SPRING	SUMMER	AUTUMN	WINTER
PLANT				
HARVEST				

PLANTING

Although it is possible to grow strawberries from seed it is much easier to buy healthy, disease-free plants or runners. Runners will either be fresh and dug up just before purchase, or will have been cold-stored – kept at just below freezing point until they are thawed out and ready to sell.

Plant out fresh summer-bearing and perpetual types mid- to late summer; cold-stored runners between late spring and early summer, and plant day-neutral types at any time of year.

Strawberries prefer a sunny, site with free-draining soil, and they will tolerate slightly acidic conditions. They can also be grown in a variety of containers (see tip box on p.119).

Firm plants in gently after planting.

Dig in well-rotted manure or compost before planting, to improve the soil structure and increase its fertility.

Ensure that crops have enough space – they need about 45cm (18in) between plants, and about 75cm (30in) between rows. When planting, ensure that the crown of the plants are kept above soil level, and water in well.

Strawberries are commonly grown through plastic sheeting as this warms the soil, prevents the fruits being splashed with mud, and also suppresses weeds. Create a 1m (3ft) wide mound of soil the length of your row. Lay a sheet of plastic over it and then bury the edges so that it is weighed down tight. Cut slits and plant the runners through them.

Protect young plants with a cloche.

If there is a risk of frost, cover young plants with a cloche (see image, right) or cold frame. To fruit year-round strawberries, they will need to be brought under cover in autumn.

CROP CARE

Ensure that plants are kept well-watered – especially those in containers as their soil will dry out much faster than those planted in the ground. However, be careful not to over-water the plants. Take care not to splash the berries when watering as this may encourage them to rot. Feed plants with a general fertilizer in early to mid-spring.

To prevent fruits from sitting directly in the soil it is common

TIP   MULCHING

Mulching around your plants with straw serves many useful purposes: it deters slugs and snails, keeps fruits ventilated and dry, and also protects them from getting covered with soil.

- Carefully lift the leaves and fruits and tuck a thick layer of clean, dry straw underneath them.
- Place strawberry mats around plant stems. Mats can be dried, brushed off, and re-used the following year.

Keeping fruits dry and cushioned minimizes the chance of them spoiling.

to mulch around them with straw, or use fibre mats around the base of plants (see tip box, left).

Rotate your strawberry crops every few years to prevent a build up of diseases in the soil. Plants should last for about two to three years, their yields decreasing year-on-year, so plant replacements in a fresh bed, and do not re-use the original plot for several years, for either strawberries or raspberries.

HARVESTING AND STORING

Strawberries are relatively quick to ripen and are ready to pick when the fruits have become fully red. They do not store well however, so be prepared to eat them or use them for cooking as soon as possible after harvesting.

PESTS AND DISEASES

Strawberries are most commonly afflicted by viruses, grey mould, slugs and snails, and birds. Buy plants that are healthy and disease-free, and rotate every few years to reduce the risk of diseases spreading. Do not wet the fruits or foliage, and keep plants well-ventilated to prevent grey mould. Mulching with straw helps to improve ventilation and it will deter slugs and snails, too. Use fine netting to deter birds.

TIP CONTAINERS

Strawberry plants will grow happily in containers as long as you ensure that their soil is well-drained and that they have enough root space. Give plants full sun, and make sure that containers do not dry out. Why not experiment and grow strawberries in unusual recycled containers (see p.15).

- It is fairly common to see strawberries planted in hanging baskets, which has the added advantage of keeping the plants out of the path of slugs and snails.
- Growing bags are useful since they come with their own form of "plastic sheeting".
- Special strawberry planters are also commonly used – place a plant in each of the "cups". These are both space-efficient and ornamental.

Move your strawberry pots to give your plants the best possible conditions. They need protection against late frosts, and full sun when fruits are ripening.

'Albion'

'Albion'

This new variety is popular with organic growers because of its excellent disease resistance and high yields. This perpetual strawberry produces mouth-wateringly sweet, large, bright red berries from early summer right into the autumn.

- suitable for containers
- late spring to late summer
- good resistance
- hardy
- self-fertile
- early summer to late autumn

'Malling Opal'

This is considered one of the best perpetual-fruiting strawberries. The plants have good disease resistance and bear consistently heavy yields of large, red, sugar-sweet berries over a long season, cropping earlier than most and continuing into the autumn.

- suitable for containers
- late spring to late summer
- good resistance
- hardy
- self-fertile
- early summer to mid-autumn

'Alpine'

This US-only variety bears small fruits with an intense wild-strawberry flavour. A compact habit, all-season production, and few runners make this wild strawberry an excellent choice for growing in a container.

- suitable for containers
- late spring to late summer
- some resistance
- hardy
- self-fertile
- early summer to autumn

'Malling Pearl'

This vigorous perpetual variety is a heavy cropper, producing good yields of large, attractive, red fruits, with a juicy texture and sweet flavour. The fruits appear from midsummer until mid-autumn and store well.

- suitable for containers
- late spring to late summer
- some resistance
- hardy
- self-fertile
- midsummer to mid-autumn

'Aromel' ♀

This traditional favourite is a perpetual-fruiting variety that is still popular today. Moderate yields of medium–large, bright red, juicy fruits are borne over a long season in small flushes. The berries produced have an outstanding flavour.

- suitable for containers
- late spring to late summer
- some resistance
- hardy
- self-fertile
- midsummer

'Mara des Bois'

This traditional variety combines the flavour of wild fruits with the size of modern hybrids. A perpetual fruiter, it bears good yields over a long period; when fully ripe the delicious, aromatic berries are deep red.

- suitable for containers
- late spring to late summer
- good resistance
- hardy
- self-fertile
- mid-spring to late summer

'Tristar'

This US-only variety bears a steady, all-season yield of deep red, flavourful, medium-sized fruits. These disease-resistant and widely adaptable plants can be grown in pots indoors for a longer harvest.

- suitable for containers
- late spring to late summer
- good resistance
- hardy
- self-fertile
- spring to autumn

'Mae'

One of the earliest summer-bearing varieties, 'Mae' can produce decent crops in mid-spring if grown under cloches, or a couple of weeks later if grown unprotected. The large, red berries have an excellent sweet flavour and a firm, juicy texture.

- suitable for containers
- late spring to late summer
- good resistance
- hardy
- self-fertile
- mid- to late spring

'Elsanta'

A Dutch summer-bearing variety, this is considered to be an improvement on 'Cambridge Favourite'. It produces an abundance of attractive fruits that are a glossy orange-red colour, with a very good flavour, and which store exceptionally well.

- suitable for containers
- late spring to late summer
- good resistance
- hardy
- self-fertile
- midsummer

'Cambridge Favourite'

A traditional summer-bearing variety that is easy to grow, reliable, and has a long life. It is susceptible to a few diseases but will produce heavy yields of juicy, orange-red fruits with an excellent flavour early in the season.

- suitable for containers
- late spring to late summer
- some resistance
- hardy
- self-fertile
- midsummer

'Hapil'

A high-yielding and vigorous summer-bearing variety that produces large, firm, bright red fruits that are full of flavour, mid-season. It is a good choice for light soils and dry conditions but it is prone to verticillium wilt.

- suitable for containers
- late spring to late summer
- some resistance
- hardy
- self-fertile
- midsummer

'Symphony' ♔

This strong-growing variety is vigorous even in colder conditions and has excellent disease resistance. The large, bright, glossy fruits have a wonderful flavour and a firm, juicy texture. They are produced in mid-season and store well.

- suitable for containers
- late spring to late summer
- good resistance
- hardy
- self-fertile
- mid- to late summer

'Pegasus' ♔

This reliable cropper has possibly the best disease resistance of the late season strawberries – it is particularly resistant to mildew and verticillium wilt. It is a popular variety that produces heavy crops of sweet, red berries, with a firm but juicy texture.

- suitable for containers
- late spring to late summer
- good resistance
- hardy
- self-fertile
- late summer

'Florence'

These vigorous plants are prolific croppers and have outstanding resistance to many fungal leaf diseases. The large, firm, glossy, dark red fruits have a very good, sweet flavour and are produced late in the season.

- suitable for containers
- late spring to late summer
- excellent resistance
- hardy
- self-fertile
- late summer

'Sonata'

A new, high-quality, mid-season variety that is becoming popular with commercial growers. It can tolerate hot weather and heavy rain, and still produce good yields of large, uniformly-shaped, juicy, red fruits with excellent flavour.

- suitable for containers
- late spring to late summer
- good resistance
- hardy
- self-fertile
- midsummer

'Honeoye' ♛

This early season strawberry
is the most popular variety
amongst commercial growers.
It bears heavy crops of bright
red, medium-sized, very firm
fruits with a superb flavour.
It tolerates colder conditions but
is susceptible to verticillium wilt.

- suitable for containers
- late spring to late summer
- some resistance
- hardy
- self-fertile
- midsummer

'Rhapsody' ♛

This late summer variety is
favoured by pick-your-own
growers for its good disease
resistance and large yields; it also
grows well in colder areas. The
medium–large, conical fruits are
glossy red with a sweet flavour.

- suitable for containers
- late spring to late summer
- good resistance
- hardy
- self-fertile
- late summer

'Alice' ♛

Considered one of the best
mid-season varieties for its good
disease resistance and its easy
picking. Plants produce heavy
crops of medium to large, bright
orange-red berries with a juicy
texture and sweet flavour.

- suitable for containers
- late spring to late summer
- some resistance
- hardy
- self-fertile
- early to midsummer

RASPBERRIES *Rubus idaeus*

Fresh, juicy raspberries are both tangy and delicious, perfect for eating fresh or using in jams or puddings. Since they are happy to grow in large containers, they can be accommodated in almost any garden. There are two main types: summer-fruiting and autumn-fruiting. For pruning purposes it is important to keep the two types separate; summer types fruit on the previous year's canes, and autumn types on new growth.

	SPRING	SUMMER	AUTUMN	WINTER
PLANT				
HARVEST				

PLANTING

Raspberry plants are supplied as canes, and although they look very small and neat at this early stage, it won't be long before they become large and trailing, so ensure that you allocate them enough space in your plot or container. Raspberries need a good support system, so prepare this before planting in the ground (see tip box, p.129) – use sturdy posts and horizontal wires, as plants can grow quite heavy.

Raspberries need full sun and a sheltered location to protect the upright plants from the wind. They prefer a well-drained, fertile soil, so dig in some well-rotted manure or compost before planting. They prefer a pH of between 6 and 6.5.

Canes will produce leafy growth in spring.

Plant raspberry canes at a depth of about 5–8cm (2–3in), and then cut the cane down to a height of approximately 30cm (12in). Leave 40cm (16in) between each cane, and 2m (6ft) between rows.

It may be easier to provide the required acidic conditions if you grow the canes in containers, although they will not produce

as large a crop. Container-grown canes will also need support – consider growing them against trellis or insert several bamboo canes, and secure plants with string or garden twine. Plant two or three canes per 30cm (12in) container.

Tie developing stems in to bamboo canes

CROP CARE

Keep canes well-watered, especially during fruiting, bearing in mind that container-grown plants will dry out more quickly than those planted directly in the ground.

Feed with a balanced fertilizer in early spring and then mulch with well-rotted manure or compost. Mulch again with straw in early summer. When canes reach about 75cm (30in) in height, thin them out. Remove any weak or diseased looking canes first. You may need to construct netting to protect the fruits from birds, which can strip a bush in no time.

Prune summer-fruiting types in late summer, as for blackberries (see p.132), after harvesting. Tie in the new growth and lightly

PESTS AND DISEASES

Although cane spot and fungal leaf spots are a potential problem for raspberries, resistant cultivars are available. Other problems include:
■ Birds – use netting to deter them.
■ Raspberry beetle and raspberry leaf and bud mite – hoe around the soil to bring them to the soil surface, and cut down stems after fruiting.
■ Raspberry viruses – remove and destroy infected canes. Rotate crops.

Raspberry cane spot virus creates purple, white-centred spots on leaves.

prune. Leave the fruited canes of autumn-fruiting varieties in the ground over winter. They should be cut right back in late winter–early spring. New canes will appear in spring. Do not prune container-grown raspberries.

HARVESTING

Raspberries will either be a summer- or autumn-fruiting variety, and will be ready to harvest accordingly. When berries are plump and juicy, pull them off the plant leaving the core attached to the bush. Eat them as soon as possible.

Once stems have fruited, cut summer-fruiting canes to ground level and cover with compost to help them decompose – this helps to prevent infection from entering the plant. If growth has been particularly good you may need to thin out the remaining stems to leave one approximately every 10cm (4in). New plants can be propagated from healthy, disease-free suckers or new canes, which should be carefully removed from the rootball with their roots intact, and then re-planted.

STORING

Raspberries will not keep long after they ripen. Freeze them to prevent them spoiling.

TIP   TRAINING

There are two good reasons for training raspberries: firstly, it is important that they receive adequate space and ventilation, and are not allowed to trail on the ground, where they become easy prey for pests and diseases. Secondly, it is much easier and much less painful to harvest berries from a well-trained plant.

There are many different ways to train your canes. Using lines of posts with horizontal wires fixed between them. Canes can be planted along the bottom of each line of posts and trained upwards (known as the hedgerow system), or planted down the middle of a set of two, then drawn upwards and diagonally out from the centre (this is known as the Scandinavian system).

When raspberries reach full height, arch them over and tie in. Plants are kept tidy, are less prone to damage, and fruits are easier to harvest.

'Tulameen' ♀

Long canes bear large, red, glossy, conical-shaped fruit with an excellent flavour, over a very long season. The highest yields are produced in midsummer. This variety has good winter hardiness and its fruits are resistant to wet weather.

- suitable for containers
- autumn to early spring
- good resistance
- hardy
- self-fertile
- mid- to late summer

'Valentina'

This early summer-fruiting variety bears heavy crops of succulent, bright pink-apricot fruits, with an excellent flavour. The upright, spine-free canes have very good pest and disease resistance, especially to aphids.

- suitable for containers
- autumn to early spring
- good resistance
- hardy
- self-fertile
- early to midsummer

'Glen Prosen' ♀

This new, popular, summer-fruiting variety bears heavy yields of exceptionally firm, round, red fruits that are full of flavour. The spine-free canes have good resistance to aphids and some viruses, and are easy to train.

- suitable for containers
- autumn to early spring
- good resistance
- hardy
- self-fertile
- midsummer

'Joan J' ♀

A new, spine-free, autumn-fruiting variety. The berries are produced in plentiful supply over a very long picking season – from midsummer until the first frosts. The large red fruits have an excellent flavour, which is preserved well when frozen.

- suitable for containers
- autumn to early spring
- good resistance
- hardy
- self-fertile
- late summer to early autumn

'All Gold' ♀

Developed from a sport of 'Autumn Bliss', this variety, also known as 'Fall Gold', bears large, golden-yellow berries. Like its parent plant, the fruits are ready in autumn and have a superior flavour to any red variety.

- suitable for containers
- autumn to early spring
- excellent resistance
- hardy
- self-fertile
- late summer to mid-autumn

BLACKBERRIES AND
HYBRID BERRIES *Rubus fruticosus* and various

Blackberries and their many hybrids, such as loganberries and tayberries,
are all descended from wild brambles and will need careful training
to prevent them from trailing on the ground or taking over your plot.
However, the taste of these sweet, juicy berries is well worth the effort.

	SPRING	SUMMER	AUTUMN	WINTER
PLANT				
HARVEST				

PLANTING

Prepare your site in advance –
dig in some well-rotted manure
or compost, and weed well.
Blackberries and other hybrid
berries will need plenty of space
and a good support system –
both for the health of the plant,
and for easy picking. There are
several options – train them over
an arch, or insert posts along
the length of your row and fix
horizontal wires between them
(see raspberries). The trailing
stems can then be looped over
the wires and tied in.

Blackberries and hybrid
berries prefer soil that is well
drained, and need shelter from
the wind, but while blackberries
will tolerate partial shade, hybrid
berries need full sun. Plant canes

Train your blackberries over wires.

to the depth of their existing soil
marks, leaving 3–5m (10–15ft)
between plants, depending on
the variety chosen.

CROP CARE

Mulch plants with straw in early
spring and pull up any suckers
that appear. Cut down canes once
they have fruited. New canes will
grow in the second year. The
plants are generally undamaged

by frosts since they flower relatively late in the year.

HARVESTING

Harvest berries every few days when they are plump, taking the core with them. Do not leave them too long or they will spoil.

STORING

The berries will not keep long, so freeze them if necessary. To prevent them forming a solid mass, space them out on a baking sheet and place in the freezer. When frozen, transfer to a container. They will keep their shape and can be used singly.

PESTS AND DISEASES

Blackberries and hybrid berries suffer the same problems as other cane fruits, especially raspberry spur blight, raspberry beetle, and grey mould. Practise good garden hygiene when pruning, and destroy infected canes.

Grey mould shrivels and rots fruits.

'Silvan' ♀

This thorny variety produces the first blackberries of the season. The large, long, dark purple-black fruits ripen in mid- to late summer and have a superb, sweet flavour. It is fairly tolerant of drought and has excellent disease resistance.

- 🪣 unsuitable for containers
- 🍂 autumn to early spring
- 🐛 excellent resistance
- ❄ hardy
- 🌸 self-fertile
- 🔒 midsummer to early autumn

'Black Butte'

This new, compact variety is notable for the exceptional size of its fruits – twice the size of other varieties. Heavy yields of rich, full-flavoured berries are borne on thorny canes, and the open habit makes picking easy.

- 🪣 unsuitable for containers
- 🍂 autumn to early spring
- 🐛 good resistance
- ❄ hardy
- 🌸 self-fertile
- 🔒 mid- to late summer

'Black Satin'

A recent introduction from the US, this thorn-free variety bears good crops of berries earlier in the season than other thornless varieties. The attractive, glossy, black fruits are very juicy and have a slightly sharp flavour.

- unsuitable for containers
- autumn to early spring
- good resistance
- hardy
- self-fertile
- late summer to early autumn

Tayberry

A blackberry and raspberry hybrid, the fruits produced are long, dark red, and juicy, with a sharp flavour. Heavy crops are borne in late summer, and since it is late-flowering it copes well with colder conditions.

- unsuitable for containers
- autumn to early spring
- good resistance
- hardy
- self-fertile
- late summer to early autumn

'Ly 654' ♀

A raspberry and blackberry cross, this loganberry has thornless canes that bear heavy crops of large, elongated, red fruits over a long period. The sharp, juicy berries are best when they have ripened to a dark red.

- suitable for containers
- autumn to early spring
- good resistance
- hardy
- self-fertile
- mid- to late summer

GOOSEBERRIES *Ribes uva-crispa*

If like most people, you've only tasted shop-bought fruits,
home-grown gooseberries are often much sweeter than you might
imagine. Dessert varieties are delicious eaten fresh from the bush;
culinary types make excellent jams and puddings; or grow dual-purpose
berries and enjoy the best of both worlds. Easy to grow, and happily
trained into cordons or fans, gooseberries are an asset to any garden.

	SPRING	SUMMER	AUTUMN	WINTER
PLANT				
HARVEST				

PLANTING

Plant bare-root gooseberries
between autumn and early
spring, and container-grown
plants at any time. Ensure
that container-grown plants
have not become pot-bound,
and select bushes that have a
clear 15cm (6in) of stem between
the roots and young branches.

Gooseberries need a well-
drained soil, so dig in some
well-rotted manure or compost
to improve the structure if
necessary; they prefer a slightly
acid pH. Bushes will need frost
protection since they produce
blossom early in the year, so
site them carefully, avoiding
frost pockets, or grow them
in pots so they can be moved
under cover in colder months.

Prune new side-shoots in summer.

Gooseberries are self-fertile, so
you will only need one plant to
produce a crop; if you grow more
than one, bushes will need 1.5m
(5ft) space. Plant single-stemmed
cordons 35cm (14in) apart.

CROP CARE

Stake young plants and protect
against frost. Ensure that bushes
have plenty of water, apply a
general fertilizer, and mulch in

early spring. Net against birds. Prune bushes hard in summer and winter – aim to create an open, well-ventilated structure.

HARVESTING AND STORING

Staggering your harvest by picking alternate berries will allow those left on the bush to grow larger and juicier; begin in late spring and continue throughout the summer. Early dual-purpose berries should be used for cooking; later ones for eating fresh. Gooseberries will store for a couple of weeks in the fridge, or they can be frozen for later use.

PESTS AND DISEASES

Gooseberries are vulnerable to a number of pests and diseases, particularly gooseberry sawfly and gooseberry mildew. Remove affected fruits or foliage and spray with insecticide. Use netting to deter birds.

Gooseberry sawfly eat foliage.

'Hinnonmaki Red'

This vigorous, very hardy variety produces heavy crops of large, dark red fruits with an excellent flavour, suitable for both dessert and culinary purposes. Berries are similar to 'Whinham's Industry', but have a greater resistance to mildew.

- suitable for containers
- late autumn to early spring
- good resistance
- hardy
- self-fertile
- midsummer

'Leveller' ♥

This culinary and dessert variety bears exceptionally flavourful, very large, downy, yellow-green fruits that are borne in abundance. It has a spreading, slightly drooping habit, and requires fertile, well-drained soil.

- suitable for containers
- late autumn to early spring
- some resistance
- hardy
- self-fertile
- early to midsummer

'Pax'

The sweet, rounded, dark red fruits are suitable for both culinary and dessert use. While young plants have some thorns, in maturity this is a thornless bush with a spreading habit. It is moderately mildew-resistant.

- suitable for containers
- late autumn to early spring
- some resistance
- hardy
- self-fertile
- midsummer

'Hinnonmaki Yellow'

Heavy crops of variably-sized, yellow fruits, from medium to very large, are produced from early to midsummer on vigorous, spreading bushes. A dual-purpose variety with a lovely flavour, it is suitable for organic growers as it has some resistance to mildew.

- suitable for containers
- late autumn to early spring
- good resistance
- hardy
- self-fertile
- early to midsummer

'Langley Gage'

The greenish-white, translucent-skinned fruits of this dessert variety are exceptionally sweet. It makes a strong-growing bush that will need pruning, as fruits are borne in the centre and can be difficult to pick.

- suitable for containers
- late autumn to early spring
- poor resistance
- hardy
- self-fertile
- midsummer

'Rokula'

This early-fruiting dessert variety has attractive, dark red berries with a sweet flavour. Bushes are moderately vigorous with a drooping habit. It is mildew-resistant, but fruit is prone to cracking if rainfall is erratic.

- suitable for containers
- late autumn to early spring
- good resistance
- hardy
- self-fertile
- early summer

'Careless' ♀

A fast-growing, heavy-cropping variety with thorny stems, it bears smooth, large berries that ripen to a milky greenish-white. Picked early, they are excellent for culinary use; ripe, they are delicious dessert berries. It is susceptible to mildew.

- suitable for containers
- late autumn to early spring
- some resistance
- hardy
- self-fertile
- midsummer

'Invicta' ♀

A fast-growing, mildew-resistant variety for both dessert and culinary use, it bears abundant large, yellowish-green fruits with a good flavour. Its very thorny stems are amenable to training against a wall, and it is tolerant of shade and most soil types.

- suitable for containers
- late autumn to early spring
- good resistance
- hardy
- self-fertile
- midsummer

'Lancashire Lad'

This variety has been popular since the early 19th century for its reliable crops of large berries, which can be cooked while green in early summer, or left to ripen to dark red for dessert use. It is a strong-growing, compact bush.

- suitable for containers
- late autumn to early spring
- good resistance
- hardy
- self-fertile
- early to midsummer

'Whinham's Industry' ♀

Large, dark red fruits, good for cooking and with lovely dessert flavour, are borne by this variety. It has more tolerance of shade and heavy or poor soils than most varieties, but it is very susceptible to mildew.

- suitable for containers
- late autumn to early spring
- some resistance
- hardy
- self-fertile
- midsummer

'Invicta'

BLACK-, WHITE-, AND REDCURRANTS *Ribes nigrum and R. rubrum*

Delicious used in puddings, pies, or jams, these beautiful berries are an eye-catching addition to any garden. Currants are fully hardy, very tough, and tolerant of most soil types, although blackcurrants prefer a more fertile soil, and more direct sunlight than white- and redcurrants.

	SPRING	SUMMER	AUTUMN	WINTER
PLANT				
HARVEST				

PLANTING

Ensure that you buy certified disease-free, one- or two-year-old plants, and ensure that container-grown plants have not become pot-bound. These can be planted at any time of year, as long as you give them enough water, but bare-root types should be planted in autumn to early spring.

Bushes can become quite large, so make sure that you give them enough space – about 1.5m (5ft) between plants. White- and redcurrants can also be trained into cordons or fans, requiring less ground space. All currants are self-fertile, so will fruit with only one plant.

Dig in well-rotted manure or compost just before planting, and site in a sheltered, frost-free spot.

Mulch currant bushes in early spring.

Remove any weeds, and if necessary double-dig the site to improve the drainage. Blackcurrant plants need to be planted 5cm (2in) lower than they were in their original pot, to encourage the plant to produce strong new stems. All currants have relatively shallow roots so can be planted in containers if need be, and then moved undercover in colder months.

CROP CARE

Currants need plenty of water and should not be allowed to dry out. Feed with a general fertilizer and mulch in early spring. Bushes will need careful pruning; red- and whitecurrants in spring and summer; blackcurrants in winter.

HARVESTING

White- and redcurrants will be ready to harvest from early summer. They are delicate fruits, so cut the whole strig loose when they are ripe. Blackcurrants can be harvested this way too in midsummer, or later as individual berries, when fully ripe.

PESTS AND DISEASES

Birds can strip a bush of its currants, so use netting to deter them. Other common problems include currant blister, aphids, grey mould, American gooseberry mildew, and reversion disease. Practise good garden hygiene.

Currant blister aphids distort leaves.

'Ben Sarek'

A dwarf bush, reaching only 1.2m (4ft), it is ideal for containers and small gardens and bears heavy crops mid-season. The large, black berries have an excellent flavour and are so abundant that the branches will need support.

- suitable for containers
- autumn to early spring
- good resistance
- hardy
- self-fertile
- midsummer

'Titania'

This new blackcurrant variety from Sweden is possibly the most frost-resistant and has excellent disease resistance. Large, black berries with a high juice content and lots of flavour keep well on the bush over a long season.

- suitable for containers
- autumn to early spring
- excellent resistance
- hardy
- self-fertile
- midsummer to mid-autumn

'Baldwin'

An old and still popular variety, this compact bush bears heavy crops in mid- to late season. The medium–large, black, tart berries are very high in vitamin C, and keep well on the plant without splitting.

- suitable for containers
- autumn to early spring
- good resistance
- hardy
- self-fertile
- mid- to late summer

'Ben Lomond' ♛

A popular variety, this upright, fairly compact bush flowers late and so has some frost resistance. As a result, very heavy yields of large, short-stalked, sweet but acidic-flavoured blackcurrants are borne later in the season.

 suitable for containers
autumn to early spring
good resistance
hardy
self-fertile
late summer

'Ben Connan' ♛

A compact but high-yielding blackcurrant, this variety is ideal for small gardens. The bush bears unusually large fruits with an excellent, rich flavour that are easy to pick. It has good mildew resistance and is tolerant of frost.

suitable for containers
autumn to early spring
good resistance
hardy
self-fertile
midsummer

'Ben Gairn'

A new, compact variety ideal for small gardens. Although one of the earliest to flower and ripen, it is not completely frost-tolerant but is resistant to reversion virus. The large, black, very juicy fruits have an excellent flavour.

suitable for containers
autumn to early spring
good resistance
hardy
self-fertile
midsummer

'Blanka'

This new, reliable variety produces the heaviest yields of all whitecurrants over a long season. The large, almost transparent, ivory-white berries have the best and sweetest flavour, and are borne on long strings that make picking easy.

🪣	suitable for containers
🍂	autumn to early spring
🕷	good resistance
❄	hardy
⬆	self-fertile
🔒	mid to late summer

'White Versailles'

This old favourite reliably bears the earliest whitecurrants of the season. The vigorous, upright, bushy plants produce heavy yields of large, shiny, pale yellow-white berries on long strings that have an excellent sweet flavour.

🪣	suitable for containers
🍂	autumn to early spring
🕷	good resistance
❄	hardy
⬆	self-fertile
🔒	midsummer

'Rovada'

Considered by many to be the best redcurrant variety, these bushes produce a profusion of fruits late in the season over a long picking period. The large berries are borne on long strings and have an outstanding flavour.

🪣	suitable for containers
🍂	autumn to early spring
🕷	good resistance
❄	hardy
⬆	self-fertile
🔒	mid- to late summer

'Red Lake' ♀

A well-established, popular variety that starts off the redcurrant picking season. Large bushes produce heavy yields of big, juicy, red berries with an excellent flavour. The fruits are borne on long strings, which makes picking easier.

- suitable for containers
- autumn to early spring
- good resistance
- hardy
- self-fertile
- midsummer

'Jonkheer van Tets' ♀

An established, reliable variety, it is also one of the earliest redcurrants to ripen. The heavy crops of large, bright red, juicy berries have an excellent, tart flavour. The fruits are borne on long strings, so are easier to pick.

- suitable for containers
- autumn to early spring
- good resistance
- hardy
- self-fertile
- midsummer

BLUEBERRIES *Vaccinium corymbosum*

Deliciously sweet and packed with vitamins and antioxidants, blueberries are often described as a "superfood". Eaten fresh, cooked in pies, or used to make jams and jellies, they will not disappoint. Grow at least two or three plants to ensure effective pollination and high yields, and buy two- or three-year-old plants if possible, as blueberries do not reach their full cropping potential until they are about five years old.

	SPRING	SUMMER	AUTUMN	WINTER
PLANT				
HARVEST				

PLANTING

Container-grown plants will establish more readily than bare-root types, but ensure that they have not become pot-bound. Plant both types between late autumn and early spring, as long as the ground is not frozen. Blueberries need an acidic soil in order to thrive – a pH of between 4 and 5.5 – so if necessary, prepare your soil in advance, or plant in a container, where you can easily control the growing conditions. Plant in a sheltered location, protected from strong winds, with plenty of sunshine in the summer months.

Most blueberries are self-fertile, but like most crops, their yield is increased and improved if pollinated by another variety.

Protect the early flowers against frost.

CROP CARE

If plants flower early in spring they may need protection against frost; use horticultural fleece, or bring container-grown plants under cover. Blueberries need a lot of water during growth, but use rainwater in order to maintain acidic soil conditions. Mulch around plants with bark or pine needles, and apply a general fertilizer after pruning.

HARVESTING AND STORING

Pick ripe berries once their blue skins have developed a whitish tinge. They can be harvested from midsummer through to early autumn, depending on the variety – some fruit early and some fruit late. Once picked, blueberries can be stored in the fridge for over a week, or frozen.

PESTS AND DISEASES

Ripening fruits are most at risk from birds, so use netting to protect bushes if necessary. Generally, provided that they have the right conditions, they are relatively problem free.

TIP CONTAINERS

Provide them with ericaceous compost, and blueberries will happily grow in pots or containers. Water regularly and do not allow the soil dry out. After a few years you may need to transfer your blueberry plant into a larger pot.

Place containers in a sunny location.

'Berkeley'

This popular garden variety bears attractive, powder-blue fruits with a mild flavour. It is easy to grow and has good disease resistance. In mild climates one bush will bear decent-sized yields, but it will be less productive in frost pockets.

🪣	suitable for containers
🔨	spring
✳️	good resistance
❄️	hardy
🔒	self-fertile (mid)
🔒	midsummer

'Coville'

A vigorous and spreading variety that reliably bears large, deep blue berries with a sweet flavour, very late in the season. The fruits can be left on the bush for a long time before they fall.

🪣	suitable for containers
🔨	spring
✳️	good resistance
❄️	hardy
🔒	self-fertile (late)
🔒	mid- to late summer

'Herbert'

This late-season variety is considered by many to produce the most flavoursome blueberries. A vigorous, upright bush, it bears heavy, compact clusters of very large, firm, dark blue berries that have an exceptional, sweet flavour.

- suitable for containers
- spring
- good resistance
- hardy
- self-fertile (late)
- mid- to late summer

'Duke' ♀

One of the most consistent and heaviest producers, this variety bears medium-sized, light blue, firm berries with a mild, sweet flavour. Although late-flowering, it crops early, so it is ideal for areas where the season is short.

- suitable for containers
- spring
- good resistance
- hardy
- self-fertile (early)
- midsummer

'Patriot'

A vigorous variety that produces high yields of fruits early in the season. The medium–large, dark blue berries have firm flesh and an excellent flavour. It is very hardy and is tolerant of colder locations and heavier, wetter soils.

- suitable for containers
- spring
- good resistance
- hardy
- self-fertile (early)
- midsummer

'Spartan' ♀

An early to mid-season variety that bears very large, light blue fruits with a tangy, sweet flavour. For the best crops, plant another variety nearby. The upright habit makes harvesting easy; do so before the leaves turn bright red in autumn.

🪣	suitable for containers
🌱	spring
🐛	good resistance
❄️	hardy
🔓	self-fertile (early)
🔒	midsummer

'Jersey'

One of the oldest and most reliable blueberry varieties, each bush produces large crops of dark blue, small- to medium-sized berries with a mild, sweet flavour. In autumn the leaves turn a fiery yellow-orange colour.

🪣	suitable for containers
🌱	spring
🐛	good resistance
❄️	hardy
👥	needs 1 pollinator (early)
🔒	midsummer

'Bluetta'

A vigorous and very productive variety that bears good crops of medium-sized, light blue berries with a sweet flavour. It has a compact habit, so it is good for containers, and flowers late, making it ideal for colder areas.

 suitable for containers

spring

good resistance

hardy

self-fertile (late)

early summer

'Bluecrop'

A popular, mid-season variety that bears high yields of large, firm, light blue fruits with a good flavour. It is a vigorous plant, drought- and frost-resistant, and also has attractive, fiery orange and copper leaves in autumn.

suitable for containers

spring

good resistance

hardy

self-fertile (mid)

mid- to late summer

'Earliblue'

As the name suggests, this is one of the earliest ripening varieties. The large, light blue, sweet fruits are borne in neat clusters. It is an attractive plant, with red, upright stems and dramatic crimson leaves in autumn.

suitable for containers

spring

good resistance

hardy

self-fertile (early)

mid- to late summer

CRANBERRIES *Vaccinium macrocarpon*

Cranberries are native to North American moorlands, where they thrive in boggy, slightly acidic conditions, and as long as you can provide them with the same conditions in your garden these attractive, spreading bushes will thrive. Although European varieties are generally too sharp to eat fresh from the bush, they are excellent used in cooking, especially in juices, jams, and of course, cranberry sauce.

	SPRING	SUMMER	AUTUMN	WINTER
PLANT				
HARVEST				

PLANTING

Cranberries need a constantly wet, although not waterlogged, soil with an acidic pH of between 4–5.5. It is, perhaps, unlikely that you will find these conditions naturally occurring in your garden, so consider growing cranberries in a container, where you can easily control their soil pH and moisture levels, or dig a dedicated cranberry bed, 15–20cm (6–8in) deep, and line the insides with polythene mesh or perforated plastic sheeting.

Cranberries are self-fertile, so you will only need one plant to produce a crop. Plants are supplied container-grown, so can be planted at any time of year. Saturate the soil with rainwater, which has a more acidic pH than

Control conditions in a cranberry container.

mains tap water, and then plant out the bushes 30cm (12in) apart. Leave 30cm (12in) between rows. Mulch around the plants with about 2.5cm (1in) of sand.

CROP CARE

Water the bushes regularly with rainwater, ensuring that the soil is always kept moist. Cranberries are low, spreading plants and may need pruning,

either after harvesting or in spring, if their growth gets out of hand. Trim back any excess stems. Careful pruning will encourage bushier growth.

HARVESTING

Cranberries should be ready to harvest from early autumn. They do not need to be picked immediately and can be left on the bush for several months.

STORING

Fruits will keep longer than most other berries – up to three months in the fridge – and they can also be frozen or made into sauce.

PESTS AND DISEASES

Cranberries are under threat from relatively few pests and diseases – if need be, construct netting to deter birds. You may find that they suffer from lime-induced chlorosis, caused by high levels of calcium in very alkaline soils, which prevents plants absorbing iron – leaves will turn yellow and then brown, before withering. Acidify the soil or add iron to it to combat the problem. Practise good garden hygiene when pruning bushes, and try to encourage strong, open growth and a well-ventilated structure.

'Pilgrim'

The lax habit of this plant makes it suitable as a trailing plant in a container. It bears pinkish-red flowers, followed by the largest berries of all the varieties, produced late in the season and sometimes persisting into winter.

- suitable for containers
- year round
- poor resistance
- hardy
- self-fertile
- mid-autumn

'Early Black'

This is one of the easiest varieties to grow as it is disease and frost resistant. The large, bell-shaped fruits are such a dark red they are almost black; they have a relatively sweet flavour. In autumn the blunt-tipped foliage turns a deep red.

- suitable for containers
- year round
- good resistance
- hardy
- self-fertile
- late summer to early autumn

'CN'

One of the heaviest croppers of all cranberry varieties, 'CN' produces large red fruits that produce a dark red juice. Plants have a moderately spreading habit, and are ideal for growing in a container on a patio.

- suitable for containers
- year round
- good resistance
- hardy
- self-fertile
- early autumn

'Franklin'

While it is not a vigorous plant and is slow to spread, 'Franklin' is worth growing since it is resistant to most diseases. It bears heavy crops of large to medium, round berries that are red to dark red in colour.

- suitable for containers
- year round
- good resistance
- hardy
- self-fertile
- early autumn

'Early Black'

MELONS *Cucumis melo*

Although melons are close relatives of the cucumber, in the cool, temperate climate of the UK it is almost inevitable that you will have to grow them under glass as they need high temperatures and high humidity to thrive. Melons fall into two main categories: sweet melons, such as canteloupes, honeydews, and musk melons, which have dense, juicy flesh, and watermelons, which have crisp, pink, "watery" flesh.

	SPRING	SUMMER	AUTUMN	WINTER
SOW/PLANT				
HARVEST				

SOWING

Sow seed under cover in mid-spring and then plant on in midsummer – keep the pots or trays warm, as the seed needs a temperature of at least 16°C (60°F) to germinate. Do not sow too early or the plants may become pot-bound. In warm climates, melons can be grown outdoors, provided that you cover them with a cloche or cold frame and site them in a warm and sunny position. Place cloches in position a few weeks prior to planting to warm up the soil. Be vigilant when there is any risk of frost.

Melons prefer a rich, well-draining soil with a neutral pH. Dig in well-rotted manure or compost prior to planting.

Sow three seeds to a pot in mid-spring.

CROP CARE

Keep plants well-watered but take care to wet the soil and not the stems. Open the greenhouse windows while the plants are in flower to assist pollination. Apply tomato feed weekly.

HARVESTING AND STORING

Melons should be ready for harvesting in late summer and early autumn. As ripening occurs,

the stems will begin to crack, the fruits will soften, and their sweet smell will grow stronger. Cut the stems with a sharp knife. They will keep fresh for a few weeks in the fridge once harvested.

PESTS AND DISEASES

Melons are at risk from general greenhouse pests and diseases, such as red spider mite and whitefly, as well as powdery mildew and cucumber mosaic virus. Combat these by practising good garden hygiene, and ensure that plants are well-spaced and well-ventilated. Try to prevent stem rot by keeping them dry.

TIP SUPPORT FRUITS

Ripening melons can become very heavy, and if you have trained your plants to climb there is a risk of fruit falling and becoming damaged. Tie netting or a string bag to the wire supports to take their weight.

Support heavy fruits with netting.

'Edonis' ♀

An early ripening hybrid that produces fruits of up to 600g (1¼lb) in weight, it is ideal outdoors in areas that experience colder conditions. The oval fruits have dark green grooves, and the pale orange flesh has a refreshing, delicate flavour.

🪴	unsuitable for containers
🌱	late spring
✳	good resistance
❄	not hardy
🌼	self-fertile
🔒	midsummer to early autumn

'Minnesota Midget'

An ideal cantaloupe for small spaces or containers, this very early variety produces good yields of 10cm (4in) long fruits on compact vines. The melons have a dark green, grooved skin and sweet, orange, fragrant flesh.

🪴	suitable for containers
🌱	late spring
✳	good resistance
❄	not hardy
🌼	self-fertile
🔒	late summer

'Galia'

A popular commercial variety that can be grown outdoors, this vigorous plant bears good, successive yields of fruits, which mature early in the season. The greeny-yellow skin has a "netted" appearance, and the pale green flesh is succulent and sweet.

- unsuitable for containers
- late spring
- good resistance
- not hardy
- self-fertile
- midsummer

'Emir' ♀

This early charentais-type variety was bred for the northern European climate, so it is fast-maturing and tolerant of cooler growing conditions. It bears good yields of yellow-green fruits with dark orange, sweet, juicy flesh.

- unsuitable for containers
- late spring
- good resistance
- not hardy
- self-fertile
- late summer to early autumn

'Magenta'

This hybrid charentais melon is a recent introduction, and similar in shape and size to 'Alvaro'. The variety gets its name from its reddish flesh, encased in "netted" skins with dark green stripes, which has a very sweet flavour.

- unsuitable for containers
- late spring
- good resistance
- not hardy
- self-fertile
- early autumn

'Sweetheart' ♀

A favourite variety, 'Sweetheart' is more tolerant of lower temperatures than other melons and reliably produces good yields, even in colder conditions. The charantais-type fruits have a smooth, grey-green skin and very sweet, aromatic, orange flesh.

- unsuitable for containers
- late spring
- good resistance
- not hardy
- self-fertile
- late summer to early autumn

'Ogen' ♀

This very popular variety bears fruits of up to 2kg (4½lb) in weight, with a superb, unrivalled flavour. As the melons mature the skin turns from green to golden-yellow, beneath which is a pale green, rich, aromatic and sweet flesh.

- unsuitable for containers
- late spring
- good resistance
- not hardy
- self-fertile
- late summer

'Outdoor Wonder'

A new introduction to the UK, this melon has been bred to grow outdoors even in cooler climates, and will do so happily, producing good yields of medium-sized, light green, "netted" fruits with a sweet flesh.

- unsuitable for containers
- late spring
- good resistance
- not hardy
- self-fertile
- early autumn

'Melba'

This vigorous variety is adaptable and fairly hardy, and can be grown either outdoors or in a greenhouse. 'Melba' produces fragrant, sweet, tasty fruits that have pale green, "netted" skin and rich, orange-coloured flesh.

- unsuitable for containers
- late spring
- good resistance
- not hardy
- self-fertile
- late summer to early autumn

'Ogen'

'Charentais'

This very old variety is commonly grown commercially but can also be grown under cover by less-experienced gardeners. The medium-sized, round fruits have a smooth, pale green-grey skin, and very juicy, sweet flesh that is deep orange in colour.

- unsuitable for containers
- late spring
- good resistance
- not hardy
- self-fertile
- early autumn

'Antalya'

This vigorous and productive galia type bears melons of up to 1.3kg (3lb). Fruits have an orange-yellow skin, and pale green, sweet, aromatic flesh. It is ideal for growing under cover as it resists many greenhouse diseases.

- unsuitable for containers
- late spring
- good resistance
- not hardy
- self-fertile
- late summer to early autumn

'Alvaro' ♀

This charentais-type melon bears sweet-smelling fruits up to 1kg (2lb 4oz) in weight, with dark-striped, pale green skin and orange flesh. They can be grown indoors or out, and have excellent pest and disease resistance.

- unsuitable for containers
- late spring
- excellent resistance
- not hardy
- self-fertile
- late summer to early autumn

'Blenheim Orange'

This old favourite is still popular for its sweet, musk flavour. The fruits can become up to 1kg (2lb 4oz) in weight, and have a green, "netted" skin, with flesh that is quite red. Grow under cover for the best yields.

- unsuitable for containers
- late spring
- good resistance
- not hardy
- self-fertile
- late summer to early autumn

'Moon and Stars'

This beautiful heirloom watermelon bears fruits with dark green skin, speckled with bright yellow spots of varying sizes, reminiscent of moons and stars. The sweet flesh can be pink or bright red.

- unsuitable for containers
- late spring
- good resistance
- not hardy
- self-fertile
- early autumn

'Sugar Baby'

This modern, early variety bears small watermelons with a smooth, dark green skin that turns almost black when ripe. The fine-textured red flesh is delicious and very sweet. It has short vines, so is ideal for small gardens.

- unsuitable for containers
- late spring
- good resistance
- not hardy
- self-fertile
- late summer to early autumn

Vegetables

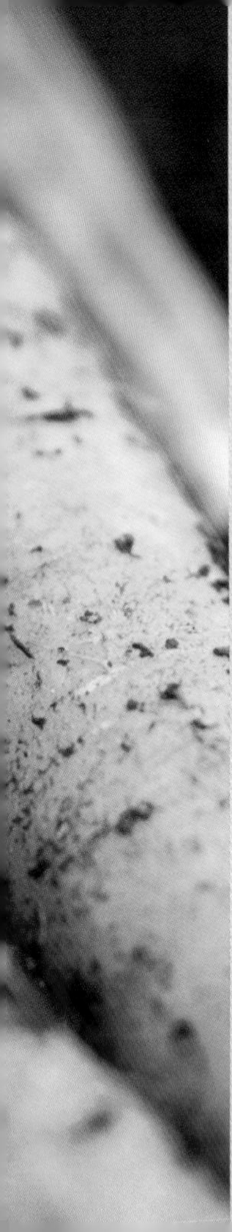

Roots

- Potatoes
- Carrots
- Parsnips
- Beetroot
- Sweet potatoes
- Swedes
- Radishes
- Turnips
- Salsify and Scorzonera
- Jerusalem artichokes

POTATOES *Solanum tuberosum*

Potatoes are a useful, adaptable kitchen vegetable, and are easy to grow, even in small spaces. They are classified by how long they take to mature: "earlies", or new potatoes, should be lifted first and are the smallest, sweetest types; "second earlies", as the name suggests are ready shortly after; and "maincrop" potatoes, which take the longest to mature, and produce large tubers excellent for mashing or roasting.

	SPRING	SUMMER	AUTUMN	WINTER
PLANT				
HARVEST				

CHITTING

Although it is not absolutely necessary, chitting your early potatoes before you plant them out will give you a headstart over the winter months, and should result in a quicker harvest. Place your seed potatoes, with their "eyes" facing upwards, in trays or egg boxes in a warm, light location. They will sprout short, green shoots or "chits". Move them to a cooler position about six weeks before planting, when the chits are 5–10mm (¼–½in) long.

PLANTING

Potatoes prefer an open, sunny, frost-free site, in well-drained soil with a pH of 5–6. Practise crop rotation, and do not plant your crop where you have grown

Plant chitted potatoes "eyes" up.

potatoes, onions, or other root vegetables the previous year.

Dig some organic matter, such as compost or well-rotted manure, into the soil in the autumn before planting. Just before you plant, apply a general fertilizer on the soil surface and work it in well. Alternatively, spread fertilizer along the drills when planting.

In early spring once there's no risk of severe frost, plant out your

early varieties. Plant second earlies in mid-spring and maincrops in mid- to late spring. If you are planting tubers out individually, plant 10–15cm (4–6in) deep and cover each with 2.5cm (1in) of soil. If planting in drills, dig a shallow trench about 15cm (6in) deep, and press tubers into the soil with chits facing upwards. Space early potatoes 30cm (12in) apart and maincrop potatoes 38cm (15in) apart. Cover with at least 2.5cm (1in) of soil. Leave about 60cm (24in) space between drills of earlies, or 75cm (30in) between maincrops.

Earth up your potatoes as they grow.

CROP CARE

Water your potatoes and keep them free from weeds. Early types will need watering while they are young; later varieties need less attention until the tubers have started to develop. Applying a liquid feed or a top-dressing of fertilizer may help to the yield.

Potato plants need "earthing up" as they grow, to ensure that no light reaches the tubers, otherwise they will turn green

TIP GROWING POTATOES IN CONTAINERS

If space is limited, or you want to protect early potatoes under cover, plant them in containers or sacks.

- Check there are drainage holes and add 20cm (8in) of soil-based compost.
- Place one or two chitted potatoes on top. Cover with about 10cm (4in) of compost, and water in well.
- Earth up with compost at intervals and water regularly. Harvest when leaves start to die back.

Potatoes will grow in a variety of containers, such as strong sacks or tubs.

and spoil. When the stems reach about 23cm (9in) tall, pile soil up around them, leaving about 10cm (4in) of foliage above the surface. You may need to repeat this process a couple of times, depending on how tall the plants grow. Cut back the stems of maincrops in early autumn, to about 5cm (2in) above the soil.

HARVESTING

Early potatoes should be ready to harvest in 50–110 days, second earlies in 110–120 days, and maincrops in 125–140 days. Check that tubers are ready to harvest by scraping back some of the earth and examining them. It is best to lift potatoes on a dry day, and then leave them out in the sun for a few hours before storing. Ensure that no tubers are left in the soil or they are likely to re-grow the following year.

STORING

Potatoes will store well in double-layered paper or hessian sacks, in a cool, dry, well-ventilated place, or in a homemade clamp. Ensure that they are properly dried out – the drier they are when you store them, the better they'll keep. Also check that potatoes are completely covered, with no light reaching them.

PESTS AND DISEASES

Pests that may damage your potatoes include cutworms, wireworms, slugs, and potato cyst eelworms. The best ways to prevent these are to control weeds, defend crops against slugs and snails, and try not to leave tubers in the ground longer than necessary.

The most serious disease is potato blight, an airborne fungus that infects plants in warm, wet weather, and usually affects maincrops at the end of the summer. The stems and leaves wither and tubers rot. Other diseases include potato common scab, potato blackleg, and powdery scab.

Include potatoes in a three year crop rotation to avoid common pests and diseases persisting in the soil. Plant potatoes where you have grown beans or peas in the previous year.

Colorado beetles (left) is a serious pest in Europe and should be reported if seen in the UK. Potato blight (right) causes plants to shrivel and die.

'Swift'

Possibly the earliest variety available, a good crop of white-skinned, waxy potatoes is ready for harvest just seven weeks after planting. The cream-coloured flesh has a delicate, new potato flavour. This is a good variety for growing in containers.

- 🪴 suitable for containers
- 🌱 mid-spring after chitting
- 🐛 good resistance
- ❄ fairly hardy
- 🔒 early to midsummer

'Arran Pilot'

This established, popular variety produces good yields of oval, white-skinned potatoes. The white, firm, waxy flesh has the best flavour when eaten fresh from the ground. The tubers grow well in all soil conditions and show resistance to slugs.

- 🪴 suitable for containers
- 🌱 early spring after chitting
- 🐛 excellent resistance
- ❄ fairly hardy
- 🔒 early to midsummer

'Duke of York'

This traditional variety is appreciated for having a good, pronounced flavour. The pale yellow tubers can be lifted as first earlies and used as new potatoes, or left to mature to be used as good general-purpose potatoes.

- 🪴 suitable for containers
- 🌱 early spring after chitting
- 🐛 good resistance
- ❄ fairly hardy
- 🔒 early to midsummer

'Red Duke of York' ♀

A sport of 'Duke of York', these distinctive red-skinned potatoes have a light, yellow flesh that has a firm texture when cooked. 'Red Duke of York' can be left to mature as a second early to produce bigger tubers.

- suitable for containers
- mid-spring after chitting
- excellent resistance
- fairly hardy
- early to midsummer

'Accent' ♀

These yellow-skinned new potatoes are an established favourite. Their pale yellow flesh is waxy and firm once boiled and has an excellent flavour. The tubers are produced in heavy yields, and show resistance to potato cyst eelworm and slugs.

- suitable for containers
- mid-spring after chitting
- good resistance
- fairly hardy
- early to midsummer

'Epicure'

This traditional variety of new potato is popular for its white-skinned tubers with creamy white flesh. The floury potatoes are good boiled, mashed, or in salads. Moderate yields are produced even in exposed areas, and have good slug resistance.

- suitable for containers
- early spring after chitting
- good resistance
- hardy
- midsummer

'Maxine' ♀

A heavy cropper, 'Maxine' produces an abundance of round potatoes with smooth, bright red skin, that store well. The white, waxy flesh has an excellent flavour and stays firm when cooked, making these ideal for boiling, roasting, or baking.

🪣 suitable for containers
🔪 mid-spring after chitting
🐛 good resistance
❄ fairly hardy
🔒 midsummer

'Foremost'

This classic early variety produces good yields of short, oval, white-skinned potatoes that have white flesh, with a firm, waxy texture and excellent flavour. The tubers have good resistance to scab and slugs, and store well once harvested.

🪣 suitable for containers
🔪 early spring after chitting
🐛 excellent resistance
❄ fairly hardy
🔒 midsummer

'Lady Christl' ♀

An early variety that produces good yields of yellow-skinned, oval tubers of a medium size. The waxy, yellow flesh is good for boiling and has a creamy taste. The tubers have good disease resistance and are particularly good for containers.

🪣 suitable for containers
🔪 mid-spring after chitting
🐛 excellent resistance
❄ fairly hardy
🔒 early to midsummer

'Orla' ♀

These creamy-skinned potatoes can be grown as second earlies or early maincrops, depending on the size of tuber you prefer. The pale yellow flesh has a good flavour. This variety is ideal for organic growers as it is has very good resistance to blight.

 suitable for containers
mid-spring after chitting
good resistance
fairly hardy
midsummer

'Estima'

This modern second early variety produces heavy yields of potatoes that are suitable for baking. The oval, light yellow-skinned tubers have a firm, moist, yellow flesh, with a mild flavour. They show good slug resistance and do well in most soils.

 suitable for containers
mid-spring after chitting
good resistance
fairly hardy
midsummer

'Roseval' ♀

This second early variety produces high yields of uniform, long, oval tubers. The potatoes are best boiled, baked, or roasted unpeeled, as the deep red skin retains its colour when cooked. The contrasting yellow, waxy flesh has an excellent flavour.

suitable for containers
mid-spring after chitting
good resistance
fairly hardy
midsummer

'Belle de Fontenay'

This French, second early salad variety is popular for its exceptional flavour, which improves on storage. It produces small, smooth, kidney-shaped, light yellow tubers, with a creamy yellow, waxy flesh. Preserve their flavour by steaming.

- suitable for containers
- mid-spring after chitting
- good resistance
- fairly hardy
- midsummer

'Kestrel'

A gardeners' favourite, this second early is a versatile and attractive potato. The tubers produced are well-shaped, with a smooth, white skin, and purple rings around the eyes. The cream-coloured flesh has a slightly waxy, floury texture and a good flavour.

- suitable for containers
- mid-spring after chitting
- good resistance
- fairly hardy
- midsummer

'Pentland Javelin'

Cropping later than other early potatoes, this variety will produce a higher yield if left to mature as a second early. The heavy crops of oval, white-skinned potatoes have a white, waxy flesh with a creamy texture, and are ideal for boiling.

 suitable for containers

early spring after chitting

good resistance

fairly hardy

midsummer

'British Queen' ♀

This traditional second early variety, over 100 years old, is popular for its heavy and uniform crops. The white-skinned potatoes have white flesh with a floury texture. They have a delicious flavour and are excellent for all types of cooking.

suitable for containers

mid-spring after chitting

good resistance

fairly hardy

midsummer

'Picasso' ♀

This second early variety produces heavy crops of excellent potatoes, ideal for storing. The tubers are very versatile and have waxy flesh, smooth white skins, and pink eyes. It has good all-round disease resistance but can be prone to slug damage.

suitable for containers

mid-spring after chitting

good resistance

fairly hardy

midsummer

'Blue Danube'

Also known as 'Adam Blue', this modern Sarpo introduction produces spectacular blue-skinned, oval tubers with bright white flesh. The large potatoes have a good flavour and are ideal for baking. Tubers have good disease resistance.

- suitable for containers
- mid-spring
- good resistance
- fairly hardy
- midsummer

'King Edward'

An established favourite, the red-skinned tubers of this variety have a distinctively-flavoured, creamy white flesh. They are an excellent all-rounder but are particularly good roasted. Plants produce reasonable yields and show good resistance to slugs.

- suitable for containers
- mid-spring
- good resistance
- fairly hardy
- early autumn

'Maris Piper'

This potato is widely-grown commercially for its high yields of well-flavoured tubers. The potatoes have a light yellow skin, and their flesh has a firm texture when cooked. It is an excellent all-rounder, and is the connoisseur's choice for chips.

- suitable for containers
- mid-spring
- excellent resistance
- fairly hardy
- early autumn

'Kerr's Pink'

The "pink" in 'Kerr's Pink' refers to the colour of the tubers, which are short and oval. The creamy-white flesh has a dry and floury texture when cooked, and is good for mashing and roasting. The potatoes have good blight resistance and keep well.

- suitable for containers
- mid-spring
- good resistance
- fairly hardy
- midsummer

'Salad Blue'

This variety has intensely blue skin and flesh. The short, oval tubers are good for mashing, but despite its name they are not recommended for using in salads, as the mildly-flavoured flesh becomes fluffy and disintegrates when cooked.

- suitable for containers
- mid-spring
- excellent resistance
- fairly hardy
- early autumn

'Sarpo Una'

A high-quality variety that produces large yields of pink-skinned, oval tubers with waxy flesh. Use as a salad potato or leave to mature for baking. Like other Sarpo potatoes, the tubers have outstanding blight resistance.

- suitable for containers
- mid-spring
- excellent resistance
- fairly hardy
- early to mid-autumn

'Desiree'

This popular, scab-resistant variety produces heavy crops even in dry conditions. The red-skinned potatoes have a pale yellow flesh, with a waxy texture and excellent flavour. They are good for baking and mashing, and once harvested, store well.

- 🪣 suitable for containers
- 🌱 early to mid-spring
- 🌼 good resistance
- ❄️ fairly hardy
- 🔒 late summer to mid-autumn

'Cara'

Each plant bears an abundance of neatly rounded, white potatoes with pinkish-red eyes and floury white flesh. This variety has excellent disease resistance and tolerates drought conditions. Once harvested, the all-purpose potatoes store well.

- 🪣 suitable for containers
- 🌱 mid to late spring
- 🌼 excellent resistance
- ❄️ fairly hardy
- 🔒 early to mid-autumn

'Sarpo Axona'

A new introduction, and an excellent all-rounder, the pink-skinned potatoes of this variety are similar to 'Sarpo Mira', but have a more uniform shape, a more creamy flesh, and a superb flavour. The tubers have outstanding blight resistance.

- 🪣 suitable for containers
- 🌱 mid to late spring
- 🌼 excellent resistance
- ❄️ fairly hardy
- 🔒 early to mid-autumn

'Pink Fir Apple'

This old variety produces unusual-looking, long, knobbly, pink-skinned potatoes; their yellow, waxy flesh has the best flavour of any salad variety. The yields are not heavy, but the tubers will store until early winter if left in the ground.

 suitable for containers
mid-spring
good resistance
fairly hardy
late summer to early winter

'Sarpo Mira'

This outstanding modern potato bears huge yields of floury, pink-skinned tubers in most soil conditions, and also has outstanding resistance to blight and slugs. The potatoes have a good flavour and store well.

suitable for containers
mid to late spring
excellent resistance
fairly hardy
early to mid-autumn

'Dunbar Standard'

An established potato, 'Dunbar Standard' bears good yields of white-skinned tubers with light cream, firm flesh and a strong, earthy flavour. An excellent all-purpose potato, it is a good choice for heavy soils, in which it grows happily.

suitable for containers
mid to late spring
some resistance
fairly hardy
early to mid-autumn

CARROTS *Daucus carota*

An allotment favourite, carrots are a mainstay in the kitchen and are one of the most popular and easy vegetables to grow. They come in a variety of shapes, sizes, and colours, but usually fall into one of two categories – early varieties, sown from autumn, and maincrops, which are sown and harvested later and take slightly longer to mature. Carrot fly can be a major problem, so growing crops in a raised container is ideal.

	SPRING	SUMMER	AUTUMN	WINTER
PLANT				
HARVEST				

SOWING

Carrots favour open, dry sites and a light soil with a pH of 6.5–7.5. Ensure that the soil is free from stones so that roots have space to develop and do not become constricted or malformed. Dig in plenty of well-rotted manure or compost before planting.

Seed should be sown directly into the ground from mid-autumn through to midsummer, as carrots are difficult to pot on and transplant. Sow the seeds 1–2cm ($\frac{1}{2}$–$\frac{3}{4}$in) deep and space around 10cm (4in) apart, leaving 15cm (6in) between each row. By sowing successively every few weeks it is possible to have a continuous harvest throughout the summer and autumn.

Pinch out carrot leaves when thinning.

CROP CARE

Weed the area regularly by hand while the carrots are small, until their leafy canopy has grown sufficiently dense to suppress any competition. Water them during dry spells, especially if the soil starts to harden, but remember that carrots don't need as much water as some other crops; do not over water them or they will become too leafy.

HARVESTING

Thin out the carrots as they grow, eating some as baby vegetables, while allowing the others to continue growing. Early crops should be ready to harvest seven weeks after sowing, maincrops in ten to eleven weeks. Gently pull out by hand, or if the soil is too hard, ease out with a fork.

STORING

Carrots can generally be left in the ground until they are needed, or stored in big wooden boxes filled with damp sand, in order to protect them from frosts through the winter months.

PESTS AND DISEASES

Carrot flies lay eggs in the soil and their larvae tunnel into roots, causing them to rot. Intercrop with onions to disguise the scent, erect a fine mesh fence, or grow in containers above 45cm (18in): higher than they can fly.

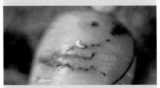

Damage caused by the carrot fly.

'Early Nantes'

The blunt-ended, deep orange roots of this variety are 13–15cm (5–6in) long, with only a minimal core and sweet, crunchy flesh. Fast-maturing, they can be picked at finger-size. 'Early Nantes' can be sown in late winter under glass or cloches.

🪴	suitable for containers
🌱	mid-spring to late summer
🐛	poor resistance
❄️	hardy
🔒	midsummer to mid-autumn

'Adelaide' ♀

This is one of the earliest varieties to mature and can be sown under cloches in mid- to late winter for a head start. The roots, ready for harvesting nine weeks after sowing, are 9cm (3½in) long, bright orange, and nearly coreless.

🪴	suitable for containers
🌱	mid-spring to late summer
🐛	some resistance
❄️	hardy
🔒	early summer to mid-autumn

'Early Scarlet Horn'

This reliable early variety, dating from the 17th century, produces 13–15cm (5–6in) long, stump-rooted carrots, ideal for shallow or stony soils where longer-rooted carrots would struggle to thrive. They have a good flavour and freeze well.

🪴	suitable for containers
🌱	late winter to mid-spring
🐛	poor resistance
❄️	hardy
🔒	late spring to midsummer

'Parano' ♀

A very early Nantes hybrid, 'Parano' produces smooth-skinned, cylindrical, blunt-ended roots with good colour and flavour, up to 15–18cm (6–7in) long. They are excellent raw, juiced, or cooked. This variety is suitable for growing under glass and for successional sowings.

 suitable for containers
late winter to mid-spring
some resistance
hardy
early to midsummer

'Amsterdam Forcing' ♀

Heavy-yielding and fast-maturing, 'Amsterdam Forcing' can be sown early in a cold frame or under cloches. Successional sowing will produce slim, very sweet, deep orange, finger-size carrots, for harvesting within 12–14 weeks over a long period.

 suitable for containers
late winter to late summer
some resistance
hardy
early summer to late autumn

'Nairobi' ♀

This heavy-cropping, Nantes type, F1 hybrid carrot has uniformly long, smooth, stump-ended roots with little core; the flavour is among the best of all carrot varieties and is very sweet, especially if the roots are pulled young to use as finger carrots.

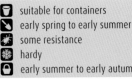 suitable for containers
early spring to early summer
some resistance
hardy
early summer to early autumn

'Parmex' ♀

The tender, sweet roots of this variety are round, measuring only 3–5cm (1½–2in) in diameter. It is ideal for containers, shallow soils, and growing bags, and can be sown under glass or cloches in mid- to late winter for earlier crops.

- suitable for containers
- early to late spring
- some resistance
- hardy
- late spring to early autumn

'Mokum' ♀

This high-yielding early variety produces almost coreless, very juicy, sweet, and crunchy roots that are good pulled young as baby carrots or allowed to mature to 15–18cm (6–7in) long. It can be sown under glass from midwinter onwards.

- suitable for containers
- late winter to mid-spring
- some resistance
- hardy
- early to midsummer

'Nelson Hybrid'

This early Nantes hybrid has 15cm (6in) long, smooth, blunt-ended, cylindrical roots that are deep orange in colour and excellent in flavour. They can be harvested young as baby carrots. Very productive, it is resistant to greentop and cracking.

- suitable for containers
- late winter to mid-spring
- poor resistance
- hardy
- early to midsummer

'Trevor' ♀

This F1 hybrid, Nantes-type
variety produces heavy yields
of cylindrical roots with a good
orange colour. The roots can
be grown for early or maincrop
harvests and have a sweet flavour
and firm texture. The plants have
good bolt resistance.

🪣 suitable for containers
🔰 mid-spring to late summer
🦠 some resistance
❄ hardy
🔒 midsummer to autumn

'Tendersnax Hybrid'

The slightly tapered roots of
'Tendersnax' are 13–15cm (5–6in)
long, blunt-ended, rich orange,
and smooth-skinned. The flesh is
exceptionally tender and juicy,
delicious cooked or raw, and is
high in beta-carotene. It is a
disease-resistant variety.

🪣 suitable for containers
🔰 mid-spring to midsummer
🦠 good resistance
❄ hardy
🔒 midsummer to late autumn

'Ideal' ♀

This early Nantes type is fast-
maturing and the rich orange
roots can be pulled for use as
tender finger carrots when they
are 5mm ($^{1}/_{4}$in) in diameter.
Left to mature, they become
medium length, well-filled
roots with strong top growth.

🪣 suitable for containers
🔰 late winter to midsummer
🦠 some resistance
❄ hardy
🔒 early summer to late autumn

'Touchon'

This heirloom Nantes carrot produces smooth, cylindrical, stump-ended roots measuring 18–20cm (7–8in) long, with no core. They are crisp, sweet, and notably juicy, retaining these qualities well during winter storage. Excellent raw or juiced, the roots also freeze well.

- suitable for containers
- mid- to late spring
- poor resistance
- hardy
- midsummer to mid-autumn

'Rainbow Hybrid'

The aptly-named roots of this variety are diverse in colour, both in the skin and the flesh, ranging from white, through yellow, to orange. They are tapered, growing to about 18–23cm (7–9in) long, with a sweet flavour and juicy, tender texture.

- unsuitable for containers
- mid-spring to early summer
- poor resistance
- hardy
- midsummer to early autumn

'Bolero'

A heavy-yielding variety with 18cm (7in) long, conical, deep orange roots and outstanding flavour, 'Bolero' is very resistant to powdery mildew and alternaria leaf spot. The roots are sweet and crunchy, retaining these qualities well, even in long term storage.

- suitable for containers
- mid-spring to midsummer
- good resistance
- hardy
- early to late autumn

'Red Samurai'

The bright red skin and pinkish flesh of this striking variety from Japan retain their beautiful colour after cooking. The tapering roots are 25–28cm (10–11in) long, sweet and strong in flavour, and possess a crisp texture.

- unsuitable for containers
- early spring to midsummer
- poor resistance
- hardy
- early summer to early autumn

'Crème de Lite'

The cream-coloured, tapering roots of 'Crème de lite' have sweet, juicy flesh, and are equally good raw and cooked; they do not need to be peeled. It prefers moist, rich, well-drained soils, and is resistant to greentop, alternaria leaf spot, and powdery mildew.

- unsuitable for containers
- mid-spring to early summer
- good resistance
- hardy
- midsummer to mid-autumn

'Danvers Half Long'

This 19th-century American variety has roots up to 23cm (9in) long and 5cm (2in) in diameter, with sweet, tender, and crunchy flesh that retains these qualities during storage. It performs well in any soil, including clay and other heavy types.

- unsuitable for containers
- mid-spring to early summer
- poor resistance
- hardy
- early summer to mid-autumn

'Carson' ♀

A Chantenay type of carrot, 'Carson' has 13cm (5in) long, smooth, conical roots with a rich orange core and particularly good flavour; they store well for winter use. Because of their shorter roots, this variety is a good choice for heavy soils.

- suitable for containers
- early spring to midsummer
- some resistance
- hardy
- late spring to mid-autumn

'Barcelona' ♀

A reliable F1 hybrid maincrop variety, 'Barcelona' has long, smooth-skinned, cylindrical roots of a deep orange colour, with strong and healthy tops. It is resistant to mildew and is a good choice for storing over winter.

- unsuitable for containers
- late spring to midsummer
- some resistance
- hardy
- late summer to mid-autumn

'Purple Haze'

A new variety with striking purple skin, 'Purple Haze' has bright orange, tender, crunchy flesh. To preserve the skin's colour it is best to eat the roots raw or only cook them lightly. Given protection, the roots can overwinter in the soil.

- suitable for containers
- early spring to early summer
- poor resistance
- hardy
- early summer to late winter

'Cosmic Purple'

The roots of this variety are 18cm (7in) long and purple-skinned, with coreless, orange flesh and a high sugar content, which gives them a sweet flavour. The attractive colour is retained after cooking. Seed can be sown under cloches from early spring.

- 🪣 suitable for containers
- 🍃 late spring to midsummer
- ✸ poor resistance
- ❄ hardy
- 🔒 late summer to mid-autumn

'Danvers 126'

The deep orange roots of this improved version of 'Danvers Half Long' reach about 15–20cm (6–8in) long, and are blunt or slightly tapered, nearly coreless, sweet, and crunchy. It is vigorous and heavy-cropping, and tolerant of different soil types.

- 🪣 suitable for containers
- 🍃 mid-spring to early summer
- ✸ poor resistance
- ❄ hardy
- 🔒 early summer to mid-autumn

'Kingston' ♀

This new 'Autumn King' hybrid produces large, pointed roots with a strong, attractive colour and very good flavour. It is easy to grow, high-yielding, and has strong tops that make the roots easy to lift; it also stores well over winter.

- 🪣 unsuitable for containers
- 🍃 late spring to midsummer
- ✸ some resistance
- ❄ hardy
- 🔒 late summer to late autumn

'Berlicum'

Renowned for the excellent flavour of its deep orange roots, 'Berlicum' also has the advantage of keeping well over winter. The roots are slender, up to 20cm (8in) long and with small cores. They are not prone to woodiness.

	unsuitable for containers
	mid-spring to early summer
	poor resistance
	hardy
	early autumn to mid-spring

'Flyaway' ♀

A maincrop F1 hybrid, 'Flyaway' is relatively unattractive to carrot fly. The roots are 13–15cm (5–6in) long, blunt ended, with smooth skin, attractive colour, and a sweet flavour. They are equally good harvested young or allowed to mature for storage in autumn.

	suitable for containers
	mid-spring to midsummer
	good resistance
	hardy
	midsummer to mid-autumn

'Ulysses'

This variety produces top-quality, deep orange, cylindrical roots, 18–20cm (7–8in) long, with strong tops. It is resistant to splitting and bolting, and will overwinter well in the ground or in storage. Sow under protection in late winter or early spring for earlier crops.

	unsuitable for containers
	mid- to late spring
	good resistance
	hardy
	midsummer to mid-autumn

'Chantenay Red Cored'

This old variety produces
blunt, deep orange roots
that reach 15cm (6in) long,
and are now often pulled at
about 8–10cm (3–4in) for use
as very sweet-flavoured baby
carrots. It is tolerant of heavy
soils and stores well.

- suitable for containers
- early spring to early summer
- poor resistance
- hardy
- early summer to late autumn

'Infinity'

A new Imperator F1 hybrid
variety, 'Infinity' produces
long, slender, uniformly orange
roots with sweet, juicy flesh.
Maturing 12 weeks after sowing,
it will store well over winter.
It is excellent cooked in stews
or served raw with dips.

- unsuitable for containers
- late spring to early summer
- poor resistance
- hardy
- late summer to mid-autumn

'Yellowstone'

Canary yellow and 23–25cm
(9–10in) long, the roots of this
variety are distinctive and retain
their colour throughout cooking.
The flavour is mild, and is sweetest
when they are eaten raw. Sow
under protection in mid- to
late winter for earlier crops.

- unsuitable for containers
- early spring to early summer
- poor resistance
- hardy
- midsummer to early winter

PARSNIPS *Pastinaca sativa*

Sweet, delicious parsnips are excellent cooked in soups or stews, or roasted like potatoes. Although they are fairly slow to germinate, once established they are a relatively low-maintenance crop, and will reliably bear roots as long as they are sufficiently watered and have enough space. Roots are available in different shapes, sizes, and even colours, so try a slightly unusual variety.

	SPRING	SUMMER	AUTUMN	WINTER
SOW				
HARVEST				

SOWING

Parsnips thrive in an open, sunny position, in light, sandy soil, with a slightly acidic pH of 6.5. They come in a range of shapes and sizes, so make sure that your soil is deep enough for whichever type you choose. Dig well-rotted manure into the soil the previous autumn, and ensure that it is not compacted.

Wait until mid- to late spring before sowing any seed. Sow directly into the soil about 2cm (³⁄₄in) deep, either thinly along the row, or with two or three seeds together as parsnips often germinate unreliably. Once the seedlings are established, thin to 10–14cm (4–6in) apart for medium roots, and 20cm (12in) for large.

Sow thinly to increase chances of success.

CROP CARE

Water your seeds regularly while they are germinating, then only water the developing roots if the ground is very dry. Roots may split if they are allowed to dry out and are then watered. Parsnips do not normally need feeding, but give them a liquid feed if growth is poor. Weed your parsnips carefully until they are established.

HARVESTING

Parsnips can be harvested in the summer when young or left in the ground until the first frosts, which improves the flavour.

STORING

Spread moist sand in the bottom of a wooden box and place a layer of parsnips on top, ensuring that they are not touching. Cover with sand and store in a cool, dry place. The sand will prevent the roots from shrivelling or rotting. Alternatively, parsnips can be left in the ground until you need them. Cover with a layer of straw if the weather turns cold.

PESTS AND DISEASES

Parsnips are vulnerable to pests such as carrot fly and celery root miner. Female carrot flies lay eggs in the soil near to plants, which hatch and tunnel into the roots, rotting them. Use fine mesh to deter them (see carrots pp.184–5). There is no cure, so dig up affected roots. Celery leaf miner causes brown spots on leaves, but may not be fatal if prompt action is taken.

Diseases include parsnip canker and downy mildew. Choose canker-resistant varieties, and keep plants well watered to prevent mildew.

'Gladiator' ♔

With fast-maturing, tapering roots that have smooth, white skin and a fine, sweet flavour, this consistently high-quality, F1 hybrid variety is popular for both exhibition purposes and the table. It is resistant to canker and is easy to clean for cooking.

- unsuitable for containers
- early to late spring
- good resistance
- hardy
- early autumn to early spring

'Cobham Improved Marrow' ♔

Medium-sized roots with a tapering, elegant shape and smooth white skin make this a good variety for exhibition; they also have a fine, sweet flavour. They mature in 32–36 weeks and are resistant to canker.

- unsuitable for containers
- late winter to late spring
- good resistance
- hardy
- early autumn to mid-spring

'Hollow Crown'

This popular 19th-century variety has tapering roots up to 30cm (12in) long and 7.5cm (3in) in diameter, with hollow crowns and sweet, mellow-flavoured flesh. It is very high-yielding and is resistant to canker.

- unsuitable for containers
- late winter to mid-spring
- good resistance
- hardy
- early autumn to late winter

'Albion' ♀

This variety has uniformly long, smooth, tapering roots with whiter skin than most parsnips. The flavour is very sweet, becoming more so after the first frosts. It is an F1 hybrid, bred for resistance to canker and other diseases.

- 🪣 unsuitable for containers
- 🌱 late winter to mid-spring
- 🕷 good resistance
- ❄ hardy
- 🔒 early autumn to late winter

'Javelin' ♀

An F1 hybrid variety giving a high yield, 'Javelin' produces long, slender, tapering roots with smooth, easy to wash skins, and a good flavour. Their uniformity makes the roots good for the show bench too. It is resistant to pests and diseases.

- 🪣 unsuitable for containers
- 🌱 late winter to mid-spring
- 🕷 good resistance
- ❄ hardy
- 🔒 mid-autumn to late winter

'Lancer' ♀

With short, slender, wedge-shaped roots, this variety is ideal for planting in small plots, and for use as a baby vegetable. The roots have smooth, white skins and good-flavoured flesh. 'Lancer' is very hardy and is resistant to canker.

- 🪣 unsuitable for containers
- 🌱 late winter to early summer
- 🕷 good resistance
- ❄ hardy
- 🔒 early summer to late autumn

'Countess' ♀

This variety has smooth, cream-skinned, conical roots with shallow crowns, which can be lifted as late as mid-spring with no loss of quality. They mature about 32–36 weeks after sowing, with increasing sweetness over time. 'Countess' is a vigorous and disease-resistant variety.

🪣	unsuitable for containers
🡇	early to late spring
❋	good resistance
❄	hardy
🔒	mid-autumn to mid-spring

'Panache' ♀

A new and vigorous hybrid, 'Panache' has smooth, white-skinned roots with creamy, sweet-flavoured flesh; they are uniformly large and wedge-shaped, with shallow crowns. It is very resistant to canker and has good storage qualities.

🪣	unsuitable for containers
🡇	mid-spring to early summer
❋	good resistance
❄	hardy
🔒	early autumn to late winter

'Archer' ♀

A strong-growing variety, easy to germinate, with uniform, tapering, long, white roots and smooth, unblemished skin, 'Archer' is an excellent variety for exhibition displays as well as for the table. In the UK it is best harvested before midwinter.

🪣	unsuitable for containers
🡇	late winter to late spring
❋	some resistance
❄	hardy
🔒	early autumn to late winter

'White Gem'

This high-yielding variety has comparatively short roots, making it suitable for shallow soils. It is tolerant of most soil types and has good resistance to canker. The roots are broad-shouldered, with a smooth, white skin and excellent flavour.

- unsuitable for containers
- late winter to late spring
- good resistance
- hardy
- early autumn to mid-spring

'Excaliber' ♀

The roots of 'Excalibur' are shallow-crowned, smooth, and white-skinned, with an excellent, sweet flavour; they can be lifted from early autumn, and store well. It has some resistance to canker, which is improved by sowing from mid-spring onwards.

- unsuitable for containers
- mid- to late spring
- good resistance
- hardy
- early autumn to late winter

'Tender and True' ♀

Smooth-skinned, long-tapering roots make this a good variety for exhibition use, and it rates well for its flavour too. The roots are large, measuring 7.5cm (3in) at the shoulder, and have only a small core. This variety is resistant to canker.

- unsuitable for containers
- late winter to late spring
- good resistance
- hardy
- mid-autumn to late winter

BEETROOT *Beta vulgaris*

Beetroot is a highly underrated vegetable, being not only simple to grow, but also a delicious, versatile culinary crop. Grow roots for pickling or eating fresh in salads, and harvest the bright, beautiful leaves when young, to be eaten raw or cooked like spinach. Roots come in a multitude of sizes, shapes and colours, from the standard purple globes, to tiny baby beets, in a range of colours from orange or white, to pink-and-white striped.

	SPRING	SUMMER	AUTUMN	WINTER
SOW				
HARVEST				

SOWING

Beetroot will grow almost anywhere, but it prefers a sunny, open site and light, sandy soil with a pH of around 6.5–7. It can sometimes be difficult to encourage beetroot seeds to germinate, so soak them in warm water for about an hour before planting – this will remove any traces of germination inhibitor.

Sow early, bolt-resistant seed under the cover of a cloche or cold frame while there's still risk of frost, or directly into the ground between late spring and summer. Sow standard-sized beetroot 10cm (4in) apart, and smaller varieties about 5cm (2in) apart, at a depth of 2.5cm (1in), with 15cm (6in) between rows. Thin seedlings if necessary.

Thin out seedlings as they develop.

CROP CARE

Protect seedlings and young plants against frosts and pests as necessary. Once established, water in moderation; too much water will encourage leafy growth but no root, while too little will turn the root woody. Spray with a foliar, seaweed-based fertilizer once or twice during growth to boost levels of manganese and boron in the soil.

HARVESTING AND STORING

Begin to harvest roots when they are about 5cm (2in) wide. Spring-sown beetroot will be ready in summer; summer-sown beetroot in autumn. The longer you leave the roots in the ground, the larger they will become, so thinning them as you harvest will encourage remaining crops to grow bigger.

Beetroot can be overwintered by leaving it in the ground and covering with a 15cm (6in) layer of straw. Alternatively, pull up the roots, twist off the leaves, and store in a box of moist sand in a cool, dark place.

PESTS AND DISEASES

Beetroot is usually relatively trouble free, but may fall victim to aphids or cutworms. Seedlings may be at risk of damping off; protect against this by maintaining good garden hygiene, and giving plants enough light and space.

Beetroot leaf infested with aphids.

'Red Ace'

This hybrid, globe variety produces high-quality, oval roots that are dark red in colour, with red, ringless flesh, and an excellent flavour. The roots grow well in all soils, even dry conditions, and are a favourite with exhibition growers.

🪣	suitable for containers
🌱	early spring
✴	good resistance
❄	hardy
🔒	midsummer to late autumn

'Bull's Blood'

Although often grown as an ornamental plant, the young, deep burgundy leaves of this variety have a sweet, mild flavour and are a great addition to salads. The roots are best harvested when young, and have a candy-striped flesh.

🪣	suitable for containers
🌱	early spring to midsummer
✴	good resistance
❄	fairly hardy
🔒	early summer to mid-autumn

'Kestrel'

This fast-maturing globe variety reliably produces good-quality, smooth, round, dark red beets. The sweet flavour of the deep red flesh is particularly good when the roots are harvested young. It has good resistance to disease and bolting.

🪣	suitable for containers
🌱	early spring to mid-summer
✴	good resistance
❄	hardy
🔒	midsummer to late autumn

'Chioggia'

A striking globe variety from Italy, its large, round, red roots mature very early in the season, and when sliced, the flesh reveals attractive red and white rings which fade to light pink when cooked. The young leaves can be cooked like spinach.

- suitable for containers
- early spring to midsummer
- good resistance
- fairly hardy
- late spring to late summer

'Pronto' ♀

This globe variety is bolt-resistant and can be sown early in the season and successively throughout the summer. Roots are round, purple, and smooth-skinned, and have the best sweet flavour as baby beets. The leaves are ideal for picking for salads.

- suitable for containers
- early spring to midsummer
- good resistance
- hardy
- midsummer to late autumn

'Albina Vereduna'

This unusual, heirloom, globe variety produces round roots with white skin and flesh that doesn't bleed when cut. Roots have a good flavour and are best eaten fresh as they do not store. The leaves can be cooked like spinach.

- suitable for containers
- early spring
- good resistance
- hardy
- midsummer to late autumn

'Moneta'

This globe variety can be sown early without the risk of bolting. Each seed reliably produces one plant, beetroot normally produce up to four plants per seed, so less thinning out will be required. The uniform, round, smooth-skinned roots have crimson flesh with an excellent flavour.

- suitable for containers
- early spring
- good resistance
- hardy
- midsummer to late autumn

'Cylindra'

This late-ripening variety produces sturdy, dark red, long cylindrical roots that are perfect for slicing. They keep their sweet flavour all season and store well for a long period once harvested. They are slow to bolt and have good disease resistance.

- suitable for containers
- early spring
- good resistance
- fairly hardy
- mid to late summer

'Mr Crosby's Egyptian'

This is one of the earliest-maturing, larger varieties, and has good resistance to bolting. A rapid-grower, it produces deep red, smooth, rounded, but slightly flattened, roots with an excellent flavour. The beets can be lifted young or when mature.

- suitable for containers
- early spring
- good resistance
- fairly hardy
- late spring to late summer

'Action' ♀

This variety reliably produces good crops of well-flavoured, round, baby roots with a smooth skin; the red-coloured flesh has no rings and is tender when young. This variety is ideal for growing in containers or growing bags.

 suitable for containers

early spring to midsummer

good resistance

hardy

midsummer to late autumn

'Bonel' ♀

This globe variety produces round, purple beets with a red, smooth flesh and no rings. It is bolt-resistant so can be sown early in the season. The upright foliage makes it easier to thin seedlings and harvest young leaves.

suitable for containers

early spring to midsummer

good resistance

hardy

early summer to late autumn

'Yellow Cylindrical'

A rare, European, heirloom variety which, as the name suggests, has elongated, cylindrical roots with an unusual, yellow skin. The flesh is white and crisp and has an excellent flavour, which is sweeter if picked when roots are young.

suitable for containers

early spring

good resistance

hardy

midsummer to late autumn

'Solo' ♀

This British variety is easy to grow and requires no thinning as it reliably produces one plant per seed. It produces good yields of uniform, round, medium-sized beets that have a smooth, red skin and sweet flesh. This variety is ideal for growing as baby beets.

 suitable for containers
early spring to late summer
good resistance
hardy
midsummer to late autumn

'Detroit Globe 2'

An improved version of 'Detroit', this variety produces uniform, round roots with smooth, dark red skins. The flesh is dark red with no rings, and has a good texture and flavour. The beets are good for successional sowing.

suitable for containers
early spring to midsummer
good resistance
hardy
early summer to late autumn

'Boro' ♀

This good-quality, globe variety produces crops with a dark red, smooth skin. They can be used as baby beets or allowed to mature. Seeds sown later in the growing season can be lifted in mid-autumn to store.

 suitable for containers
early spring to mid-summer
good resistance
fairly hardy
midsummer to autumn

'Alto'

A very popular, early-maturing hybrid, 'Alto' produces good crops of uniform, cylindrical roots that are perfect for slicing. Under the smooth red skin is a ringless red flesh, which has a very sweet flavour.

- suitable for containers
- early spring
- good resistance
- hardy
- early summer to late autumn

'Burpee's Golden'

This unusual variety has orange flesh that turns yellow when cooked, and doesn't bleed and stain when cut. The beets have an outstanding flavour and are best harvested when small. The spinach-like leaves can be steamed or boiled.

- suitable for containers
- early spring to midsummer
- good resistance
- fairly hardy
- early summer to mid-autumn

'Forono'

A high-yielding beetroot with long, deep red, cylindrical roots, 'Forono' has an outstanding flavour, which is at its best when the beets are eaten young and tender. Sow slightly later than other varieties to prevent bolting. The roots store well.

- suitable for containers
- mid-spring
- good resistance
- fairly hardy
- late summer to late autumn

SWEET POTATOES *Ipomoea batatas*

Sweet potatoes are not related to potatoes at all but are actually members of the bindweed family. Like potatoes though, their orange or white flesh is delicious roasted, baked, or mashed. They originate from tropical or sub-tropical climates so will only produce a good crop during a very warm summer, or if grown in a greenhouse. Seed can be raised under cover and then planted out, but using rooted cuttings called "slips" is more common.

	SPRING	SUMMER	AUTUMN	WINTER
SOW/PLANT				
HARVEST				

SOWING & PLANTING

Sweet potatoes need a warm, sheltered site, with sandy, highly fertile soil and a pH range of 5.5–6.5. Sow indoors in trays or pots at a depth of 2.5cm (1in) in early to mid-spring. Harden off and transplant once the young plants reach a height of about 10–15cm (4–6in). If growing from slips, plant out in late spring.

Create a 30cm (12in) high ridge in the soil and plant seedlings or slips at least 25–30cm (10–12in) apart; plant slips 5–8cm (2–3in) deep. Bear in mind that sweet potatoes grow very large, and will need plenty of space – at least 75cm (30in) between rows. Consider trimming foliage or training it up wire supports to keep your plot looking tidy.

Trim the foliage to keep it under control.

CROP CARE

Sweet potatoes require a lot of water, especially during their early growth period. Consider sinking the tops of cut-off plastic bottles upside down into the soil around your crops, as pouring water into these will ensure that it reaches right down to the roots. Give your sweet potatoes a feed with general-purpose fertilizer every two to three weeks.

HARVESTING

Pick the leaves as you require them – they can be cooked and eaten like spinach. The tubers should be ready to harvest from early autumn, and you should finish lifting them before the first frosts. Take care not to split or damage the sweet potatoes when digging them up as the skins are delicate.

STORING

Roots can be stored inside for several months, but they will need to be "cured" first; leave in the sunshine for four to seven days to toughen their skins.

PESTS AND DISEASES

Red spider mite, aphids, and whitefly might affect your crops, as well as other general fungal diseases and viruses. Practise good garden hygiene to minimize the risks, and check plants regularly for symptoms. If these spread, treat accordingly.

Mottling may indicate red spider mite.

'Centennial'

Uniformly cylindrical roots with copper skin and orange flesh are produced in abundance and are ready to harvest about 18 weeks after planting, or 14 weeks for smaller, tender roots. 'Centennial' is suitable for heavy soils and is resistant to viral disease.

- unsuitable for containers
- mid-spring to early summer
- good resistance
- not hardy
- mid-autumn

'Carolina Ruby'

This excellent US-only variety, bred by North Carolina Agricultural Research Service, is resistant to fusarium wilt but susceptible to root-knot eelworm. Garnet-coloured roots mature in about 12 weeks. The moist, tasty flesh is an attractive bright orange.

- unsuitable for containers
- late spring
- some resistance
- not hardy
- late summer to early autumn

'Hernandez'

Red-orange skinned 'Hernandez' is an adaptable US-only variety, good for both northern and southern gardens. Plants exhibit fair resistance to bacterial and fungal diseases. The orange-fleshed roots are very moist when cooked.

- unsuitable for containers
- late spring
- some resistance
- not hardy
- late summer to early autumn

'Jewel'

This variety offers above-average yields, producing medium-sized, orange-skinned roots with sweet, moist, light orange flesh. It has an excellent flavour and soft texture. It is resistant to cracking and root-knot eelworm, but is intolerant of cold, wet soil.

- unsuitable for containers
- mid-spring to early summer
- some resistance
- not hardy
- mid-autumn

'Beauregard'

This vigorous variety is one of the fastest to mature, at 12–13 weeks, and is high-yielding. The roots have a red-coppery skin and moist, sweet, soft orange flesh. They are resistant to cracking and root-knot eelworm, and store well after harvesting.

- unsuitable for containers
- mid-spring to early summer
- good resistance
- not hardy
- mid-autumn

'Vardaman'

Released in 1981, US-only 'Vardaman' is known for producing small, deep orange roots with outstanding flavour. The plant grows in a compact bush form and has attractive foliage, making it an excellent choice for the ornamental garden.

- unsuitable for containers
- late spring
- some resistance
- not hardy
- late summer to early autumn

'Nancy Hall'

This US-only, heirloom variety is a favourite of gardeners because of the sweet flavour and firm texture of its yellow flesh. The pale-coloured roots do not have the disease resistance of the newer varieties, and are generally smaller. The roots store well.

- unsuitable for containers
- late spring
- poor resistance
- not hardy
- late summer to early autumn

'Vineless Puerto Rico'

This vineless, or bush, variety is a favourite of gardeners with limited space. The roots have copper skin and reddish-orange flesh with a rich flavour and a smooth texture. An older variety, it is susceptible to fusarium wilt and root-knot eelworm.

- unsuitable for containers
- late spring
- poor resistance
- not hardy
- late summer to early autumn

'O'Henry'

Ready to lift in around 14 weeks, the prolific roots of 'O'Henry' have cream-coloured flesh and skin. The tubers have a drier texture than other varieties, but their flavour is sweet and delicious. Roots develop in a cluster beneath the plant allowing easy picking.

- unsuitable for containers
- late spring
- some resistance
- not hardy
- late summer to early autumn

'White Yam'

Also called 'White Triumph', this US-only, heirloom variety is one of the oldest available sweet potatoes. The vines produce good yields of tan-skinned, white-fleshed roots that sweeten with storage, and have a drier, firmer texture than orange-fleshed varieties.

- unsuitable for containers
- late spring
- some resistance
- not hardy
- late summer to early autumn

'Violetta'

This vining, US-only, heirloom variety produces above-average yields of bright purple roots with white flesh. The tubers mature earlier than most sweet potatoes and are very flavourful, but vines lack the disease resistance of more recent varieties.

- unsuitable for containers
- late spring
- poor resistance
- not hardy
- late summer to early autumn

'T65'

This reliable, vigorous sweet potato will produce the largest yields of any UK variety. Its large, reddish-pink tubers have white-golden flesh, with a good flavour and creamy texture. They are excellent for culinary use.

- unsuitable for containers
- late spring
- some resistance
- not hardy
- late summer to early autumn

'Allgold'

High-yielding, US-only 'Allgold', was developed in Oklahoma in 1952, and produces moist, orange-fleshed roots that store well. This vigorous variety resists a variety of common diseases but is susceptible to root-knot eelworm.

- unsuitable for containers
- late spring
- some resistance
- not hardy
- late summer to early autumn

'Georgia Jet'

A reliable, heavy-cropping, and early-maturing variety, 'Georgia Jet' has deep purplish-red skin and deep orange, moist flesh with an excellent flavour. Ready to harvest 12 weeks after planting, the roots will store well in a warm place at the end of the season.

- unsuitable for containers
- mid-spring to early summer
- poor resistance
- not hardy
- mid-autumn

'Nemagold'

A variety from Oklahoma, 'Nemagold' has dark orange skin and dry orange flesh, which has a high carotene content. It is resistant to root-knot eelworm and some common diseases, making it a good choice for the organic gardener.

- unsuitable for containers
- mid-spring to early summer
- some resistance
- not hardy
- mid-autumn

'Covington'

Orange, flavourful flesh, consistently good yields, and resistance to fusarium wilt and root-knot eelworm have made 'Covington' a favourite among US growers. The reddish-skinned roots are high in fibre and betacarotene.

- unsuitable for containers
- late spring
- good resistance
- not hardy
- late summer to early autumn

SWEDES *Brassica napus* Napobrassica Group

First introduced as "Swedish turnips", but also known as turnips or "neeps" in Scotland, and rutabaga in the United States, swedes are a staple of many soups, stews, and casseroles. Their sweet orange or yellow flesh is also delicious mashed. This very hardy root vegetable is actually a member of the brassica family and is well worth growing, despite its slow growth, and the number of pests and diseases that can affect crops.

	SPRING	SUMMER	AUTUMN	WINTER
SOW/PLANT				
HARVEST				

SOWING

Prepare your plot the previous autumn by digging in well-rotted manure or compost. Swedes like a sunny position in a light soil with a pH above 6.8. Relatively slow-growing, they can take up to six months before they are ready to harvest, so sow as soon as the soil has warmed up, and protect with fleece, cold frames, or cloches if the weather turns cold.

Sow in pots and transplant, or sow directly into shallow drills that are 2cm (³⁄₄in) deep, and at least 38cm (15in) apart. Once the seedlings have established, thin to about 23cm (9in) apart.

CROP CARE

Weed and water regularly and be vigilant against pests.

Cut away the leafy stems before storing.

HARVESTING

Swedes should be ready to harvest in autumn or early winter when they are about 10–15cm (4–6in) in diameter. They can be left in the ground for as long as needed, even over winter, although bear in mind that they risk turning woody the longer they are left, and will need a protective layer of straw if the weather turns cold.

STORING IN A CLAMP

Swedes can be left in the ground over winter, or when harvested, can be stored in boxes packed with moist sand. Traditionally however, swedes are stored in "clamps". To make a clamp spread a layer of straw 20cm (8in) thick on the ground in a sheltered spot. Arrange your swedes in a pyramid, twice as wide than tall, with the largest at the bottom and their necks facing outward. Cover with a 20cm (8in) layer of straw, and, if the weather is particularly cold, a layer of soil as well. Firm down, and check occasionally for signs of pests or damage.

PESTS AND DISEASES

Swedes are prone to the pests and diseases that affect members of the cabbage family, including cabbage root fly, clubroot, flea beetle, mealy cabbage aphids, and mildew (see pp.246–7). Try using fine netting to deter cabbage root fly and flea beetles.

Aphids can cause blistering on leaves.

'Brora'

A popular, fast-growing variety that develops an attractive reddish-purple skin. The fine-grained, creamy-yellow flesh has a good flavour and no bitterness. It is resistant to clubroot and powdery mildew, has good winter hardiness, and stores well.

- suitable for containers
- early summer
- good resistance
- hardy
- early autumn

'Marian'

An old favourite, which bears heavy crops of uniform, purple, globe-shaped roots with cream-coloured bases. The yellow flesh is of a fine texture and an excellent flavour. This variety is resistant to both clubroot and powdery mildew.

- suitable for containers
- early summer
- good resistance
- hardy
- early autumn

'Best of All'

A popular variety, 'Best of All' is easily grown and is a reliable cropper. It bears medium-sized roots with a purple skin and yellow flesh, which has a mild flavour and smooth texture. It has good winter hardiness and stores well.

- suitable for containers
- early summer
- good resistance
- hardy
- early autumn

'Helenor'

A large, purple, globe-shaped swede with a cream-coloured base and a deep yellow flesh that has a smooth texture and sweet flavour. This variety is resistant to mildew, has excellent winter hardiness, and stores well once harvested.

 suitable for containers

early summer

good resistance

hardy

early autumn

'Ruby' ♀

The globe-shaped, slightly elongated roots have an attractive, dark purple skin. The creamy-yellow flesh deepens in colour when cooked, and has an outstanding, extra sweet flavour. It is resistant to powdery mildew and is winter hardy.

suitable for containers

early summer

good resistance

hardy

early autumn

'Wilhelmsburger' ♀

This heirloom variety bears roots of a uniform, rounded shape, with a green skin that is unusual amongst swedes. The creamy, golden-white flesh is firm and free from bitterness. It is resistant to clubroot and stores well.

suitable for containers

early summer

good resistance

hardy

early autumn

RADISHES *Raphanus sativus*

You may be surprised to discover that there are hundreds of different types of radish, not just the familiar small, red salad types. If you fancy some variety, try the large, white Oriental mooli (or daikon) radishes that can grow as long as 60cm (24in) and weigh up to 2kg (4½lb), or grow winter radishes in rainbow shades of black, purple, yellow, or green, and eat these raw, or cook in the same way as swedes or tunips.

	SPRING	SUMMER	AUTUMN	WINTER
SOW				
HARVEST				

SOWING

Radishes are a versatile crop and will grow in almost any location. They will tolerate partial shade, and are happy interplanted with other crops or grown in containers, but dislike recently manured soil.

Radishes can be grown successionally to provide a year-round crop; very early radishes can be sown indoors before planting out; summer radishes should be sown directly in the ground in early spring; and winter radishes in mid- to late summer. By sowing seed every few weeks you can achieve a continuous harvest. Sow at a depth of 1cm (½in) in rows or blocks, thinning summer radishes to 2.5cm (1in) apart,

Interplant with slow-growing crops.

and winter radishes to 15cm (6in) apart, once crops are establised.

CROP CARE

Water regularly but be careful not to overwater or you will simply encourage too much leafy growth.

HARVESTING

Summer radishes grow very quickly and some may be ready to eat in as little as one month.

Harvest promptly as they tend to bolt and become woody. Winter radishes can be harvested from autumn until the following spring. Their seed pods are also edible, so leave the roots in the ground over winter and they will produce a flowering stem and juicy seed pods.

STORING

As with other root crops, radishes can be stored in boxes packed with moist sand. Alternatively winter radishes can be left in the ground over winter, although they may need protection from hard frosts.

PESTS AND DISEASES

Try to prevent flea beetles, slugs, and snails from targeting radish leaves by using fine netting around plants. Practise strict crop rotation to help prevent diseases such as clubroot, which is an incurable fungus that can persist in the soil for up to 20 years.

Flea beetles create ragged leaf holes.

'Saxa 2'

An early variety with roots that mature within just three weeks of sowing outdoors, 'Saxa' can also be sown under glass or cloches for an even earlier crop. The round roots are bright red, with crisp, mild, white flesh.

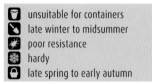

	unsuitable for containers
	late winter to midsummer
	poor resistance
	hardy
	late spring to early autumn

'April Cross'

The white, cylindrical roots of this daikon radish grow up to 38cm (15in) long and 5cm (2in) in diameter. The roots have crisp, fine-textured flesh with a mild flavour, good for cooking or for salads. This variety is slow to bolt and stores well.

	unsuitable for containers
	early to late summer
	poor resistance
	hardy
	late summer to late autumn

'Minowase Summer Cross'

The white, tapering roots of this daikon radish have a crisp texture and mild, sweet flavour. They grow up to 50cm (20in) long and can be used raw or cooked. Its good resistance to viruses, fusarium wilt, and heat is an added advantage.

	unsuitable for containers
	early to late summer
	good resistance
	hardy
	mid to late autumn

'Amethyst'

Shiny, deep purple skins
and crisp white flesh make
this new variety attractive for
its appearance as well as its
flavour. The roots retain their
crispness well, and the strong
tops allow roots to be easily
pulled from the ground.

 suitable for containers
early spring to early autumn
some resistance
hardy
late spring to midwinter

'Giant of Sicily'

An heirloom radish from Sicily,
this variety has bright red-
skinned roots, up to 5cm (2in)
across, with tender, crisp white
flesh with a good flavour. Roots
mature 45 days after sowing.
It is easy to grow and shows
some resistance to clubroot.

unsuitable for containers
early spring to early autumn
good resistance
hardy
late spring to mid-autumn

'White Icicle'

This 16th-century Italian
variety has smooth, tapering
roots about 10–12cm (4–5in)
long, with crisp, mild flesh.
It is at its best harvested 30
days after sowing, but retains
its mildness in maturity and
is slow to become pithy.

unsuitable for containers
early spring to early autumn
poor resistance
hardy
mid-spring to mid-autumn

'Scarlet Globe' ♀

Bright red, round roots with crisp, white, mild flesh are produced on an adaptable plant that will do well even in poor soils. It can be grown under cloches for early cropping – roots will be ready to pull in four to six weeks.

- unsuitable for containers
- late winter to early autumn
- some resistance
- hardy
- early spring to mid-autumn

'München Bier'

This radish is grown for its 7.5cm (3in) green pods, as well as for its turnip-like white roots, both of which are good in salads and stir-fries. Sow in spring for the pods, or summer and autumn for the roots.

- unsuitable for containers
- early spring to early autumn
- poor resistance
- hardy
- late spring to late autumn

'Pink Beauty' ♀

Even when large, the roots of 'Pink Beauty' retain their sweet, mild flavour, and resist the onset of pithiness longer than most varieties. They are round, with rose-pink skins and crisp white flesh. This variety is also slow to bolt.

- unsuitable for containers
- late winter to early autumn
- some resistance
- hardy
- late spring to mid-autumn

'French Breakfast' ♀

Elongated, bright scarlet roots with white tips identify this classic variety. It is one of the fast-growing radishes, but also one of the quickest to turn pithy. The flavour is mild and sweet when young, becoming hotter as roots mature.

 suitable for containers
late winter to early autumn
some resistance
hardy
late spring to mid-autumn

'Purple Plum'

A striking variety with purple skin and crisp, white, sweet, and mild flesh, this radish tolerates heat well. It is slow to pithiness and is hardy, adaptable, and fast-maturing, good in containers as well as in the vegetable bed.

suitable for containers
late winter to early autumn
poor resistance
hardy
late spring to mid-autumn

'Rudolf'

This early and fast-growing radish has strong, upright foliage and large, round, red roots that are uniform in shape and colour. It can be sown under glass for earlier crops and shows resistance to most of the pests and diseases that afflict radishes.

unsuitable for containers
early spring to midsummer
good resistance
hardy
late spring to mid-autumn

'Cherry Belle' ♈

This early, fast-growing variety is cherry-shaped, with a bright red skin and mild-favoured, crisp, white flesh that is slow to become pithy in maturity. Sow under cloches for an early crop; the roots are ready to pull only 24 days later.

- unsuitable for containers
- early spring to early summer
- some resistance
- hardy
- mid-spring to midsummer

'Sparkler' ♈

The bright red, spherical roots of this reliable Victorian variety are attractively white-tipped. They have crunchy flesh with a mildly peppery flavour and are slow to pithiness. Sow in a moist, cool position; early sowings can be made under glass or cloches.

- unsuitable for containers
- late winter to early autumn
- some resistance
- hardy
- late spring to mid-autumn

'Zlata'

Unusual for their golden skin, the roots of 'Zlata' are round to plum-shaped, with crunchy white flesh, a juicy texture, and a strong, mildly spicy flavour – excellent in salads. This Polish variety is resistant to both bolting and pithiness.

- unsuitable for containers
- early spring to early autumn
- poor resistance
- hardy
- late spring to late autumn

'China Rose'

The oblong roots of this winter variety have pinkish-red skin and white flesh, with a hot, pungent flavour. Best harvested when 10–15cm (4–6in) long, they keep especially well if stored in dry sand. The leaves are also good to eat.

 unsuitable for containers

early to midsummer

poor resistance

hardy

late summer to mid-autumn

'Long Black Spanish'

This winter radish has black skin and white flesh. Roots can reach a length of 20cm (8in), and are more pungent than round types, with a fiery taste. The roots can be used cooked or raw, and can be left in the ground until needed, or stored in sand.

unsuitable for containers

early summer to early autumn

poor resistance

hardy

early autumn to midwinter

'Mantanghong'

This Chinese-type winter radish has greenish-white skin and crisp, bright magenta flesh, which tastes sweet and slightly nutty – good in salads or as a winter vegetable. They can grow to 35cm (14in) long and can be left in the ground until needed.

unsuitable for containers

early to late summer

poor resistance

hardy

early autumn to midwinter

TURNIPS *Brassica rapa* Rapifera Group

Grown like root vegetables but members of the brassica family, turnips are an often overlooked crop. Harvested young, their roots have a delicious nutty flavour and are excellent cooked or eaten raw. Also try harvesting the spicy young leaves, or "turnip tops", and cook as spring greens. There are many unusual varieties that are well worth trying, in a variety of striking colours, including black, purple, and white.

	SPRING	SUMMER	AUTUMN	WINTER
SOW/PLANT				
HARVEST				

SOWING

Turnips will grow well in most soils but they require high levels of nitrogen and a pH of between 5.5–7.5. Dig in some well-rotted manure or compost the autumn before planting.

Sow four seeds to a cell in module trays and transplant each group when seedlings have grown two or three leaves each. Protect seedlings from frost. Alternatively, sow seed directly into the ground in early spring; they are less likely to germinate in later months when the weather warms up. To avoid a glut, sow successively every few weeks. Scatter seed thinly along rows 23–30cm (9–12in) apart, or in blocks spaced 15cm (6in) apart. Cover with 2cm (³/₄in) of soil and

Plant out module-grown crops in spring.

water in. Thin seedlings to 10–15cm (4–6in) apart before they are more than 2.5cm (1in) tall. For turnip tops, sow in late summer, early autumn, or early spring.

CROP CARE

Keep plants weeded and well-watered, especially during the summer, to prevent them from bolting. Turnips should not need an additional feed during growth.

HARVESTING

Early turnips will be ready to harvest within about five to six weeks, and larger maincrop varieties in about ten. Harvest by late autumn as the roots risk becoming woody if left in the ground for too long. Pick the "turnip tops" when leaves are still young, about 13–15cm (5–6in) tall. If kept well-watered, the tops will usually crop a couple of times.

STORING

Turnips have a relatively high water content and do not store well. Harvest as needed and use them as soon as possible.

PESTS AND DISEASES

Like swedes, turnips are members of the brassica family and fall prey to the same pests and diseases (see pp.246-7). Sow seed under fine mesh to prevent attack from cabbage root fly and flea beetles. Also watch out for diseases such as clubroot and downy mildew.

Clubroot stunts growth and kills crops.

'Golden Ball'

A dwarf variety popular since the 19th century, this very hardy turnip has deep yellow roots with soft flesh and a sweet flavour. Round while young, they flatten a little at their mature size of 7.5–10cm (3–4in). They store particularly well.

- unsuitable for containers
- late spring to late summer
- poor resistance
- hardy
- midsummer to late autumn

'Oasis' ♀

Eaten raw, this unusual turnip has a flavour like that of a melon; cooked, it tastes like a turnip but with a more delicate flavour. The conical white roots are fast-maturing and can be picked at any size. It has good resistance to viruses.

- unsuitable for containers
- mid-spring to midsummer
- good resistance
- hardy
- late spring to early autumn

'Tokyo Cross' ♀

This early, fast-growing variety is often harvested at about 2.5cm (1in) in diameter, when it can be eaten raw and tastes not unlike a radish. Equally, it can be left in the ground to mature and has smooth, sweet flesh when cooked.

- unsuitable for containers
- mid-spring to midsummer
- some resistance
- hardy
- late spring to mid-autumn

'Purple Top Milan'

This 19th-century turnip has
flattened roots, purple at the
top and white below ground.
It is useful for early crops
when sown under protection
of cloches. It does not store
well and is best pulled when the
roots are 5–7.5cm (2–3in) across.

- 🪣 unsuitable for containers
- 🕐 late spring to midsummer
- ✳ poor resistance
- ❄ hardy
- 🔒 midsummer to early autumn

'Snowball'

A fast-growing variety, 'Snowball'
can be brought to harvesting
point even earlier by sowing
under cloches. The roots have
white skin and their tender flesh
has a mild and sweet flavour.
They can be pulled at six to eight
weeks for use as baby vegetables.

- 🪣 unsuitable for containers
- 🕐 early spring to midsummer
- ✳ poor resistance
- ❄ hardy
- 🔒 late spring to mid-autumn

'Primera' ♀

The roots of this variety are
small and flattened, with
purple tops, smooth skin, and
succulent, sweet flesh. Harvest
them when they are the size
of golf balls, about five weeks
after sowing, and use them
either raw or cooked.

- 🪣 unsuitable for containers
- 🕐 mid-spring to late summer
- ✳ some resistance
- ❄ hardy
- 🔒 late spring to mid-autum

'Atlantic' ♔

This variety crops over a long period, producing flattened, round, white roots with purple crowns that can be harvested from the time they reach golf ball size. The upright leaves can be cooked as a green vegetable and will resprout after cutting.

- suitable for containers
- early spring to late summer
- some resistance
- hardy
- late spring to early winter

'Ivory' ♔

This variety produces uniform, white roots that are long and cylindrical with a smooth skin. Their flavour is sweet and delicious. If growing for the tops, sow in early spring, late summer, or early autumn, and they will be ready to harvest a month later.

- unsuitable for containers
- late winter to late summer
- some resistance
- hardy
- late winter to late summer

'Tokyo Top' ♔

Like 'Tokyo Cross', this variety can be harvested young to be eaten raw in salads, or allowed to mature for cooking. The roots are uniformly small, round, and white. It is resistant to virus and downy mildew, and is slow to bolt.

- unsuitable for containers
- mid-spring to midsummer
- good resistance
- hardy
- early summer to late autumn

'Blanc de Croissy'

An old, easy-to-grow, French variety, 'Blanc de Croissy' produces unusual, oblong, white roots that have a sweet, pungent flavour and crisp texture. They grow up to 15cm (6in) long and 4cm (1½in) across, maturing 45–60 days after sowing.

- unsuitable for containers
- late winter to early summer
- poor resistance
- hardy
- mid-spring to late summer

'Tiny Pal' ♀

The roots of 'Tiny Pal' are the size of golf balls, round, and white with a good flavour. They grow very fast; successional sowings will give you crops over a long harvesting period. They will do well in a container.

- suitable for containers
- early spring to late summer
- some resistance
- hardy
- late spring to mid-autumn

'Market Express' ♀

This very hardy, fast-maturing variety has pure white, globe-shaped roots with a mild, sweet flavour. They are best harvested at 4–5cm (1½–2in), within about 50 days. Sow seed little and often for a constant supply over a long cropping period.

- unsuitable for containers
- mid- to late spring
- some resistance
- hardy
- late spring to mid-autumn

SALSIFY AND SCORZONERA

Tragopogon porrifolius and *Scorzonera hispanica*

Salsify and scorzonera, sometimes called black salsify, are root crops that are relatively uncommon but well worth growing if you have the space. Similar in texture to a parsnip but with an oyster-like flavour, salsify can be cooked in stews or soups, and the young leaves can be used in salads. Scorzonera is similar, but has black skin and larger leaves.

	SPRING	SUMMER	AUTUMN	WINTER
SOW				
HARVEST				

SOWING

Both salsify and scorzonera will develop long, tapering roots, so ensure that you sow them in deep, light soil where there are no root-obstructing stones. Both crops prefer a pH range of 6–7.5 and an open, sunny position. It is important to use fresh salsify seed every year as old seed declines in quality and is less likely to germinate.

Sow seed directly into the ground in mid- to late spring, as soon as the soil warms up. Sow thinly in drills at a depth of 1cm (½in), allowing both salsify and scorzonera 15–30cm (6–12in) between rows. Scorzonera can also be sown in late summer to be harvested the following autumn; it is slow-growing

Keep the leafy crops well weeded.

and can be left in the ground for up to 18 months if necessary. Both crops can be overwintered.

CROP CARE

Keep plants well-watered and ensure that they are kept free from weeds. Either apply a mulch, such as black plastic sheeting, to suppress them, or weed by hand; using a hoe may damage the roots.

HARVESTING

Both crops can be harvested for their roots or leaves. When roots have reached the desired size, dig them out carefully as they can be quite brittle; scorzonera roots are prone to "bleed" if damaged.

Roots left in the ground over winter they will sprout again in spring. Cover the plants with a layer of straw or leaves to blanch new growth. Salsify produces tasty shoots, and will re-sprout two or three times. Scorzonera leaves should be cut when they reach 10cm (4in) long. The flowerbuds can also be harvested and eaten.

PESTS AND DISEASES

Both salsify and scorzonera have excellent general pest and disease resistance but are sometimes prone to white blister disease. This fungus causes white patches to appear on the underside of leaves and creates yellowish patches on the top, causing leaves and flowers to become misshapen. Ensuring that plants are well ventilated, with enough air and space, will help to prevent the spread of this disease. Practise crop rotation to prevent a build up in the soil. Resistant varieties are available.

'Sandwich Island Mammoth'

This heirloom variety bears some of the finest-tasting salsify. The long, tapered, white roots have a sweet, tender, white flesh, with an outstanding oyster-like flavour. This variety keeps well, and can also be overwintered in the soil until mid-spring.

🪣	unsuitable for containers
🌱	mid-spring
❄	good resistance
❄	hardy
🔒	mid-autumn to mid-spring

'Giant'

This popular, widely available salsify variety reliably produces long, slender, elongated white roots with a good flavour. As with other varieties, roots can be lifted in autumn for storing, or left to overwinter in the soil until mid-spring.

🪣	unsuitable for containers
🌱	mid-spring
❄	good resistance
❄	hardy
🔒	mid-autumn to mid-spring

'Scorzobianca'

A popular salsify variety, 'Scorzobianca' bears white-skinned, white-fleshed roots that have an excellent flavour. As with other varieties, they store well or can be overwintered in the ground and lifted when needed.

🪣	unsuitable for containers
🌱	mid-spring
❄	good resistance
❄	hardy
🔒	mid-autumn to mid-spring

'Long Black Maxima'

This modern variety of scorzonera produces long, black-skinned roots that have a delicate flavour. It produces heavy yields and also has good resistance to bolting. The roots can be harvested in autumn or left to overwinter in the ground.

 unsuitable for containers
mid-spring
good resistance
hardy
mid-autumn to mid-spring

'Russian Giant'

Also known as 'Geante Noire de Russie', this is the most popular and widely available of scorzonera varieties. The long, slender, black roots have white flesh and a delicate flavour. The leaves can also be used in salads.

unsuitable for containers
mid-spring
good resistance
hardy
mid-autumn to mid-spring

'Belstar Super'

This US-only scorzonera is grown for its 23–28cm (9–11in) long, straight, black-skinned, white-fleshed roots that are eaten boiled, baked, or in soups and stews. 'Belstar Super' is a vigorous, early-maturing strain that is free of side-roots.

unsuitable for containers
early to late spring
good resistance
hardy
mid- to late autumn

JERUSALEM ARTICHOKES

Helianthus tuberosus

A relative of the sunflower, Jerusalem artichokes are tall and stately plants that can produce bright yellow, sunflower-like blooms. The knobbly tubers develop in the soil in autumn, and can be eaten raw or cooked, but beware – they are notorious for producing flatulence. Don't be put off, as the tubers are a delicious vegetable.

	SPRING	SUMMER	AUTUMN	WINTER
PLANT				
HARVEST				

PLANTING TUBERS

Jerusalem artichokes will grow almost anywhere as long as the soil is not water-logged, but they prefer alkaline conditions, so add lime to the soil if its pH is below 5. Plants can grow to about 3m (10ft) tall, so site them carefully – they can be grown to form natural screens or windbreaks.

Either obtain tubers fresh from a nursery, or use saved tubers from previous years. Apply a soil improver before planting to encourage larger tubers. Plant when the soil has warmed up in early spring. Dig a drill 10–15cm (4–6in) deep and place tubers along it at intervals of 30–45cm (12–18in), before covering over with soil.

The vibrant flowers add a splash of colour.

CROP CARE

Weed well, and water during dry spells. Plants will need to be earthed up as they grow, with about 4–10cm (1½–4in) of soil, and supported with canes or wires. This provides the tall stems with stability, which is especially useful if they are planted in an exposed or windy position. In mid- to late summer cut the plant down to 1.5m (5ft),

and remove any flowers. This will encourage the plant to divert its energy and attention into producing tubers. Remove any yellowing foliage in autumn, and cut the stem back to about 10cm (4in) above ground level.

HARVESTING

Jerusalem artichoke tubers should be left in the ground and harvested as required – they don't keep very well once lifted. Ensure that all tubers are removed from the ground at the end of the season as they will grow again the following year, and may become invasive.

PESTS AND DISEASES

Jerusalem artichokes are generally a problem-free crop, but they may come under attack from slugs and snails. To deter these, use pellets, place beer traps around your plot, and lay a ring of sharp gravel, crushed eggshells, or copper tape as a barrier.

More rarely, white blister may affect crops. It causes whitish patches on the underside of leaves, with yellow patches on the top. There is no cure for this fungus, so remove and destroy any affected plants, improve ventilation, and practise crop rotation.

'Common'

This variety of Jerusalem artichoke has knobbly, irregular-shaped tubers with a pale purple-brown skin that needs peeling before cooking. Despite this extra preparation, its flavour is as good as that of the other varieties.

- 🪣 unsuitable for containers
- 🌱 early spring
- 🕷 good resistance
- ❄ hardy
- 🔒 mid-autumn to mid-spring

'Fuseau'

This is perhaps the most popular variety because of its large, smooth-skinned tubers, which are easier to peel than other, more knobbly types. The white flesh has a nutty flavour and is good roasted, boiled, or baked.

- 🪣 unsuitable for containers
- 🌱 early spring
- 🕷 good resistance
- ❄ hardy
- 🔒 mid-autumn to mid-spring

'Dwarf Sunray'

As the name suggests, this is a more compact variety, with shorter stems, and makes an attractive ornamental plant. The tubers have a good flavour and their white skin is thinner than that of other varieties, so does not need peeling.

- 🪣 unsuitable for containers
- 🌱 early spring
- 🕷 good resistance
- ❄ hardy
- 🔒 mid-autumn to mid-spring

'Stampede'

Recommended for areas with early frosts, 'Stampede' flowers and matures a month earlier than other varieties. Plants are 2–2.5m (6–8ft) tall, and the tubers are white and rounded, weighing as much as 225g (8oz) each.

- 🪣 unsuitable for containers
- 🌱 early spring
- 🕷 good resistance
- ❄ hardy
- 🔒 mid- to late autumn

'Fuseau'

Brassicas and Leafy Vegetables

- Cabbages
- Brussels sprouts
- Cauliflowers
- Broccoli
- Kale
- Spinach
- Swiss chard
- Kohl rabi
- Pak choi
- Chinese cabbage

CABBAGE *Brassica oleracea* Capitata Group

Cabbages are usually classified according to when they are harvested, and by planting a number of different varieties you can ensure a year-round supply. Spring and summer cabbages are round or pointed in shape, and need to be eaten soon after picking. Autumn and winter cabbages are generally larger in size, with denser heads, and are hardy. They can be stored for months once harvested.

	SPRING	SUMMER	AUTUMN	WINTER
SOW/PLANT				
HARVEST				

SOWING

Dig in well-rotted manure or compost in the autumn before planting, and add some lime to the soil in winter if its pH is less than 6.8. Most importantly, the soil needs to be firm, as some cabbages will grow very heavy and their roots will need to support their weight. Ensure that you have a crop rotation system in place as cabbages should not be planted where brassicas have grown within the last three years.

Although summer and winter cabbages need sowing at different times of year, the method is still the same – sow in pots or modules at a depth of 2cm (¾in). Sow summer, autumn, and red cabbages in early spring; sow

Thin seedlings to give them room to grow.

winter cabbages in mid- to late spring; and sow spring cabbages in summer, ready for harvesting the following year.

PLANTING OUT

Plant out your seedlings when they have four leaves. Plant in rows 40–60cm (16–24in) apart, with 30–45cm (12–18in) between plants. Dig holes about 15cm (6in) deep, and water before gently

planting the seedlings. Fit your seedlings with a brassica collar (see pests, right) to deter cabbage root fly, which will attack the roots. At all stages of growth cabbages will be irresistible to birds and cabbage white butterflies, so put mesh or netting over your crop.

Net cabbages to deter butterflies.

CROP CARE

Weed seedlings thoroughly. Water regularly, daily if necessary when young, and then once a week when plants are more established. As cabbages grow you will need to earth up the soil around them to support the weight of their growing heads. Trim off any dead outer leaves. Apply a high-nitrogen fertilizer or organic liquid feed to summer-sown cabbages in winter; feed autumn-sown cabbages in spring.

HARVESTING

Spring or early summer cabbages can be harvested when they are still loose and leafy, before their leaves develop into a firm head; these are known as "spring

DISEASES

Cabbages are under threat from diseases such as downy and powdery mildew and white blister, but there are few as serious as clubroot – a disease to which all brassicas are prone. This fungus attacks the plants' roots, rotting and eventually killing them. There is no cure – so good garden hygiene, crop rotation, and digging up and destroying infected plants are absolutely essential.

Plants cannot be cured of clubroot. It can persist in the soil for up to 20 years.

greens". Once cut, you might be able to persuade the remaining stumps to produce a second crop: with a sharp knife, make a cross-cut pattern on the stump, and water as normal. Alternatively, wait for your cabbages to develop dense hearts, and then cut the head from the roots with a sharp knife. Use spring and summer types as soon as possible after harvesting as they don't keep well.

Harvest autumn and winter cabbages as needed. Winter cabbages are frost hardy and slow to bolt – they can be left in the ground over winter, so there is no rush to harvest them. As with spring and summer cabbages, cut the heads from the roots with a sharp knife, or dig the entire cabbage up. To reduce the risk of diseases persisting in the soil, dig up all remaining roots shortly after harvesting.

STORING

Autumn and winter cabbages can be stored for months if they are harvested before the first frosts, but ensure that they are cut with at least a 15cm (6in) stem. Hang them in net bags in a cool, dark place, or lay them on wooden slats and cover them with straw or newspaper, to protect them if the weather turns cold.

PESTS

You may find your cabbages under threat from a range of pests, and you may have to use more than one different measure during the crop's growth. When seedlings are young or first planted out, use a collar to prevent cabbage root flies from laying eggs next to the vulnerable plants. You can make your own using a small square of cardboard or carpet underlay.

Consider using a cloche or the cut-off top of a plastic bottle for protection against pests such as cabbage white caterpillars and mealy cabbage aphids; these may also be a problem at later stages of growth.

Use netting to deter birds and cabbage white butterflies. Construct a wooden or wire frame over your plants and fix the netting to it.

Cabbage white butterfly caterpillars will swarm a cabbage, stripping its leaves. Pick the caterpillars off by hand. If necessary spray with an insecticide.

'Ruby Ball'

This ruby-red, summer variety is an excellent cabbage. Quick to grow from a spring sowing, it produces a dense, compact head with colourful, tasty leaves. Add vinegar to the water when cooking to retain the colour. It can also be used in salads and coleslaw.

- unsuitable for containers
- mid-spring
- poor resistance
- fairly hardy
- late summer to autumn

'Integro'

This excellent, quick-growing, tasty cabbage produces a rosette of large, red-veined, greyish, leaves. Right in the centre is a tight, crisp ball of shiny, ruby-red leaves that are ideal for colourful salads, coleslaw, and pickling.

- unsuitable for containers
- mid-spring
- poor resistance
- fairly hardy
- late summer to autumn

'Red Jewel'

A top choice, this hardy variety produces large, tightly packed, round, purple-red heads, set off by their wide rosettes of leaves. Sow it in mid-spring for cutting from mid-autumn, or leave it in the ground over winter for harvesting when it is required.

- unsuitable for containers
- mid-spring
- poor resistance
- hardy
- early to mid-autumn

'Savoy King'

One of the best winter Savoys, this variety produces light green leaves and one of the biggest heads – it is ideal for feeding large families. Sow in spring for a tasty, early autumn crop that will stand well over the winter months without splitting.

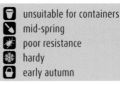

- unsuitable for containers
- mid-spring
- poor resistance
- hardy
- early autumn

'Ruby Perfection'

A good choice for containers and small plots because of its upright habit, 'Ruby Perfection' puts on quick growth from a spring sowing. The tight, round, red heads can be harvested from late summer, and are excellent used in salads or coleslaws.

- suitable for containers
- mid-spring
- poor resistance
- fairly hardy
- late summer to autumn

'Super Red 80'

The round, rich burgundy heads of this US-only variety are produced about 80 days after transplanting. Protected by thick, tough outer leaves, the hearts have a peppery taste, and hold up well in hot and cold weather.

- unsuitable for containers
- mid-spring to midsummer
- some resistance
- fairly hardy
- midsummer to mid-autumn

'Red Drumhead'

This variety is a good choice for small gardens due to its compact size, and for the kitchen because of its dark red, solid, round heads. It is good for adding colour to salads, or used finely shredded in coleslaws and pickles. Sow in mid-spring for an autumn harvest.

- unsuitable for containers
- mid-spring
- poor resistance
- fairly hardy
- early to mid-autumn

'Duncan' ♀

This versatile cabbage has a range of sowing options: sow in late summer for a spring crop; sow in early summer for an autumn crop; or sow in late summer for a late autumn crop of leafy greens. It has excellent flavour and won't split when left in the ground.

- 🪣 unsuitable for containers
- 🌱 early to late summer
- ✳ some resistance
- ❄ hardy
- 🔒 spring to late autumn

'Tundra' ♀

This excellent, sweet-tasting, frost-hardy, Savoy cabbage is sown in late spring, ready for cutting from autumn to mid-spring the following year. The solid, dark green cabbages keep well when left in the ground.

- 🪣 unsuitable for containers
- 🌱 late spring
- ✳ some resistance
- ❄ hardy
- 🔒 mid-autumn to mid-spring

'Durham Early'

This very popular, tasty cabbage has a pointed, firm shape. It is worth growing for fresh spring crops from an autumn sowing. It can also be grown to produce tasty late winter–early spring greens, if cabbages are closely planted the previous summer.

- unsuitable for containers
- mid- to late summer
- poor resistance
- hardy
- mid- to late spring

'Early Jersey Wakefield'

Regarded by many gardeners as one of the tastiest cabbages, this established, US-only variety dates back to the mid-19th century. Compact plants produce solid, conical heads, maturing 60 to 65 days from transplanting.

- unsuitable for containers
- mid-spring to midsummer
- poor resistance
- fairly hardy
- midsummer to mid-autumn

'Myatt's Early Offenham'

This attractive variety adds striking, wide, dark green leaves to the kitchen garden. If seed is sown in autumn, spring greens can be harvested in early spring, or leave them to develop a head and harvest in late spring.

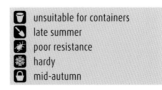

- unsuitable for containers
- late summer
- poor resistance
- hardy
- mid-autumn

'Pixie' ♔

This pointy-headed, compact cabbage is ideal for close planting, so is a great choice for a small garden. The outer leaves can be picked for spring greens, added to roasts, or sautéed. Sow in late summer for an early spring crop.

 unsuitable for containers
mid- to late summer
some resistance
fairly hardy
mid-autumn

'Wheeler's Imperial'

Grown for at least 100 years, this compact, dwarf variety produces dark green, dense heads in autumn from a spring sowing. With few outer leaves, plants can be set just 30cm (12in) apart. Closer planting in late summer will generate an abundance of fresh spring greens.

unsuitable for containers
mid-spring
poor resistance
hardy
early autumn

'Spring Hero'

This variety is grown for its solid, dark green, round heads, each weighing up to 1kg (2lb 4oz), and with a crisp, white, tasty heart. The cabbages are ideal for use in salads, stews, coleslaws, or pickles. Sow in late summer, no earlier, for a spring crop.

 unsuitable for containers
late summer
poor resistance
hardy
spring

'Savoy Express Baby'

One petite, yellow-green head of US-only 'Savoy Express' is the right size for a single meal. The sweet flavour of this attractive crinkled hybrid, combined with its extra early ripening time, earned it an All America Selections award in 2000.

unsuitable for containers
mid-spring to midsummer
poor resistance
fairly hardy
early summer to autumn

'Wheeler's Imperial'

'Stonehead' ♀

This variety gets its name from the solid, round, packed-tight, crisp heads, growing on short, thick stalks. It is an ideal choice for small gardens as cabbages can be planted just 30cm (12in) apart. Sow in early spring for cropping after midsummer, or sow later for an autumn crop.

- unsuitable for containers
- early to late spring
- some resistance
- fairly hardy
- midsummer to autumn

'Hispi' ♀

This compact variety is an excellent cabbage for a small garden. It can be sown year round. Sow in the winter greenhouse for a tasty early summer crop, or in mid-spring for a midsummer harvest. It can be left in the ground without splitting.

- unsuitable for containers
- mid-spring
- some resistance
- fairly hardy
- midsummer

'Minicole' ♀

This variety produces small, crisp, tightly-packed, greenish-white heads that are ideal for a small garden. They grow quickly from spring to autumn, and can be left standing for up to four months without deteriorating. They are ideal for use in salads and coleslaws.

- unsuitable for containers
- late spring
- some resistance
- hardy
- early autumn to early winter

'Famosa'

This quick-growing, fast-maturing, F1 Savoy type is grown for its compact, solid heads, which are ready for cutting from late summer. It produces an excellent crop of attractive, fresh green, crinkly leaves that are packed with flavour.

- unsuitable for containers
- mid-spring
- poor resistance
- fairly hardy
- late sumer to early autumn

'Brunswick'

This large, quick-growing variety dates back to the 1870s and even earlier. It produces dense, solid, 23cm (9in) wide heads, each weighing up to 4kg (9lb). The cabbages are borne in the centre of a 75cm (30in) wide ruff of green outer leaves.

- unsuitable for containers
- mid-spring
- poor resistance
- fairly hardy
- late summer to early autumn

'Winningstadt'

This dual-purpose, pointy-headed cabbage, originally from America, dates back to the mid-19th century. The cabbages have a sweet flavour, and can be grown for an autumn crop of solid hearts when sown in spring, or alternatively, leafy greens if sown in late summer.

- unsuitable for containers
- mid- to late spring
- poor resistance
- fairly hardy
- early to late autumn

'Elisa' ♀

This sweet, summer-cropping F1 cabbage produces compact, round, shiny heads. It is a useful crop as it can be left standing for longer than most varieties, without danger of splitting or bolting. It is excellent in salads and stir-fries, and for steaming.

- unsuitable for containers
- mid-spring
- some resistance
- fairly hardy
- late summer

'Derby Day' ♀

One of the best early ball-head types, this variety is ready for harvesting from midsummer. It grows quickly, producing light green, tasty heads, with very good resistance to bolting. They can be sautéed, steamed, or shredded in salads.

- unsuitable for containers
- mid-spring
- some resistance
- fairly hardy
- mid- to late summer

'Farao F1'

This short-season, US-only hybrid yields dense, round, deep green heads that can reach 1.6kg (3½lb) or more, and have a crisp texture and peppery, sweet taste. Plants are resistant thrips and hold well in summer heat.

- unsuitable for containers
- mid-spring to midsummer
- good resistance
- fairly hardy
- midsummer to mid-autumn

'Caraflex Pointed-Head'

This hybrid US-only variety produces small, pointed, very uniform heads, with tight outer leaves that protect the tender insides from insects. It is crunchy and sweet, and stores well. The plants are resistant to fusarium wilt.

- unsuitable for containers
- mid-spring to midsummer
- good resistance
- fairly hardy
- midsummer to mid-autumn

'January King' ♀

This very attractive, crispy, ball-headed winter variety reliably reddens up in the cold. It is excellent when gently sautéed or used in stir-fries or risottos. A late-spring sowing gives a crop ready for harvest from late autumn into midwinter.

- unsuitable for containers
- late spring
- some resistance
- hardy
- late autumn to midwinter

'Protovoy' ♀

A spring sowing of 'Protovoy' gives an autumn crop of small, pointed heads, about the size of tennis balls, perched on top of short, stout stalks. This makes them perfect for use in stir-fries, or for use as baby vegetables; they can be steamed or eaten raw.

- unsuitable for containers
- mid-spring
- some resistance
- fairly hardy
- early to mid-autumn

'Celtic' ♀

One of the best winter cabbages, this F1 hybrid is produced from a cross between winter-white and Savoy types. The round, hard heads can stand outside for months over winter without danger of splitting. They are excellent in soups and stews.

- unsuitable for containers
- late spring
- some resistance
- hardy
- late autumn to midwinter

'Tarvoy'

This remarkably useful Savoy cabbage lasts well in the ground over winter, with no ill effects. The dense, green head grows tucked inside its wide, puckered, dark green outer leaves. Sow in late spring for a late autumn to winter crop.

- unsuitable for containers
- late spring
- poor resistance
- hardy
- autumn to winter

'Premium Late Flat Dutch'

This German, US-only, heirloom variety produces huge, flattened oval heads that keep well into the winter. It grows slowly, requiring three to four months to mature, and is considered one of the best late season cabbages.

- unsuitable for containers
- spring to early summer
- poor resistance
- fairly hardy
- mid- to late autumn

'Celtic'

BRUSSELS SPROUTS

Brassica oleracea Gemmifera Group

Love them or hate them, this Christmas dinner staple resists indifference. Sprouts have a delicious, sweet, nutty taste when picked and cooked young, and their flavour is enhanced if harvested after a frost. Try growing one of the more unusual purple or red types and interplant with fast-growing crops like lettuces, to make the most of your space.

	SPRING	SUMMER	AUTUMN	WINTER
SOW/PLANT				
HARVEST				

SOWING

Sprouts need a soil with a pH of at least 6.8, so apply some lime if necessary. Dig in some well-rotted manure or compost in the autumn before planting, and ensure that the soil is firm – the plants will become quite heavy and need to support their own weight. Make sure that you have rotated your crops and that you are not planting sprouts where brassicas have been grown in the last three years.

Sow seeds in trays or modules at a depth of 2cm (¾in), or sow directly into the ground and protect with a cloche or fleece against frost. After about four or five weeks the seedlings should be ready to plant out. For autumn or late winter crops, plant

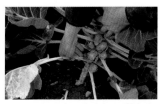

Harvest sprouts from the bottom upwards.

seedlings in early or mid-spring; for late summer–early autumn crops, sow seeds under cover in winter and plant out in spring. Space large plants 60cm (24in) apart, and dwarf varieties 45cm (18in). Plant them deeply, with the lowest leaves touching the soil.

CROP CARE

Fit a brassica collar around the seedlings to deter cabbage root

fly, and cover with netting. Keep plants weeded and well-watered, and earth up around the stems to provide extra support. Feed with a nitrogenous fertilizer or organic liquid feed in summer.

HARVESTING AND STORING

Harvest sprouts from the bottom of the plant first, and either cut them off with a knife, or snap them off. You could also dig up the whole plant, hang the stem in cool, frost-free place, or stand in a bucket of water and pick sprouts from it as you need them. The youngest leaves can also be picked and eaten as spring greens.

PESTS AND DISEASES

Covering your Brussels sprouts with fine netting or horticultural fleece and giving them a brassica collar will minimize the risk of bird and insect damage (see pp.246-7). Deter cabbage root fly as far as possible as once these appear they are difficult to get rid of. They will attack plant roots and cause them to rot. Brussels sprouts are also prone to mealy cabbage aphids and whitefly, which target leaves and will cause them to shrivel. Spray infected plants with insecticidal soap or use a suitable insecticide.

'Diablo' ♀

This variety produces sweet-tasting sprouts that are of uniform size and all mature at the same time, so the whole crop can be picked in one harvest if required. 'Diablo' grows vigorously and is resistant to fusarium wilt.

- unsuitable for containers
- early to mid-spring
- some resistance
- hardy
- autumn to winter

'Cascade' ♀

A very hardy variety, 'Cascade' withstands bad weather and can be harvested throughout the winter. The solid, dark green sprouts, borne in large quantities, are of excellent quality and have a fine taste. It has good resistance to powdery mildew.

- unsuitable for containers
- early to late spring
- good resistance
- hardy
- winter

'Clodius' ♀

The firm, tasty sprouts produced by this variety can be harvested right through the winter, as it stands up exceptionally well to cold weather. It also has excellent resistance to disease, in particular to powdery mildew and brassica ring spot.

- unsuitable for containers
- late spring
- excellent resistance
- hardy
- winter

'Rubine'

The small purple-red sprouts of this striking plant are both decorative and good to eat. They have a nutty flavour and keep their colour during cooking if steamed rather than boiled. This variety crops early but its season may extend through to late winter.

- unsuitable for containers
- early to mid-spring
- poor resistance
- hardy
- late autumn to midwinter

'Long Island Improved'

This heirloom variety is very high yielding, despite its compact size. Its dependability has made it a long-standing garden favourite. The firm, round, dark green sprouts grow closely packed together on the stem, and have a particularly fine flavour.

- unsuitable for containers
- early spring to summer
- poor resistance
- hardy
- autumn to winter

'Igor' ♀

The tightly wrapped, dark green sprouts of this heavy-cropping variety have an excellent flavour. They can be harvested in succession as needed, but will also last well on this very frost-tolerant plant for picking in a single harvest.

- unsuitable for containers
- early to mid-spring
- some resistance
- hardy
- late autumn to winter

'Falstaff'

The colour of this gourmet variety develops as the plant matures, from green to rich purple-red when the plant is touched by frost, and is retained during light cooking. 'Falstaff' matures slowly, bearing sprouts that are milder and nuttier in flavor than many other types.

- unsuitable for containers
- early to mid-spring
- poor resistance
- hardy
- autumn to winter

'Maximus' ♀

Abundant crops of smooth, solid sprouts last well on the stem and can be harvested over an exceptionally long period. 'Maximus' produces sweet-tasting sprouts that are free from bitterness. This robust variety is noted for good disease resistance.

- unsuitable for containers
- early to late spring
- good resistance
- hardy
- autumn to late winter

'Genius' ♀

This mid- to late season sprout is a comparatively new variety that has recently become popular. It is a heavy cropper, producing an abundance of small, firm, dark green sprouts until well into the winter. This variety has good resistance to brassica ring spot.

- unsuitable for containers
- early to late spring
- good resistance
- hardy
- late autumn to winter

'Red Delicious'

The purple-red sprouts of this unusual cultivar hold their colour better during cooking than some of the older red varieties. They have a mild flavour. Well formed, these sprouts look attractive on the stem, adding welcome interest to a winter garden.

	unsuitable for containers
	spring
	poor resistance
	hardy
	winter

'Bedford Fillbasket'

This traditional variety produces some of the largest sprouts to be found. Although not as uniform in size and shape as modern hybrids, the sprouts are firm and full of flavour. The plant is a prolific cropper over a long harvesting period.

	unsuitable for containers
	late winter to early spring
	poor resistance
	hardy
	autumn to winter

'Montgomery' ♀

This excellent, mid-season variety crops heavily, bearing sprouts in time for Christmas, right through until spring. The sprouts are dark green in colour, and are round and smooth. They have good flavour and are excellent for culinary use.

	unsuitable for containers
	early to mid-spring
	some resistance
	hardy
	autumn to late winter

CAULIFLOWER *Brassica oleracea* Botrytis Group

Cauliflowers require an investment of both time and space as they can stay in the ground for up to a year, taking up a relatively large amount of ground. If you give them enough water and can persuade them not to bolt, they will produce striking white, purple, or even lime-green heads, or "curds". With careful planning you can ensure a delicious crop, which can be cooked or eaten raw in salads, all year round.

	SPRING	SUMMER	AUTUMN	WINTER
SOW/PLANT				
HARVEST				

SOWING

Cauliflowers prefer fertile soil with a pH of no less than 6.8, so add lime to the soil if necessary. Fully grown heads, or "curds", will eventually become quite heavy, so cauliflowers need a firm soil to support them. Ensure that crops are rotated, and do not plant cauliflower where any brassicas have been grown in the last three years.

Cauliflowers can be grown to produce a year-round harvest. Sow seed in autumn or winter to produce an early summer crop; sow in spring for a summer and autumn crop; sow in late spring for a winter or spring crop.

Sow in pots or module trays at a depth of 2cm (³⁄₄in) and keep indoors or under a cloche or cold

Use a cloche to protect young seedlings.

frame to protect from frost and to encourage germination.

PLANTING

Do not let seedlings grow taller than 5cm (2in) before you plant them out, or you will risk damaging the roots, which might encourage plants to bolt.

Cauliflowers need space to grow, and generally the later you plant them, the more space they

need. Leave about 60cm (24in) between summer and autumn cauliflowers, and 70cm (28in) between winter and spring varieties. If you wish to grow miniature cauliflowers, choose fast-growing, early summer varieties and plant seedlings about 15cm (6in) apart. The crowded environment will cause growth to be stunted, producing heads that are approximately 4–8cm ($1^{1}/_{2}$–3in) in width.

At this height, seedlings are ready to plant.

CROP CARE

Young seedlings are a tempting delicacy for pests, so fit brassica collars (see pests and diseases box, below) to deter cabbage root fly, and use netting to prevent birds and butterflies getting at crops. Keep cauliflowers free from weeds, but most importantly, keep them well-watered; they are thirsty crops that require a lot of water during growth. Without sufficient water they may bolt or produce small, premature heads. Give winter and spring cauliflowers an organic liquid feed or nitrogenous fertilizer in late winter or early

PESTS AND DISEASES

Cauliflowers are prone to the pests and diseases that trouble all brassicas, so take the same precautions as for cabbages (see pp.246–7). Place brassica collars around the stems of vulnerable seedlings, net plants against attack from birds, and as best you can, guard against clubroot, as this disease is incurable and can persist in the soil for decades. Cauliflowers are also prone to boron and magnesium deficiencies.

Construct a frame out of bamboo canes and fasten your netting to it.

spring. Mulching around the plants during summer will also encourage steady growth.

Cauliflowers will need protection from discolouration by the sun, which can turn their curds yellow. To prevent this, use the leaves to form a shield over the curd (see tip box, right). This method can also be used to provide protection from the cold in winter. Firm the soil around the plants to give them extra support and protection in frosty and windy weather.

HARVESTING AND STORING

Harvest cauliflowers when the curds are firm – if left in the ground, the flower buds will open and the head will deteriorate. If you are not harvesting for immediate use, cut the head from the roots leaving some of the outer leaves on the curd. This will help to protect it from damage and keep it humid.

Store summer cauliflowers by hanging them in a cool, dark place, and spray them occasionally with water. They will last for up to three weeks. Autumn and winter cauliflowers store for longer. Miniature types don't keep, so should be harvested and eaten as soon as possible.

TIP BLANCHING

The process of tying cauliflower leaves so that they cover the curds, forming a shield, should be done in summer, when it prevents the sun from reaching the curds and turning them yellow. It will also help to protect cauliflowers from frost in winter since the leaves act as a layer of effective insulation.

Once plants are large enough, simply wrap the leaves inward, making sure to completely cover the curd, and fix in place with garden string or soft twine. Ensure that plants are dry or you may encourage the cauliflower to rot. Some varieties are self-blanching, and their inner leaves will naturally fold inwards. They may still benefit from protection in winter.

Ensure that no light can reach the cauliflower curds as this would cause them to discolour. Keep the string in place until you are ready to harvest.

'Mayflower'

A very early-cropping variety, this is ready for harvest ahead of most other summer cauliflowers. It produces medium–large heads with pure white, cloud-shaped curds that are resistant to discoloration in hot weather. It has an excellent flavour.

🪣	unsuitable for containers
🌙	late winter
✳	some resistance
❄	not hardy
🔒	early summer

'Autumn Giant'

This popular late-season variety can be harvested until almost the end of the year. The gigantic, solid white heads, which may grow up to 30cm (12in) across, are well protected from colder weather by the leaves.

🪣	unsuitable for containers
🌙	spring to early summer
✳	poor resistance
❄	fairly hardy
🔒	autumn to winter

'Gypsy'

A sturdy summer variety, 'Gypsy' will tolerate poorer soils than most cauliflowers. This useful plant produces well-rounded white curds that, unlike many other summer varieties, do not develop a pinkish discoloration in hot weather.

🪣	unsuitable for containers
🌙	spring
✳	some resistance
❄	not hardy
🔒	summer

'Violet Queen'

A prolific cropper, this variety has a purple head that turns green when cooked. It is a reliable plant for late summer and autumn harvesting. In areas where heavy frosts are unlikely, it can also be overwintered for harvesting the following spring.

- unsuitable for containers
- spring
- poor resistance
- fairly hardy
- spring to autumn

'Galleon' ♀

A hardy variety with a superb flavour, this fully deserves its Award of Garden Merit. It has a long maturing period; after spring or summer plantings, it overwinters well and the firm white heads are ready for harvesting the following spring.

- unsuitable for containers
- late spring to early summer
- some resistance
- hardy
- spring

'Amazing'

Well named, this variety has some impressive qualities. The enormous, ivory-white heads can grow up to 25cm (10in) and are densely packed. It will last for an exceptionally long period in the ground without losing its excellent flavour or texture.

- unsuitable for containers
- early spring to late summer
- poor resistance
- not hardy
- late spring to autumn

'Clapton'

'Clapton' is hailed as the first cauliflower with resistance to clubroot. It is a sturdy plant, with a dense, white head, well protected by the leaves. This variety can be sown over two to three months to produce a succession of crops.

- unsuitable for containers
- spring to early summer
- good resistance
- not hardy
- late summer to late autumn

'Skywalker'

Sturdy and reliable, this variety produces solid, bright white, domed heads, and as a bonus, has good resistance to wilt. The leaves have an erect habit and wrap around well to protect the curds. Frost sweetens the flavour.

- unsuitable for containers
- spring
- good resistance
- hardy
- autumn

'Candid Charm'

Easy to grow and a consistent producer of early-maturing crops, this variety is popular with gardeners. The medium–large, attractively shaped, white heads are well protected by the stout leaves. Sow under cover in late winter.

- unsuitable for containers
- late winter to spring
- poor resistance
- not hardy
- late summer

'Graffiti' ♛

The deep purple heads of this award winner intensify in colour if left exposed to light. Its sweet flavour makes it ideal for eating raw in salads, though it is also tasty when cooked. 'Graffiti' is considered to be superior to older purple-headed varieties.

- 🪣 unsuitable for containers
- 🌱 early to late spring
- ✴ some resistance
- ❄ not hardy
- 🔒 summer to autumn

'Goodman'

This vigorous summer variety produces heavy crops. The dense curds are well protected by the dark green, upright leaves. If sown outdoors in spring, it is ready to harvest in late summer or autumn; sow under cover in winter for early summer crops.

- 🪣 unsuitable for containers
- 🌱 early spring to early summer
- ✴ poor resistance
- ❄ not hardy
- 🔒 summer to autumn

'Cheddar'

Beautiful yellow-orange heads, which contain a high level of the nutrient betacarotene, make this variety a stunning addition to the vegetable garden. The colour deepens if the heads are left unwrapped and is retained during cooking.

- 🪣 unsuitable for containers
- 🌱 spring
- ✴ poor resistance
- ❄ not hardy
- 🔒 summer to autumn

'Snowball'

This long-established variety is a compact plant with medium-sized, tightly packed, snow-white heads. Commonly sown in late spring for an autumn harvest, it can also be started indoors in late winter for a midsummer crop. It keeps well and is versatile in the kitchen.

 unsuitable for containers
late winter to spring
poor resistance
not hardy
summer to autumn

'Maystar'

After a late spring sowing, this hardy variety overwinters to mature in early summer the following year. An excellent flavour and texture make this a good all-purpose cauliflower for cooking or eating raw. The solid white curds freeze very well.

unsuitable for containers
spring
poor resistance
hardy
early summer

'Medallion'

This winter cauliflower produces a good crop early in the year following sowing. The large white curds form a round head with a full, rich flavour. Although hardy, it is less likely to overwinter well in colder areas.

unsuitable for containers
early summer
poor resistance
hardy
spring

'Snow Crown'

One of the easiest varieties to grow, 'Snow Crown' has vigorous growth and produces substantial crops. The large white heads may develop a pink tinge in hot weather, but this does not impair the mild flavour. The variety keeps well in the ground for a week or two after maturing.

- unsuitable for containers
- spring
- poor resistance
- not hardy
- summer

'Cassius F1'

This vigorous, US-only, hybrid cauliflower produces dense, self-blanching white heads 65–75 days after planting. Suitable for both spring and autumn harvests, the plants are sturdy, resistant to many diseases, and perform well in a range of conditions.

- unsuitable for containers
- mid-spring and midsummer
- some resistance
- not hardy
- early summer and autumn

'Early White Hybrid'

The solid, pure white, self-blanching heads of this US-only variety are harvestable after just 52 days after planting. One of the earliest varieties, its fast-maturing habit and excellent flavour make it an adaptable choice for summer and autumn harvests.

- unsuitable for containers
- mid-spring and late summer
- some resistance
- not hardy
- early summer and autumn

BROCCOLI *Brassica oleraceam* Italica Group

The term "broccoli" is perhaps a little misleading, since it actually encompasses two distinct types of crop: calabrese, which produce the large, rounded heads commonly referred to as "broccoli", and sprouting broccoli, which produces smaller florets on longer stalks. Calabrese is a summer to autumn crop, while sprouting broccoli can be overwintered, making it a valuable winter crop when there is little else on offer.

	SPRING	SUMMER	AUTUMN	WINTER
SOW/PLANT				
HARVEST				

SOWING

Give your broccoli a sheltered site in firm, fertile soil, with a pH of at least 6.8. Ensure that you choose a location where other brassicas have not been grown in the last three years. Dig in some well-rotted manure in the autumn prior to planting.

Calabrese seeds should be sown directly into the ground from mid-spring, successively through to early summer. Sow the seed at a depth of 2cm ($^{3}/_{4}$in), and 30cm (12in) apart. Plants will grow fairly large so space rows at a distance of 45cm (18in).

Sow sprouting broccoli seeds at a depth of 2cm ($^{3}/_{4}$in) either in trays or modules under cover, or directly in the ground in early spring, covering them until frosts

Harvest to encourage a second crop.

have passed. Alternatively, sow in mid-autumn for overwintering crops. Sprouting broccoli will grow larger than calabrese, so give them more space – 60cm (24in) between plants, and rows.

CROP CARE

Plants can become quite heavy once heads have developed, so earth up the stems as they

grow, and stake tall plants if necessary. Water and weed well while young. When established, avoid overwatering sprouting broccoli, to help it to overwinter.

HARVESTING

The central head of calabrese should be harvested before the flower buds open in late summer. Then give the plant a mulch of compost to encourage it to produce a crop of sideshoots. Harvest spears of sprouting types between winter and spring, when they reach about 15cm (6in) in length. New spears will grow back and you may get a harvest for up to two months.

PESTS AND DISEASES

Broccoli is relatively problem-free, but rotating your crops will help to prevent persistant diseases such as clubroot from attacking. Cover plants with netting to deter pests such as birds and cabbage white butterflies.

Use netting as a barrier against pests.

'Belstar' ♀

This F1 variety bears a mid-
to late season crop of attractive,
well-domed, bluish-green heads.
They have a good flavour and are
excellent boiled, lightly steamed,
or for use in stir-fries. Heads
will keep well once harvested;
the plants will go on to produce
plenty of extra sideshoots.

- unsuitable for containers
- mid- to late spring
- some resistance
- not hardy
- midsummer to mid-autumn

'Romanesco'

Resembling a cross between
a very tall broccoli and a
cauliflower, 'Romanesco' or
'Broccoflower', as it's sometimes
called, was developed in Scotland
and is grown for its outstanding
flavour and texture, and its
spiral of highly ornamental,
domed, lime-green curds.

- unsuitable for containers
- late spring
- poor resistance
- not hardy
- early winter

'Green Magic' ♀

This variety is highly rated for its
flavour and tightly packed, dark
green heads, which are followed
by a good crop of sideshoots
when the main head is harvested.
Quicker to mature than many
varieties, it makes a strong, bold
display in the kitchen garden.

- unsuitable for containers
- mid- to late spring
- some resistance
- not hardy
- midsummer to mid-autumn

'Fiesta' ♀

This impressive variety produces
numerous large, shapely, domed
heads, and bears a good number
of secondary sideshoots once
the central portion has been
removed. It is a good choice
for hot summer sites because
it withstands high temperatures.

- unsuitable for containers
- mid- to late spring
- some resistance
- not hardy
- midsummer to mid-autumn

'Romanesco'

'Red Arrow' ♀

A highly-rated purple broccoli, this variety is easy to grow and is hardy over winter. The vigorous plants bear flavourful spears that lose their purple colour on cooking, becoming green. Even so, they are good in salads and stir-fries, and should be steamed for maximum tenderness.

- 🪴 unsuitable for containers
- 🌱 mid- to late spring
- ✳ some resistance
- ❄ hardy
- 🔒 late winter to early spring

'Cardinal'

This purple-sprouting variety produces thick, sweet, flavourful spears. It crops late, bearing heavy yields on large, colourful plants, which add a strong presence to the kitchen garden. It is excellent for use in a wide range of recipes, but particularly steamed or in stir-fries.

- 🪴 unsuitable for containers
- 🌱 mid- to late spring
- ✳ poor resistance
- ❄ hardy
- 🔒 late winter to early spring

'Rudolph'

This attractive variety produces an early crop of purple-sprouting heads, ready for picking several weeks before more traditional varieties. They have a wonderful, deep colour and are thick and of high quality. The plants are large and vigorous, bearing high yields.

- 🪴 unsuitable for containers
- 🌱 early to late spring
- ✳ poor resistance
- ❄ hardy
- 🔒 late autumn to late winter

'Santee'

This purple-sprouting broccoli is ready for picking much earlier than other varieties, which tend to be picked over winter; it can crop in the same year as it is sown. It bears a good yield of tasty, tender spears, with an abundance of mini heads.

- 🪴 unsuitable for containers
- 🌱 mid- to late spring
- ✳ poor resistance
- ❄ not hardy
- 🔒 midsummer to late autumn

'Early Purple Sprouting' ♀

This variety is an essential crop for the midwinter kitchen garden, providing the striking combination of tasty purple heads tucked into bluish-green leaves. Steam it to preserve its excellent taste and texture, and add it to hot meals and salads.

- unsuitable for containers
- mid- to late spring
- some resistance
- hardy
- late winter to early spring

'Red Spear' ♀

Heavy-yielding and vigorous, this variety produces thick spears that will add striking purple colour to the kitchen garden over winter. Harvest the tender spears in late winter and use them, and the subsequent crop of sideshoots, in soups and salads.

- unsuitable for containers
- mid- to late spring
- some resistance
- hardy
- late winter to early spring

'White Star' ♀

Developed to be at its peak in mid-spring when many other varieties are past their best, 'White Star' bears a good crop of attractive, high quality, white spears, followed by numerous secondary sideshoots. The plants are reliable, bearing good yields.

- unsuitable for containers
- mid- to late spring
- some resistance
- hardy
- mid-spring

'Claret' ♀

This very tall, F1 hybrid is grown for its heavy crop of dark purple spears, ready for picking from late winter. The plants are vigorous, even when grown in poor soils. The spears make a good addition to stews and pasta dishes.

- unsuitable for containers
- mid- to late spring
- some resistance
- hardy
- late winter to early spring

'Wok Brocc'

This novel, purple-sprouting, Oriental variety was specifically developed to crop from early summer to winter, when sown in succession over several months. It has a wonderful nutty flavour, and is excellent used in stir-fries.

- unsuitable for containers
- early spring to early summer
- poor resistance
- hardy
- early summer to early winter

'White Eye' ♀

This excellent variety provides a heavy crop of sweet, delicious white broccoli at the start of the New Year. The spears are excellent steamed and added to a wide range of winter dishes. The plants look particularly striking planted alongside purple types.

- unsuitable for containers
- mid- to late spring
- some resistance
- hardy
- late winter to mid-spring

'Early White Sprouting'

One of the earliest broccolis, 'Early White Sprouting' produces a heavy crop of sweet, tender, white spears. Harvest promptly and consistently and it will crop over a long period. It is an attractive plant and makes a strong visual contrast with overwintering purple varieties.

 unsuitable for containers
mid- to late spring
poor resistance
hardy
late winter to early spring

'Bordeaux' ♛

This purple-sprouting variety does not rely on the winter cold to trigger flowering, so is ideal to sow in spring for an early crop. It produces heavy yields of thick, tender, flavourful spears, which are excellent steamed or in stir-fries.

unsuitable for containers
mid- to late spring
some resistance
not hardy
midsummer to autumn

'Late Purple Sprouting' ♛

This tall, robust, purple-sprouting variety provides a reliable crop of broccoli spears through winter; hardy, it thrives even in very cold conditions. The spears have an excellent flavour and their colour makes this variety a striking asset.

unsuitable for containers
mid- to late spring
some resistance
hardy
late winter to early spring

KALE *Brassica oleracea* Acephala Group

Kale is a hardy and adaptable plant, able to survive sub-zero winter temperatures, and in the case of some varieties, hot summers as well. Packed with high levels of vitamins and minerals, it is delicious eaten raw in salads when young and tender, or boiled or stir-fried when leaves are mature. Kale is also an ideal ornamental plant since its leaves are striking in shape and colour, and look good throughout the winter.

	SPRING	SUMMER	AUTUMN	WINTER
SOW/PLANT				
HARVEST				

SOWING

Kale plants can become relatively large, up to 90cm (3ft) high, and 60cm (2ft) wide, so they need both space to spread and firm soil to support their eventual weight. Sow seeds in early spring to produce a crop in summer, or sow in late spring to early summer to produce a crop in autumn to winter.

Sow in pots or module trays at a depth of 2cm (³⁄₄in). Plants will be ready to transplant when they are about seven weeks old; be careful not to damage the roots when planting out. Kale can be grown as a cut-and-come-again crop and planted densely, with seedlings spaced at a distance of 8–10cm (3–4in). If you plan to let kale crops grow to full size

Harvest whole kale plants when mature.

they will need to be planted 45–60cm (18–24in) apart.

CROP CARE

Keep seedlings well-weeded and give them plenty of water while young. However, when plants are established avoid overwatering as this produces lush growth that is less capable of overwintering. If the crop yellows in autumn, remove

affected leaves and feed with high-nitrogen fertilizer. Remove any flower buds that appear.

HARVESTING

Young, tender kale leaves can be harvested as required from cut-and-come-again crops, which will then re-sprout. Cut leaves when they are about 10cm (4in) in length, and harvest until plants become bitter-tasting.

Fully-grown kale can be left in the ground and harvested as required. Kale is one of the hardiest winter crops and can be left in the ground at temperatures as low as -15°C (5°F).

PESTS AND DISEASES

Kale is less susceptible to the problems that plague other brassicas (see pp.246–7), but you may find that fine netting is needed to deter birds and butterflies. Rotate crops – plant where peas or beans have previously grown.

Netting will prevent attacks from birds.

'Redbor'

This variety is a 'must-have' for the kitchen garden, or for the front of a border, where its striking purple stems and frilly green leaves will last through winter. Use it as a cut-and-come-again crop, trimming off the tender young leaves to encourage new, tasty growth.

- unsuitable for containers
- mid-spring to early summer
- some resistance
- hardy
- early autumn to mid-spring

'Winterbor'

A top choice for exposed winter gardens, this variety withstands low temperatures to produce a thicket of short, bluish-green, curly leaves. Treat it as a cut-and-come-again kale into the following spring. Cook the leaves gently to preserve their flavour.

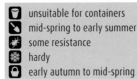

- unsuitable for containers
- mid-spring to early summer
- some resistance
- hardy
- early autumn to mid-spring

'Darkibor'

This tough variety produces a profusion of dark green, tightly curled leaves, over a long picking season. Cut the leaves from the crown, moving outwards. They should be cooked gently to preserve their flavour, and are good for use in stir-fries.

- unsuitable for containers
- mid-spring to early summer
- some resistance
- hardy
- early autumn to mid-spring

'Dwarf Green Curled'

This attractive variety produces dark green, tightly curled leaves; their good flavour is best retained through gentle cooking. It will grow to about 60cm (24in) if left to develop, or it can be harvested as a cut-and-come-again crop. It doesn't require staking and is a good choice for small plots.

- unsuitable for containers
- mid-spring to early summer
- some resistance
- hardy
- early autumn to mid-spring

'Starbor'

Grow some plants especially for their tender baby leaves, harvesting them in summer for salads, allowing other plants to mature over winter. Sow 'Starbor' in pots on a sunny windowsill, so the flavourful, fresh growth can be easily harvested in winter.

- suitable for containers
- mid-spring to early summer
- some resistance
- hardy
- early autumn to mid-spring

'Reflex' ♀

This F1 hybrid was specially bred to produce extra curly, bluish-green leaves on tall, very hardy plants. It stands well without any danger of yellowing, and can be sown successively to provide regular crops throughout the year.

- unsuitable for containers
- mid-spring to early summer
- good resistance
- hardy
- early autumn to mid-spring

'Cavolo Nero'

Also known as 'Tuscan Kale', this traditional south Italian vegetable is widely available. It has a rich flavour, and should be steamed or sautéed quickly to retain its dark green colour. It can be used in all kinds of winter dishes, from soups and stews to salads.

🗑	unsuitable for containers
🔨	mid-spring to early summer
❄	some resistance
❄	hardy
🔒	early autumn to mid-spring

'Fizz'

This unusual kale is quick-growing, producing fleshy leaves on upright stems. Harvest the tender young growth for summer recipes, adding it raw to salads, and using in stir-fries. Grow to the front of the kitchen garden for easy picking.

🗑	unsuitable for containers
🔨	mid-spring to early summer
❄	some resistance
❄	hardy
🔒	summer

'Bornick'

This F1 hybrid variety produces a quick-maturing, early crop, with curly, mid- to dark green leaves. As with all kales, use the tender young leaves before they become tough and bitter. Steam instead of boiling to retain the flavour, or use in stir-fries.

🗑	unsuitable for containers
🔨	mid-spring to early summer
❄	some resistance
❄	hardy
🔒	early autumn to mid-spring

'Red Russian'

This frilly, highly decorative kale produces grey-green leaves with striking purple stems and veins. Some of the leaves can be harvested at the baby-leaf stage for use in summer salads, leaving the rest to mature for winter. Mature leaves can be braised, steamed, or blanched.

- unsuitable for containers
- mid-spring to early summer
- some resistance
- hardy
- early autumn to mid-spring

'Ripbor'

This large kale will grow to about 60cm (24in), and is packed with frilly, dark green leaves, ready for cropping from autumn; it lasts well in the ground over winter. Remove the first leaves from the crown, moving outwards when cutting.

- unsuitable for containers
- mid-spring to early summer
- some resistance
- hardy
- early autumn to winter

'Fribor' ♀

This variety has especially good resistance to pests and diseases, and is a good choice for cold, exposed sites because it overwinters well. It produces mid- to dark green leaves with very frilly edges. Boost yields by adding organic matter to the soil.

- unsuitable for containers
- mid-spring to early summer
- good resistance
- hardy
- early autumn to mid-spring

SPINACH *Spinacia oleracea*

Packed with vitamins and minerals, spinach is nutritious and has a delicious flavour; try the traditional thicker, wrinkled varieties for cooking, and thinner, smooth-leaved varieties for eating raw in salads. Happy to grow in cooler climates and shady positions, spinach is a very accommodating vegetable, however be careful to keep it well-watered. Water more than once a day in hot, dry weather as it will readily bolt.

	SPRING	SUMMER	AUTUMN	WINTER
SOW/PLANT				
HARVEST				

SOWING

Spinach prefers a fertile soil, so apply well-rotted manure or compost the autumn before planting, or apply a general fertilizer shortly before sowing. Spinach is a very versatile plant; it will happily grow in containers as a cut-and-come-again crop and it is ideal for intercropping as it will tolerate partial shade.

Spinach can be sown all year round to provide a constant crop. Sow seed every few weeks throughout the year between midwinter and late summer. Sow at a depth of 2cm ($^3/_4$in) and space your rows 30cm (12in) apart. When seedlings have established, thin out giving them 7–15cm (3–6in) of space, depending on how big you want

Sow in pots if your space is limited.

them to grow. Sow cut-and-come-again crops in wide drills. Make a 15–20cm (6–8in) wide drill the length of your row and sow two lines of seeds within it.

CROP CARE

Keep spinach well-weeded, and most importantly, keep it well-watered to help prevent bolting. If growth is slow, feed with a high-nitrogen fertilizer.

HARVESTING

When plants reach approximately 5cm (2in) in height, harvest the outer leaves a few at a time for use in salads. When plants are about 10–12 weeks old, either cut a few leaves as and when you need them, or harvest the whole plant. Either uproot it completely, or cut the tops off about 2.5cm (1in) above the ground; this stump may re-sprout and provide you with a second crop.

STORING

Spinach does not keep well after harvesting, so sow successionally for a year-round crop instead.

PESTS AND DISEASES

Because spinach grows quickly it is usually a relatively trouble-free crop, but you may need to use netting to deter birds. Slugs and snails may target crops, and diseases such as downy mildew may be a problem. This causes white mould on the underside of leaves, with yellowish-brown patches on the top. Remove and destroy the affected leaves to prevent the spread of infection, and spray the remaining crops with a fungicide. Giving plants plenty of space will help to reduce the risk. Resistant cultivars are available.

'Bordeaux'

This attractive variety produces dark green leaves that contrast with its striking red stems and leaf veins. It is a good choice for a sweet baby spinach – excellent for use in salads. If cooking, do so gently, as it has a tendency to reduce quickly and take on a soggy texture.

- suitable for containers
- early spring to early autumn
- poor resistance
- fairly hardy
- mid-spring to mid-autumn

'Giant Noble'

This vigorous, spreading variety produces a heavy yield of large, thick, tender, hand-sized leaves over a long period. The leaves become denser towards the middle; right in the centre the tight cluster of leaves resembles the developing head of lettuce.

- suitable for containers
- early spring to early autumn
- poor resistance
- fairly hardy
- mid-spring to mid-autumn

'Atlanta'

A good cropper, this fast-maturing variety is grown for its large, round, mid-green leaves. They are thick and flavourful and excellent used in cooking. Like other varieties it needs a sunny, sheltered site with plenty of well-rotted compost.

- suitable for containers
- early spring to early autumn
- some resistance
- fairly hardy
- mid-spring to mid-autumn

'Triathlon' ♀

This mildew-resistant variety can be sown from early spring onwards to provide batches of fresh, tasty leaves. Plants grow quickly; their large, mid-green leaves can be harvested young for use in salads, or allowed to develop for culinary use.

- 🪣 suitable for containers
- 🌱 early spring to early autumn
- ❋ good resistance
- ❄ fairly hardy
- 🔒 mid-spring to mid-autumn

'Fiorano' ♀

Resisting all forms of mildew, this fast-maturing variety produces upright growth with dark green, round leaves. Use raw in salads as a baby leaf or cook it; cook quickly and gently as it has a tendency to wilt and may lose its shape and texture.

- 🪣 suitable for containers
- 🌱 early spring to early autumn
- ❋ excellent resistance
- ❄ fairly hardy
- 🔒 mid-spring to mid-autumn

'Mikado' ♀

Also known as 'Oriento', this vigorous, Oriental-type spinach has plenty of selling points: it is slow to bolt, even when dry conditions are unavoidable, and it produces a high yield of tasty, glossy, pointed leaves, borne on its many side-shoots.

- 🪣 suitable for containers
- 🌱 early spring to early autumn
- ❋ good resistance
- ❄ fairly hardy
- 🔒 mid-spring to mid-autumn

'Lazio'

This variety is often sold in supermarkets because it ticks all the right boxes: it has excellent mildew resistance; reliable and solid growth; and gives a consistently high yield of tasty, dark green leaves. Its baby leaves are very good for tossing straight into salads or risottos.

- suitable for containers
- early spring to early autumn
- excellent resistance
- fairly hardy
- mid-spring to mid-autumn

'Giant Winter'

This variety is an excellent choice for its large, lance-shaped winter leaves, which have a strong flavour. It will need some protection in cold, exposed, windy areas. It is useful for cooking, and like other varieties, it can be frozen raw or cooked.

- suitable for containers
- early spring to early autumn
- poor resistance
- fairly hardy
- mid-autumn to midwinter

'Scenic'

This variety is the ideal choice for mildew-prone sites as it has very good disease resistance. It produces dark green, upright leaves, which are best picked for use as tender young greens. Steam, braise or sautée gently, or add them to stir-fries.

- suitable for containers
- early spring to early autumn
- excellent resistance
- fairly hardy
- mid-spring to mid-autumn

'Campania' ♛

This quick-maturing, sturdy F1 hybrid is resistant to most forms of mildew. It stands up well and produces clumps of dark green leaves that can be used fresh in salads, or cooked. As with other varieties, make sure that it is well watered or it is likely to bolt.

- suitable for containers
- early spring to early autumn
- excellent resistance
- fairly hardy
- mid-spring to mid-autumn

'Hector' ♛

This F1 spinach is highly rated because it produces a generous supply of smooth, round, dark green, flavourful leaves. Use them while young and small directly in salads, or like other varieties, grow to a larger size and lightly cook.

- suitable for containers
- early spring to early autumn
- some resistance
- fairly hardy
- mid-spring to mid-autumn

'Emilia' ♛

One of the best varieties, 'Emilia' is resistant to all forms of mildew, and produces an upright cluster of slightly puckered, dark green leaves. They can be harvested when young for use in salads, or left to mature for use in cooking. It has good bolt resistance.

- suitable for containers
- early spring to early autumn
- excellent resistance
- fairly hardy
- mid-spring to mid-autumn

'Reddy'

This quick-growing F1 spinach, was especially raised for its striking mix of red stems and veins, and green leaves. Grow in a prominent position for easy picking. Use as a baby leaf; cook it gently to preserve the shape and colour.

- suitable for containers
- early spring to early autumn
- poor resistance
- fairly hardy
- mid-spring to mid-autumn

SWISS CHARD *Beta vulgaris* subsp. *cicla* var. *flavescens*

Swiss chard is often referred to as a "leaf beet" since it is related to beetroot, but produces large, delicious leaves and insignificant, inedible roots. It is an attractive plant, often grown as an ornamental as its leaf veins and stems are produced in a range of vibrant colours from vivid red and yellow, to purple. Swiss chard leaves have a peppery flavour and can be used in salads or cooked and eaten like spinach.

	SPRING	SUMMER	AUTUMN	WINTER
SOW/PLANT				
HARVEST				

SOWING

Swiss chard likes a fertile, moisture-retentive soil, so dig in some well-rotted manure or compost the autumn before sowing, or add a general fertilizer to the soil. If the pH of the soil is below 6.5, consider adding some lime to the soil as Swiss chard likes alkaline conditions. Provide crops with a sunny, sheltered position.

Seed can be sown directly into the soil, or grown in modules in a greenhouse or cold frame, and then transplanted when established. Sow at a depth of 2.5cm (1in) and space rows 45cm (18in) apart. Once seedlings are established, thin out depending on your requirements; if growing for

Leave cut stems in the ground to re-sprout.

salad crops, leave 10cm (4in) between plants; larger plants will need more space, so allow 30cm (12in) between them.

CROP CARE

Keep chard well-watered and free from weeds. Remove any flowering buds to encourage the plant to direct its energy into its leaves. If you are leaving plants in the ground to overwinter, a

cloche offers some protection. Feed once with fertilizer.

HARVESTING

Harvest with a knife, leaving the stems in the ground to re-sprout; removing the plant's leaves will encourage further growth. Harvest young leaves for use in salads and older leaves for cooking, as and when you need them. Keep harvesting from the plant until it runs to seed.

PESTS AND DISEASES

Chard is usually trouble-free. Practise crop rotation and good garden hygiene for healthy yields.

GROW IN CONTAINERS

Swiss chard grows well as a cut-and-come-again crop in a container, so why not sow in pots on the patio, or intercrop with flowers in a windowbox. Harvest leaves regularly, before they outgrow their space.

Chard grows in even the smallest space.

'Lucullus'

While it is not one of the more decorative varieties, 'Lucullus' is popular for its flavour and for the profusion of its large, deeply puckered, light green leaves and succulent white stems, which are broad and up to 50cm (20in) tall.

- suitable for containers
- mid-spring to late summer
- some resistance
- fairly hardy
- late spring to late autumn

'Vulcan'

With fiery red stems and dark green leaves, this is a highly ornamental variety with excellent flavour both when young and raw in salads and when harvested mature and served as a steamed vegetable. The leaves are sweet-tasting and tender.

- suitable for containers
- mid-spring to late summer
- poor resistance
- fairly hardy
- late spring to late autumn

'Bright Lights'

This handsome chard variety
produces stems ranging in
colour from red to pink, purple,
green, orange, and yellow, with
large green or bronze foliage.
Harvestable as baby leaves
28 days after sowing, it reaches
maturity in 50–60 days.

- 🪣 suitable for containers
- 🍴 mid-spring to late summer
- 🕷 poor resistance
- ❄ fairly hardy
- 🔒 late spring to late autumn

'Rhubarb Chard' ♀

This heirloom variety produces
heavily puckered, red-veined,
dark green or purple leaves
on deep red stems. It is both
beautiful and very good to eat;
the stems have a slight asparagus
flavour and the flower stalks can
be cooked like sprouting broccoli.

- 🪣 suitable for containers
- 🍴 mid-spring to late summer
- 🕷 some resistance
- ❄ fairly hardy
- 🔒 late spring to late autumn

'Perpetual Spinach'

This variety has dull green stems
with smooth, dark green leaves
with small midribs, resembling
spinach but coarser. It is less
likely to bolt than spinach and is
hardier than other Swiss chards,
making it easier to grow and
suitable for a long harvest season.

- 🪣 suitable for containers
- 🍴 mid-spring to late summer
- 🕷 poor resistance
- ❄ fairly hardy
- 🔒 late spring to early winter

'Bright Yellow' ♀

The broad golden stalks and large, puckered, deep green leaves of 'Bright Yellow' make it a candidate for the flower border as well as the vegetable patch. When young, the stalks can be eaten raw and are an attractive addition to a salad.

- suitable for containers
- mid-spring to late summer
- some resistance
- fairly hardy
- late spring to late autumn

'Charlotte' ♀

Dark green, waxy leaves are set against deep red stalks, making this a highly ornamental variety of chard. The baby leaves make attractive and tasty micro greens, used for garnishes and in salads. When mature, the leaves and stem are delicious steamed.

- suitable for containers
- mid-spring to late summer
- some resistance
- fairly hardy
- late spring to late autumn

'White Silver'

Described as having the best flavour of all varieties, 'White Silver' has broad, white, succulent stems with a taste like that of celery. Although early sowings tend to bolt, it is worth growing as it is disease resistant, robust, and easy to germinate.

- suitable for containers
- mid-spring to late summer
- good resistance
- fairly hardy
- late spring to late autumn

'Improved Rainbow Mix'

The reds, pinks, yellows, and oranges of this variety's thin stems intensify in colour as it matures, giving a striking display against the dark green, puckered leaves. The colours are attractive in salads and are retained even after light cooking.

- suitable for containers
- mid-spring to late summer
- poor resistance
- fairly hardy
- late spring to late autumn

'Fordhook Giant' ♀

This vigorous variety can tolerate heat, partial shade, and moderate frost and is slow to bolt. It has heavily puckered, shiny, dark green leaves, with white veins and long, broad, pale stems. Baby leaves can be picked just 25 days after sowing.

- suitable for containers
- mid-spring to late summer
- some resistance
- fairly hardy
- late spring to late autumn

'Magenta Sunset'

Beautiful in a vegetable garden, flower border, or a container, this US-only variety produces crumpled green leaves with pink to magenta ribs, and grows to 60cm (24in) in height. Baby leaves, picked at 30 days, make a tasty addition to salads.

- suitable for containers
- mid-spring to late summer
- good resistance
- not hardy
- late spring to summer

KOHLRABI *Brassica oleracea* Gongylodes Group

Kohlrabi's combination of distinctive ornamental leaves and a bulbous, alien-looking stem is both bizarre and beautiful. The swollen purple, green, or white stems have a mild, sweet flavour, and can be cooked or eaten raw in salads. This fast-growing vegetable can be grown in containers, but is ideal for use as a catch crop. It should be sown successively as it does not keep very well once harvested.

	SPRING	SUMMER	AUTUMN	WINTER
SOW/PLANT				
HARVEST				

SOWING

Kohlrabi will tolerate most soils, but it prefers a non-acidic pH, so consider adding lime to soil if the pH is below 7. Kohlrabi needs a minimum temperature of 10°C (50°F) to prevent bolting.

In early spring, sow in under cover in modules, at a depth of 2.5cm (1in), and plant the seedlings out before they reach 5cm (2in) tall, as this will also help to prevent bolting. When planting the seedlings out, ensure that you leave at least 23cm (9in) between them, and 30cm (12in) between rows. Sow directly into the ground once the soil has warmed up.

Thin out seedlings before they become too large or you risk damaging the roots. Try

Ensure that crops have space to develop.

sowing three seeds in each location, and then remove the weakest two once the seedlings have established. Plant faster-growing green and white varieties first and slower purple varieties later.

CROP CARE

Ensure that you weed and water regularly – if kohlrabi dries out it becomes woody and unpalatable.

HARVESTING

Kohlrabi is best harvested when its stems have reached the size of tennis balls, although some varieties are still worth eating if left in the ground to grow larger. Cut them at the root and remove the oldest leaves; leaving young leaves will help to keep it fresh. If the weather is mild, kohlrabi can be left in the ground in winter, but lift if frosts are forecast.

STORING

Kohlrabi can be stored in boxes full of moist sand but it is best eaten fresh, so sow successively to ensure a continuous crop.

PESTS AND DISEASES

Kohlrabi is susceptible to attack from cabbage root fly, flea beetles, aphids, and slugs and snails (see pp.246–7). Since the leaves are not eaten some damage might be tolerable. A bigger problem is clubroot; dig up and destroy affected plants, and rotate crops.

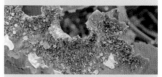

Some leaf damage can be tolerated.

'Superschmelz'

This is a giant variety, with bulbs up to 20–25cm (8–10in) across. The skins are pale green and the white flesh remains sweet and tender into maturity. It is fast-growing, ready to harvest within 60 days, and is resistant to bolting and splitting.

▢	unsuitable for containers
◣	early spring to late summer
✹	poor resistance
❋	fairly hardy
🔒	early summer to late autumn

'Quickstar' ♀

The pale green-skinned bulbs of this high-yielding F1 hybrid remain juicy and crunchy into autumn. The foliage is not large, which means that denser planting is possible to produce baby vegetables. 'Quickstar' matures quickly and is slow to bolt.

▢	unsuitable for containers
◣	early spring to late summer
✹	some resistance
❋	fairly hardy
🔒	early summer to late autumn

'Korist F1'

This very early variety, suitable for growing under glass, matures about 55 days after sowing. The bulbs are a flattened globe shape with tender, crisp, and juicy flesh that has a mild flavour, and is excellent either raw or cooked.

▢	unsuitable for containers
◣	early spring to late summer
✹	poor resistance
❋	fairly hardy
🔒	early summer to late autumn

'Kolibri' ♔

The flattened globe-shaped bulbs of this variety are 10–15cm (4–6in) across, purple-skinned, and white-fleshed. As they retain their sweetness and juiciness when most other kohlrabi have become woody, this is a good choice for a late harvest.

- 🪣 unsuitable for containers
- 🌱 early spring to late summer
- 🌼 some resistance
- ❄ fairly hardy
- 🔒 early summer to late autumn

'Kongo'

A fast-growing, high-yielding F1 hybrid with very pale green, squat bulbs measuring 10cm (4in) in diameter, 'Kongo' has sweet, moist, and tender flesh. It is best harvested young for the finest flavour, but if left to mature is slow to turn pithy.

- 🪣 unsuitable for containers
- 🌱 early spring to late summer
- 🕷 poor resistance
- ❄ fairly hardy
- 🔒 early summer to late autumn

'Rapidstar' ♔

An F1 hybrid, 'Rapidstar' has very uniform, medium to large, smooth and attractive, greenish-white bulbs that mature early, just 52 days after sowing. It is very slow to bolt and successive sowing will produce a long cropping season.

- 🪣 unsuitable for containers
- 🌱 early spring to late summer
- 🌼 some resistance
- ❄ fairly hardy
- 🔒 early summer to late autumn

PAK CHOI *Brassica rapa* Chinense Group

Pak choi – or bok choy as it is sometimes called – is a quick-growing member of the Oriental brassica family. Like Chinese cabbage, it is delicious in salads and is a useful late summer crop, but has larger, darker leaves and a more delicate taste. The leaves, stems, and flowering shoots of pak choi are all edible; harvest leaves when young for use in salads, or leave to mature for cooking lightly in stir-fries.

	SPRING	SUMMER	AUTUMN	WINTER
SOW/PLANT				
HARVEST				

SOWING

Pak choi prefers a sheltered, sunny site with fertile, moisture-retentive soil. Dig in some well-rotted manure or compost the autumn before sowing the following year. Like spinach, pak choi benefits from a top-dressing of fertilizer shortly before sowing.

Sow seed directly into the ground in late spring or summer; avoid planting earlier than this as pak choi will bolt if conditions are too cold. You can sow earlier in spring under cover in a heated greenhouse and then transplant. Sow seed at a depth of 2cm (³/₄in).

Plants will need about 30cm (12in) spacing if they are to be harvested whole, but only 10cm (4in) if you plan to harvest just the leaves. Consider

Leave the cut stems to re-sprout.

intercropping amongst other, slower-growing crops such as sweetcorn, as pak choi grows relatively quickly.

CROP CARE

Because of its shallow roots, pak choi needs to be watered regularly to ensure it doesn't dry out. It is relatively easy to grow but does have a tendency to bolt. Keep plants well-weeded.

HARVESTING

Pak choi is ready to harvest in little more than a month. The leaves, stems, and flowering shoots are all edible. Either harvest the young leaves as a cut-and-come-again crop – the plant will re-sprout several times – or uproot the whole plant when it has matured, forming a proper head. Stems and shoots can be harvested as needed when the plants are young.

STORING

Pak choi will wilt quickly after harvesting, so pick leaves as and when they are needed.

PESTS AND DISEASES

Pak choi is at risk from the same problems that affect other brassicas (see pp.246–7). Practise crop rotation and use brassica collars to protect against cabbage root fly. Make collars out of cardboard or carpet underlay.

Leaf diseases can spoil crops.

'Joi Choy'

Fast growing but slow bolting, this 30–38cm (12–15in) hybrid pak choi can be harvested leaf-by-leaf, or all at once. White-ribbed, dark green leaves are ready to eat in about 50 days, and have a crunchy, juicy texture and a mild mustard flavour.

- suitable for containers
- mid-spring to late summer
- poor resistance
- fairly hardy
- late spring and autumn

'Mei Qing Choy'

At just 20–25cm (8–10in) tall, this baby pak choi matures into a compact vase shape in about 40 days. The leaves are rich green with lighter ribs and have a crunchy texture and sweet flavour. Heads can be braised whole, or chopped for stir fries.

- suitable for containers
- mid-spring to late summer
- poor resistance
- fairly hardy
- late spring and autumn

'White Stemmed Pac Choy'

This 30cm (12in) tall variety has thick white stems rather like celery and large, rounded, glossy, dark green leaves with a mild, sweet flavour. It is fast-growing, reaching maturity in 50 days, is slow to bolt, and is cold-resistant.

- unsuitable for containers
- early spring to midsummer
- poor resistance
- hardy
- mid-spring to mid-autumn

'Purple'

Reddish-purple leaves and
purple-ribbed stems make this
an attractive garden plant. It is
also a productive salad vegetable
and produces a profusion of tasty
flowering stems. Harvest at 30
days for baby leaves or at 45–70
days to pick mature plants.

- unsuitable for containers
- early spring to midsummer
- poor resistance
- fairly hardy
- mid-spring to mid-autumn

'Hon Tsai Tai'

A Cantonese pak choi, or choy
sum, this variety produces purple
stems with green leaves and
yellow flowers. It is good in
salads if cut young or can be left
to mature for stir-frying – the
flowering shoots are most tasty
just before the flowers open.

- unsuitable for containers
- mid- to late summer
- poor resistance
- not hardy
- early to late autumn

'Black Summer'

This tasty variety produces
oval, dark green leaves on
broad, flat, light green stems,
which form a perfect broad
vase shape. At 25–30cm (10–12in)
tall, this very attractive pak
choi is slightly smaller than the
average. It is very slow to bolt.

- unsuitable for containers
- mid-spring to late summer
- poor resistance
- fairly hardy
- early summer to mid-autumn

CHINESE CABBAGE *Brassica rapa* Pekinensis Group

A member of the Oriental brassica family, Chinese cabbage has a delicate cabbage taste and succulent texture, and is excellent for use in stir-fries or eaten raw in salads. As long as you give it plenty of water, Chinese cabbage is an easy vegetable to grow and makes a good cut-and-come-again crop. It is also relatively fast-growing, so consider growing it before or between slower-growing vegetables such as turnips or parsnips.

	SPRING	SUMMER	AUTUMN	WINTER
SOW/PLANT				
HARVEST				

SOWING

Chinese cabbage needs very fertile soil in a sunny, sheltered position, so dig in plenty of well-rotted manure or compost the autumn before planting, or apply a general fertilizer.

Sow seed in late spring or early summer if sowing directly into the ground, as plants will try to bolt if sown outside earlier (bolt-resistant varieties are available). If you want to make an early start, sow under cover in module trays and transplant seedlings when the risk of frost has passed.

Sow seed thinly at a depth of 2cm (³⁄₄in) in rows 45cm (18in) apart. Once the seedlings are established, thin out to allow 30cm (12in) between plants.

Keep the fast-growing crops well weeded.

Use Chinese cabbage to intercrop between other, slower-growing plants, as it is quick to mature and will be ready to harvest within eight to ten weeks.

CROP CARE

Keep crops well weeded and make sure that they have plenty of water – like pak choi, Chinese cabbage has very short roots, and a tendency to dry out.

HARVESTING

When the head of the cabbage feels solid and well-developed, cut it off, leaving a 2.5cm (1in) stump left in the ground. Within the next few weeks this will re-sprout and provide a second crop. Young, late-sown plants can be harvested as cut-and-come-again crops when they are a couple of weeks old. Leaves from bolted plants are also edible.

STORING

Cabbage heads can be stored in the fridge for several weeks, but are best eaten fresh, so harvest them just before use.

PESTS AND DISEASES

Chinese cabbage, as with all brassicas, is susceptible to clubroot and cabbage root fly (see pp.246–7). Place a brassica collar around seedlings to deter pests, and plant seeds where you have grown peas, beans, or fruiting vegetables the previous season.

Make a collar from a piece of carpet.

'Wong Bok'

The large, barrel-shaped heads of 'Wong Bok' can reach 2.5kg (5½lb) within 10 weeks of sowing, and have light green leaves with faint, white midribs. Autumn crops will keep well for several weeks if wrapped in newspaper and stored in a cool place.

	unsuitable for containers
	mid-spring to late summer
	poor resistance
	fairly hardy
	midsummer to late autumn

'One Kilo SB' ♈

An excellent variety for both ease of cultivation and flavour, 'One Kilo SB' is named for the weight of its elongated heads. The outer leaves are dark green and the hearts yellow, with a crisp texture and sweet, fresh flavour.

	unsuitable for containers
	early to late summer
	some resistance
	fairly hardy
	early to late autumn

'Yuki' ♈

This is an easy-to-grow, very slow-bolting variety, with barrel-shaped heads weighing 1.8–2kg (4–4½lb), and medium to dark green, slightly crinkled leaves with prominent white ribs. The heart is yellow. It has an excellent flavour and is disease-resistant.

	unsuitable for containers
	mid-spring to late summer
	some resistance
	fairly hardy
	midsummer to late autumn

'Wa Wa Tsi Hybrid'

This variety can be grown closely spaced, making it ideal for a small garden. It is excellent for baby leaves in salads, or when mature, it makes a very tender, succulent, and sweet addition to stir-fries. The heads can reach a weight of 300–500g (10–18oz).

- unsuitable for containers
- mid-spring to late summer
- poor resistance
- fairly hardy
- early summer to mid-autumn

'Kasumi' ♟

This variety is a barrel-headed napa type, with solid heads about 30cm (12in) tall and attractive dark green leaves that have a mild, sweet flavour and tender texture. It is very slow bolting and is resistant to soft rot.

- unsuitable for containers
- mid-spring to early summer
- some resistance
- fairly hardy
- midsummer to late autumn

'Tokyo Bekana'

Within about 20 days of sowing, this loose-head Chinese cabbage produces sweet, tender baby leaves that will regrow for multiple cuttings. Ruffled and curled, and mature in 45 days, they are sturdy enough to use in soups and stir-fries.

- unsuitable for containers
- late spring to early autumn
- poor resistance
- not hardy
- early summer to late autumn

Onion Family

- Onions
- Shallots
- Leeks
- Garlic
- Spring and Bunching onions

ONIONS *Allium cepa*

For a low-maintenance crop, try growing onions. They are raised from seed or from sets, which are specially produced mini-bulbs. Apart from fertile soil and routine care, onions just need plenty of time to mature. If you want large bulbs, be prepared to wait. There are various onion cultivars available – most have brown or golden-yellow skins – but red-skinned onions are also popular and have a milder flavour.

	SPRING	SUMMER	AUTUMN	WINTER
PLANT				
HARVEST				

SOWING

Onions need an open, well-drained site and non-acid soil; dig in compost before sowing or planting. To grow large bulbs, sow seed in midwinter in a heated greenhouse at 10–16°C (50–60°F) and harden off the seedlings in spring for planting out. For smaller bulbs, sow in late winter or early spring, under cover but without heat. When the weather warms up, you can sow seed directly into the soil, at about 2cm (¾in) depth, in rows 30cm (12in) apart.

PLANTING

For a late summer or autumn harvest, plant sets in spring. Push them into the soil, 5–10cm (2–4in) apart, depending on size, and cover, leaving the tips showing.

Dry onions thoroughly before storing.

CROP CARE

When planted-out seedlings are well established, thin them out according to the size of onion you want – closely packed onions are more likely to be smaller on harvest. Water seedlings and sets regularly but moderately, as overwatering can delay swelling of the bulbs, and may make them more susceptible to disease. Weed the onion bed regularly.

HARVESTING

Onions are ready to harvest when their leaves die down and topple over. Carefully ease them out of the ground with a fork. If the weather is fine, leave them to dry on the ground. In wet weather, lifted onions rot quickly, so bring them indoors to dry off thoroughly on a rack or tray.

STORING

Once the skins have turned papery, store onions in a light, well-ventilated area. Plait the leaves into a rope and hang the onions up, or place them in single layers on slatted trays, or in a net.

PESTS AND DISEASES

Onions are susceptible to downy mildew in wet conditions. Other diseases include onion white rot, which affects the base, and onion neck rot, common in stored bulbs. Onion fly is a serious pest but less likely to affect onions grown from sets. Birds may target sets.

Remove and destroy infected foliage.

'Ailsa Craig'

This variety, named after a Scottish island, is over 100 years old but still popular, especially for showing at exhibitions. The bulbs are large and globe-shaped with golden skin. They have a mild flavour and keep well in storage.

- suitable for containers
- late winter to mid-spring
- poor resistance
- fairly hardy
- late summer to mid-autumn

'Copra'

This US-only, hybrid produces firm, medium-sized bulbs characterized by thin necks and dark yellow skins. The strong-flavoured cream-coloured flesh is best when cooked. This variety is highly rated for its storage capabilities.

- suitable for containers
- early spring
- some resistance
- hardy
- late summer

'Piatta di Bergamo'

This variety is from the Lombardy town of Bergamo in northern Italy. The bulbs are small and flattened, with reddish-brown skin and white flesh. They store well and are a lovely shape, so are good for cooking whole.

- suitable for containers
- late winter to mid-spring
- poor resistance
- fairly hardy
- late summer to mid-autumn

'Golden Bear' ♀

This F1 hybrid produces high-shouldered bulbs with thin, golden-brown skin. It is a vigorous grower, resistant to downy mildew, grey mould, and white rot, and has the advantage of cropping early, although it is not a good keeper.

 suitable for containers
late winter to mid-spring
good resistance
fairly hardy
late summer to mid-autumn

'Buffalo' ♀

An overwintering variety, 'Buffalo' is an F1 hybrid that produces good yields of flattened, globe-shaped bulbs with thin skins. It is a very hardy variety bred for autumn planting to give early crops the following year, but not intended for storage.

suitable for containers
early to late autumn
some resistance
hardy
early to midsummer

'Red Candy Apple Hybrid'

Sweet-tasting 'Red Candy Apple' is a popular US-only variety, excellent for use in salads in sandwiches. It is easy to grow, tolerating most conditions. The mild-flavoured, red-ringed onions grow larger in lower latitudes.

 suitable for containers
early spring
poor resistance
hardy
late summer

'Purplette'

This unusual variety produces mini bulbs that can be harvested early as a salad onion, or left until golf ball size when they are ideal for pickling or cooking whole. The skin is burgundy-red, and the bulbs turn pale pink when pickled or cooked.

- suitable for containers
- late winter to mid-spring
- poor resistance
- fairly hardy
- late spring to late summer

'Red Wethersfield'

This US-only, heirloom variety was named after the town of Wethersfield, Connecticut, where it was a valued crop in the 18th and 19th centuries. It has dark skin, pink-tinged flesh, and crisp, mild flavour. It is good for slicing and will store well.

- suitable for containers
- early spring
- poor resistance
- hardy
- late summer

'Radar'

This mild-tasting, overwintering variety produces good yields that can be used fresh from the garden in early summer, or stored into autumn. The bulbs are rounded, with pale brown skin and firm flesh.

- suitable for containers
- early to late autumn
- poor resistance
- hardy
- early to midsummer

'Sturon' ♀

This older variety is reliable and high yielding, with a good flavour. The globe-shaped bulbs are medium-sized, with slightly high shoulders and good, yellow-brown skins. It is slow to bolt in the ground and also keeps very well in storage.

- suitable for containers
- late winter to mid-spring
- some resistance
- fairly hardy
- late summer to mid-autumn

'Hygro' ♀

This F1 hybrid produces good yields of thick-skinned, straw-coloured bulbs. They are heavy and globe-shaped, and keep well in storage, staying in good condition right through to the spring.

- suitable for containers
- late winter to mid-spring
- some resistance
- fairly hardy
- late summer to mid-autumn

'Borettana'

This Italian, heirloom variety is traditionally planted at close spacing to produce small bulbs for pickling or cooking whole. It has pale, yellow-brown skin and crisp, white, sweet flesh. Grown at normal spacing it produces medium-sized, flattened bulbs.

- suitable for containers
- late winter to mid-spring
- poor resistance
- fairly hardy
- late summer to mid-autumn

'Red Brunswick'

This variety produces bulbs of medium to large size, with maroon-red skin and white flesh with purple rings. 'Red Brunswick' is a reliable cropper and stores well for use through winter and into spring.

🪣	suitable for containers
🍶	late winter to mid-spring
✳	poor resistance
❄	fairly hardy
🔒	late summer to mid-autumn

'Red Baron' ♀

This eye-catching variety has shiny, dark red skin and pale purple-tinged flesh with purple rings. They have a strong flavour and are good for cooking or for eating raw. The bulbs are globe-shaped, of medium size, and store well.

🪣	suitable for containers
🍶	late winter to mid-spring
✳	some resistance
❄	fairly hardy
🔒	late summer to mid-autumn

'Long Red Florence'

This Italian, heirloom variety is also known as 'Rossa Lunga di Firenze', and produces elongated, torpedo-shaped bulbs with red skin and a mild, sweet flavour. Can be pulled young as spring onions or left to mature and become larger.

🪣	suitable for containers
🍶	late winter to mid-spring
✳	poor resistance
❄	fairly hardy
🔒	late spring to early autumn

'Centurion' ⚜

This F1 hybrid variety has been developed from the popular 'Sturon'. It produces flattened globe-shaped bulbs, with straw-coloured skins of good thickness. It is a heavy cropper with crisp flesh, and stores well.

- suitable for containers
- late winter to mid-spring
- some resistance
- fairly hardy
- late summer to mid-autumn

'Tropea Rossa Lunga'

This variety from southern Italy produces long, torpedo-shaped bulbs with light, reddish-purple skin and pale pink flesh. They have a mild flavour and high sugar content so are ideal for eating raw, although they are also very good roasted whole.

- suitable for containers
- late winter to mid-spring
- poor resistance
- fairly hardy
- late summer to mid-autumn

'Texas Supersweet'

This sweet-tasting, US-only variety produces yellow-skinned, globe-shaped bulbs, up to 15cm (6in) across. The mild flesh can be eaten cooked or raw. Raised from seed in 110 days, it is excellent for storage.

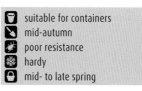

- suitable for containers
- mid-autumn
- poor resistance
- hardy
- mid- to late spring

'Setton' ♛

An F1 hybrid variety developed as an improvement to 'Sturon', 'Setton' produces attractive-looking bulbs of uniform shape, with smooth, russet-brown skin. It is a high-yielding variety that can be used fresh or stored through into spring.

🪣	suitable for containers
🌱	late winter to mid-spring
✳️	some resistance
❄️	fairly hardy
🔒	late summer to mid-autumn

'Walla Walla Sweet'

Famous for its size and sweetness, this US-only onion was named after the valley where it was first grown. The flesh is exceptionally moist and mild-tasting, and is best eaten raw. Harvest when 10cm (4in) wide and quickly – the bulbs do not store well.

🪣	suitable for containers
🌱	early spring
✳️	poor resistance
❄️	hardy
🔒	late summer

'Marco' ♛

This F1 hybrid variety produces flattened globe-shaped bulbs with golden-brown skin. It matures early – bulbs can be ripened in the late summer sun – and stores well, keeping through until spring. It has a strong flavour, so is best eaten cooked.

🪣	suitable for containers
🌱	late winter to mid-spring
✳️	some resistance
❄️	fairly hardy
🔒	late summer to mid-autumn

'Senshyu Semi-Globe Yellow'

An overwintering variety, this popular Japanese onion reliably produces heavy crops of round, straw-coloured bulbs. It is a good choice for sowing at close spacing to produce a crop of baby onions in early summer.

- suitable for containers
- early to late autumn
- poor resistance
- hardy
- early to midsummer

'White Ebenezer'

This popular, easy-to-grow, US-only variety is commonly sold as sets and can be used as a salad onion or grown on to use fresh or stored. The flattened globes mature to 6–8cm (2½–3in) and have crisp white flesh with a medium pungent taste.

- suitable for containers
- early spring
- poor resistance
- hardy
- late summer

'Ramata di Milano'

This variety from northern Italy produces bulbs that are wide at the shoulder and narrow towards the base. It has straw-brown skin, crisp white flesh, and is a good keeper. It is suitable for all culinary uses.

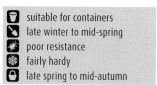

- suitable for containers
- late winter to mid-spring
- poor resistance
- fairly hardy
- late spring to mid-autumn

SHALLOTS *Allium cepa* Aggregatum Group

Small members of the onion family, shallots are less pungent than their larger relatives and are used for pickling and cooking. Shallots can be raised from seed, though the easier option is to grow them from small bulbs called sets. They need a long growing period but can be interplanted with faster-growing crops; after the companion crops are harvested, the shallots come into their own and make use of the available space.

	SPRING	SUMMER	AUTUMN	WINTER
SOW				
HARVEST				

SOWING

To raise shallots from seed, either start them off under cover in late winter, or outdoors once the soil has warmed up in spring.

Indoors, sow them in pots or trays, in good compost, and transplant them outside in mid-spring. Shallots need rich, well-drained soil. They will not thrive in very acidic soils, so check the pH levels of your plot and adjust the acidity with lime if necessary. Once the seedlings are established, thin them out to approximately 2cm (³⁄₄in) apart.

PLANTING SETS

Plant sets outside in late winter or early spring. Rake the soil over, and then make a shallow drill, about 2.5cm (1in) deep.

Plant sets out in early spring.

Push each set into the drill, spacing them 15–20cm (6–8in) apart. Cover them gently with soil, leaving the points showing above ground level.

CROP CARE

Keep the bed free from weeds, taking care not to uproot the sets or seedlings as you work. Water sparingly, unless the weather is very warm and dry.

HARVESTING

Gently lift the clumps of shallots with a fork when the tops turn yellow in mid- to late summer. In dry, sunny conditions, it is safe to leave the bulbs to dry outside on the ground. Otherwise, bring them indoors and dry them on a slatted tray or wire rack.

STORING

Store shallots once their skins have turned papery. Place them in paper bags or in single layers on trays. The storage area should be light and frost-free, with good air circulation. Small shallots can be saved as sets for next year.

PESTS AND DISEASES

Like other members of the onion family, shallots are at risk from diseases such as downy mildew, especially in wet weather, and onion neck rot. Onion fly is a major pest, but it may be deterred by placing fleece over seedlings.

Onion neck rot softens lifted bulbs.

'Pikant' ♛

Living up to its name with a strong, spicy flavour, this is a robust and prolific variety. It produces high yields of firm bulbs with dark, reddish-brown skins. They are very resistant to bolting and store well after harvest.

- 🪴 suitable for containers
- 🌱 late winter to mid-spring
- 🕷 some resistance
- ❄ fairly hardy
- 🔒 mid- to late summer

'Echalote Grise'

Despite the French name, meaning "grey shallot", this variety originated in Kazakhstan. It produces long bulbs that are easy to slice, 18 to 20 per cluster, with grey-brown skin. The flavour is intense and concentrated.

- 🪴 suitable for containers
- 🌱 late winter to mid-spring
- 🕷 poor resistance
- ❄ fairly hardy
- 🔒 mid- to late summer

'Banana'

A very long shallot, with shiny, copper-brown skin and crisp, white flesh. It has a distinctive flavour, making it a popular choice with chefs, and it stores well after harvest. Overall size can be controlled by altering the planting distance.

- 🪴 suitable for containers
- 🌱 late winter to mid-spring
- 🕷 poor resistance
- ❄ fairly hardy
- 🔒 mid- to late summer

'Jermor'

This variety produces long, coppery-brown shallots in clusters of six to eight. The flesh is pink-tinged, with a pleasant flavour. They have a good skin finish and uniform shape and size, making them suitable for exhibition.

- suitable for containers
- late winter to mid-spring
- some resistance
- fairly hardy
- mid- to late summer

'Atlantic'

This variety produces a good yield of medium to large clusters of bulbs. The skins are thin and straw-yellow, while the flesh is white, crisp, and tasty. It can be sown or planted early to crop in advance of other varieties, and has good storage potential.

- suitable for containers
- late winter to mid-spring
- some resistance
- fairly hardy
- mid- to late summer

'Mikor'

The large, elliptical bulbs of this variety have coppery-brown skin and pink-tinged flesh. They have a good flavour, and the long shape makes them easy to slice for use in soups, sauces, and stews. 'Mikor' also stores well.

- suitable for containers
- late winter to mid-spring
- poor resistance
- fairly hardy
- mid- to late summer

'Red Sun'

This attractive variety has firm, red-brown skin and solid, crisp, red-tinged flesh with a punchy taste. 'Red Sun' produces high yields, is suitable for salads, cooking, and picking, and has long storage potential.

🪣 suitable for containers
🌱 late winter to mid-spring
🕷 poor resistance
❄ fairly hardy
🔒 mid- to late summer

'Delvad' ♀

This French variety produces a uniform crop of bulbs with thick, reddish-brown skins and pink-tinged flesh. Each bulb planted will produce a cluster of eight to ten bulbs for harvesting. It is a good choice for growing in containers.

🪣 suitable for containers
🌱 late winter to mid-spring
🕷 some resistance
❄ fairly hardy
🔒 mid- to late summer

'Golden Gourmet' ♀

This reliable variety consistently produces high yields of large, good-quality, yellow-skinned bulbs. The flavour is mild, making them suitable for use in salads as well as for cooking. They have good resistance to bolting and store well after harvest.

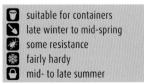

🪣 suitable for containers
🌱 late winter to mid-spring
🕷 some resistance
❄ fairly hardy
🔒 mid- to late summer

'Longor' ♀

This variety produces a good yield of long, pinky-brown bulbs uniform in size, with a consistent shape, making them a good choice for exhibition purposes. The pink-tinged flesh has a robust flavour and the bulbs store well.

- suitable for containers
- late winter to mid-spring
- some resistance
- fairly hardy
- mid- to late summer

'Picasso'

This mild-flavoured variety has red-brown skin and pink flesh, which is good for use in salads, for cooking, or for pickling. It crops early, producing uniform bulbs that show very good resistance to bolting.

- suitable for containers
- late winter to mid-spring
- poor resistance
- fairly hardy
- mid- to late summer

'Matador' ♀

This F1 hybrid produces a substantial yield of uniform bulbs. The flesh is crisp and white, and the thick, reddish-brown skins give it excellent potential for prolonged storage into spring and early summer.

- suitable for containers
- late winter to mid-spring
- some resistance
- fairly hardy
- mid- to late summer

LEEKS *Allium porrum*

Hardy, resilient leeks can be planted to provide a succession of crops from late summer right through the winter months. Early varieties are generally taller, with longer portions of blanched stem, while later crops tend to be shorter, with darker stems and a tougher texture. Delicious used in stews, casseroles, soups, or served up with white sauce, leeks are a versatile, valuable source of fresh winter vegetables.

	SPRING	SUMMER	AUTUMN	WINTER
SOW				
HARVEST				

SOWING

Although they will probably cope in any soil you care to plant them in, leeks prefer a deep, fertile soil with a slightly acidic pH. Dig in plenty of well-rotted manure or compost before planting.

Seed can be sown from as early as late winter, in trays or modules under cover. Sow at a depth of 2.5cm (1in) and harden seedlings off before you transplant them. Alternatively, sow successively into an outdoor seed bed through spring; seedlings should be ready to transplant in eight weeks, when they are about as thick as a pencil.

Trim their roots down to about 2.5cm (1in) and leaves to 15cm (6in). With a dibber, create holes about 15cm (6in) deep, and 15cm

Trim seedling roots before transplanting.

(6in) apart. Place the seedlings in the holes and water around them, allowing the water to drag the soil into the surrounding hole.

CROP CARE

Give plants a feed with a high-nitrogen fertilizer in summer but do not overwater them. To give leeks their customary white stems you will need to earth up soil around them as they grow.

HARVESTING

Within four to five months your leeks will be ready to harvest, although they can be left in the ground for longer if necessary.

STORING

Out of the ground, leeks do not store very well. If you need to use the space for planting other crops, they can be dug up and "heeled in" elsewhere.

Dig a shallow trench, deep enough to fully submerge the roots. Place the leeks in the hole, leaning them against one side. Cover the roots over with soil and then lift as required.

PESTS AND DISEASES

Leeks are prone to the same problems as other members of the onion family, most notably onion fly, leek moth, and downy mildew. They may also suffer from leek rust – remove and destroy infected leaves. Sow seed in modules to discourage fusarium wilt.

Leek moths burrow into the stem.

'Hannibal'

This early variety is quick-developing, making it a good choice for baby leeks in late summer. If left to mature it shows good resistance to "bulbing" (forming unwanted bulbs) and produces long, white shafts with healthy mid-green foliage.

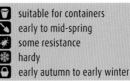

🪣 suitable for containers
🌱 early to mid-spring
🦋 some resistance
❄️ hardy
🔒 early autumn to early winter

'King Richard' ♀

This well-established, early favourite is a good choice for a quick crop of baby leeks, but will also go on to produce mature plants with very long shafts and pale green leaves. It is popular for showing and slow to bolt, with a sweet, tender flavour.

🪣 suitable for containers
🌱 early to mid-spring
🦋 some resistance
❄️ hardy
🔒 early autumn to early winter

'Lancelot'

This early variety is a good choice for producing an early crop of baby leeks and can also be left until early winter to produce a full-sized crop. It is an easy-going variety and is also good grown in containers.

🪣 suitable for containers
🌱 early to mid-spring
🦋 poor resistance
❄️ hardy
🔒 early autumn to early winter

'Bandit' ♀

This late variety produces dark blue-green leaves and has some resistance to rust disease. The leaves make an attractive contrast with the thick, white stem, which has a good flavour. 'Bandit' stands well once mature with little tendency to bolt.

 suitable for containers
early to mid-spring
some resistance
hardy
late winter to late spring

'Catalina' ♀

This maincrop variety produces thick, short, heavy stems, uniform in appearance, with dark green leaves. It stands well all winter, and will carry on cropping right into late spring, showing no tendency to bolt or go bulbous at the base.

suitable for containers
early to mid-spring
some resistance
hardy
late autumn to late spring

'Blue Solaise'

A French heirloom leek, also known as 'Bleu de Solaise', this maincrop variety has attractive deep purplish-blue leaves and thick, white, medium-length stems. It is a very hardy variety that stands well once mature, and will crop until late spring.

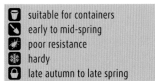 suitable for containers
early to mid-spring
poor resistance
hardy
late autumn to late spring

'Apollo'

Vigorous, high-yielding, and with uniform shafts, this maincrop F1 variety has rather pale leaves that have good resistance to leek rust. The leaves are held aloft, making it suitable for close planting.

🪴 suitable for containers
🌱 early to mid-spring
✳ good resistance
❄ hardy
🔒 late autumn to mid-spring

'Atlanta' ♀

This late variety produces healthy, blue-green foliage that stands more erect than most, making it easier to fit a greater number of plants into your vegetable bed or container. The blanched white stem is of average length.

🪴 suitable for containers
🌱 early to mid-spring
✳ some resistance
❄ hardy
🔒 late winter to late spring

'Musselburgh'

This old, maincrop variety is named after a Scottish town, and is still popular as it is very hardy and reliable. It produces rather short but sturdy stems with a good flavour. The blue-green leaves have some resistance to leek rust.

- 🪣 suitable for containers
- 🏷 early to mid-spring
- ✳ some resistance
- ❄ hardy
- 🔒 late autumn to mid-spring

'Lincoln'

Harvest US-only 'Lincoln' seeds as pencil-thin babies at 50 days, or allow them another month to develop into long, thick, white shanks. This early-maturing "summer leek" has a mild flavour that is delicate enough to eat raw.

- 🪣 suitable for containers
- 🏷 mid- to late spring
- ✳ poor resistance
- ❄ hardy
- 🔒 midsummer to autumn

'Jolant'

An early variety, 'Jolant' is one of the fastest growing leeks, producing a dense shaft with a mild flavour. A good choice for producing an abundance of baby leeks – grow them in containers as they can be planted at high density.

- 🪣 suitable for containers
- 🏷 early to mid-spring
- ✳ some resistance
- ❄ hardy
- 🔒 early autumn to early winter

'Toledo' ♀

A maincrop variety, 'Toledo' tends to be a bit late getting into its stride, but it is a good cropper, producing smooth, uniform, medium to long shafts topped by dark green leaves from early winter.

- suitable for containers
- early to mid-spring
- some resistance
- hardy
- early winter to mid-spring

'Lyon 2 – Prizetaker'

Over 100 years old, this early variety is still popular as a show leek, quickly developing long, thick, white stems with good flavour. Once mature it will stand well and tolerates low temperatures well.

- suitable for containers
- early to mid-spring
- poor resistance
- hardy
- early autumn to early winter

'Poristo' ♀

A good-looking, maincrop leek with long, clean shafts, a good length of white blanch at the base, and dark green leaves. It stays in good condition through winter and produces good yields over a long period.

- suitable for containers
- early to mid-spring
- some resistance
- hardy
- late autumn to mid-spring

'Carlton' ♀

The first F1 hybrid leek, this early variety grows quickly, producing uniform plants with long, straight shafts. The leaves are tightly packed so little soil gets trapped, and they are quick and easy to clean. However, it tends to bolt if left too long before harvest.

- 🪣 suitable for containers
- 🌱 early to mid-spring
- 🕷 some resistance
- ❄ hardy
- 🔒 early autumn to early winter

'Upton' ♀

This hybrid "summer leek" reaches a thickness of 8–10cm (3–4in) about 90 days after transplanting. Tall and vigorous, 'Upton' plants produce dark blue-green foliage of a uniformly good quality, in a variety of growing conditions.

- 🪣 suitable for containers
- 🌱 early to mid-spring
- 🕷 some resistance
- ❄ hardy
- 🔒 late summer to autumn

'Pancho' ♀

An early variety, 'Pancho' produces a good yield of medium to long, solid shafts, which have only a slight tendency to bulb. It has a crisp texture and good flavour. The leaves are mid-green and show good resistance to leek rust fungal disease.

- 🪣 suitable for containers
- 🌱 early to mid-spring
- 🕷 good resistance
- ❄ hardy
- 🔒 early autumn to early winter

GARLIC *Allium sativum* and *A. ampeloprasum*

Its distinct aroma and strong flavour make garlic a vital component of many of our everyday dishes, and it is also known for its health benefits. Despite needing a relatively long growing period, it is very easy to grow, even in cooler climates, making it a popular choice with gardeners. Soft-neck types are easier to grow and tend to have a milder flavour. Hard-neck types produce larger bulbs but do not keep as long.

	SPRING	SUMMER	AUTUMN	WINTER
PLANT				
HARVEST				

PLANTING

Garlic grows best in a sunny, open site with fertile, well-drained, and slightly alkaline soil. Plant in autumn or early winter, as garlic needs cold weather at the start of its growth. Spring-planted garlic will still succeed, but it does tend to produce smaller bulbs as there is less time for it to mature.

Create deep holes for bulbs with a dibber.

To plant, split open a bulb and divide it into individual cloves. Push these about 10cm (4in) deep into the soil with their points facing up, either directly into the ground or in modules. Space the cloves 20cm (8in) apart.

CROP CARE

Plant it in the right conditions and garlic is relatively easy to grow. Keep the plants well-weeded; keep the soil moist but be careful not to overwater them. If the weather is cold, consider giving the plants some protection with a cloche.

Watch out for signs of bolting, as this will decrease the final size of the bulb. To prevent this from happening, cut the stem down to about half its height a couple of weeks prior to harvesting.

HARVESTING

Garlic is ready to be harvested when its leaves turn yellow and start to die down. This usually happens in early summer. Alternatively, harvest while the leaves are still green and use the cloves fresh, they have a have a milder flavour but must be used quickly this way as they do not keep for long.

STORING

Hang the garlic up to dry in plaits or individually. Take care not to bruise the bulbs and they will store for up to 10 months in a well ventilated place.

PESTS AND DISEASES

Buying good-quality, disease-resistant bulbs will help to keep most diseases at bay, as will regularly rotating crops. One common problem is leek rust – orange blisters filled with powdery spores appear on leaves – remove promptly and it may not prove fatal.

A garlic leaf infected with leek rust.

'Elephant'

Although this variety is not a true garlic, and is more closely related to leeks, it looks like a giant garlic and is grown in the same way. The bulbs are huge – up to 15cm (6in) across – have a mild flavour, and are particularly good for roasting whole.

🪣	suitable for containers
🍂	autumn
🐛	poor resistance
❄	hardy
🔒	early to midsummer

'Echo' ♀

A hard-neck variety, 'Echo' is quite a late cropper, producing tidy, fat, purple-skinned cloves within a white outer skin. The yield is high with a uniform appearance and mild flavour, making it a good choice for using fresh.

🪣	suitable for containers
🍂	autumn
🐛	some resistance
❄	hardy
🔒	early to midsummer

'Arno' ♀

This soft-neck cultivar produces attractive bulbs that have a smooth, ivory-white outer skin and medium-flavour, pink-skinned cloves. It produces a good yield with uniform appearance, and stores well, making it a good all-rounder.

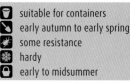

🪣	suitable for containers
🍂	early autumn to early spring
🐛	some resistance
❄	hardy
🔒	early to midsummer

'Sultop'

This hard-neck cultivar produces medium-sized bulbs with a large number of easy-to-peel, red-skinned cloves with a delicious flavour. Although hard-neck varieties are normally autumn-planted, this one does best if started in spring.

- suitable for containers
- early spring
- poor resistance
- hardy
- early to midsummer

'Lautrec Wight'

This hard neck cultivar is originally from south-west France. It has a white outer skin, and is deep pink within. The taste is subtle, smooth, and creamy. It prefers warm, dry conditions so it is sometimes best to delay planting until spring.

- suitable for containers
- autumn
- some resistance
- hardy
- early to midsummer

'Ivory' ♛

This soft-neck cultivar produces large, well-formed cloves and crops early in the season. It is suitable for all culinary purposes, and will also store well for use through the winter and on into the following spring.

- suitable for containers
- early autumn to early spring
- some resistance
- hardy
- early to midsummer

'Purple Wight'

This hard-neck cultivar crops early but still stores reasonably well, and should last until early winter. The bulbs have attractive purple stripes and the cloves have a strong taste, ideal for flavouring robust soups and stews.

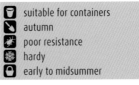

- suitable for containers
- autumn
- poor resistance
- hardy
- early to midsummer

'Mediterranean'

This soft-neck cultivar is originally from southern France. It produces large, white bulbs and is a good choice for producing 'wet' garlic for eating while still fresh and juicy. It can also be dried off and stored until late autumn.

- suitable for containers
- autumn
- poor resistance
- hardy
- early to midsummer

'Spanish Roja'

This hard-neck cultivar has excellent flavour. Its outer skin is purple-streaked and the cloves, which vary from pinky-brown to mahogany, are plump and easy to peel. However, this cultivar may perform poorly where winters are mild and wet.

- suitable for containers
- autumn
- poor resistance
- hardy
- early to midsummer

'Germidour'

A soft-neck cultivar, 'Germidour' is available as a virus-free selection for improved vigour. It tends to be late maturing, producing well-packed, purple-skinned cloves within a white outer skin. It is a reliable cropper with a mild flavour.

- suitable for containers
- early autumn to early spring
- some resistance
- hardy
- early to midsummer

'Early Wight'

This hard-neck cultivar produces a very early crop that can be ready to lift in late spring. It develops good, fat cloves that are easy to peel, and should be used soon after harvest as it does not keep well in storage.

🪣	suitable for containers
🍂	autumn
✳️	some resistance
❄️	hardy
🔒	late spring to early summer

'Albigensian Wight'

A soft-neck cultivar originating in south-west France, this variety produces a heavy crop of large, plump, white bulbs with a delicious flavour. It stores better than other Mediterranean varieties and should keep into late winter in good condition.

🪣	suitable for containers
🍂	early autumn to early spring
✳️	poor resistance
❄️	hardy
🔒	early to midsummer

'Chesnok Red'

This hard-neck cultivar has pink-striped, white outer skin, and is pink inside. It bears eight to ten good-sized cloves whose rich flavour and creamy texture are a good choice for baking whole and ideal for garlic bread.

🪣	suitable for containers
🍂	autumn
✳️	poor resistance
❄️	hardy
🔒	early to midsummer

SPRING AND BUNCHING ONIONS

Allium cepa and *A. fistulosum*

Mostly enjoyed as a salad vegetable when their stems are still
slender, spring onions will also develop into sizeable bulbs if left
to grow on. They are very easy to raise and need minimal care.
Bunching onions should be grown in the same way, and can be
harvested at spring onion size, or left to mature to the size of leeks.

	SPRING	SUMMER	AUTUMN	WINTER
SOW				
HARVEST				

SOWING

Grown from seed, spring and
bunching onions need a sunny,
fertile, well-drained site, and will
not do well on very acid soils.
Test the pH levels of your soil
and add lime if necessary. Dig
in plenty of well-rotted manure
or compost before sowing.

Sow the seed directly into
the ground from early spring.
If you want to harvest onions
throughout the summer, sow
successive batches at two-weekly
intervals until the autumn. You
can also sow hardy varieties in
the autumn for overwintering
crops that will be ready to
harvest the following spring.

Prepare shallow drills 1–2cm
(½–¾in) deep and 30cm (12in)
apart. Allow about 1cm (½in)

Pull spring onions as required.

between seeds. Carefully rake
back the soil to cover the drills.
Plants will not need thinning.

CROP CARE

Weed the bed regularly and
water if the weather is very dry,
as this can cause the onions to
become bulbous. If you live in
an area where there is a high
risk of frosts, protect early or
late crops with cloches.

HARVESTING

The longer you leave spring onions in the ground, the bigger the bulbs will grow. If you want them at their youngest and most delicate, start harvesting as soon as the onions reach approximately 15cm (6in) high. Harvest bunching onions as required, either when young and slender, or leave them to mature and become thicker.

STORING

Spring and bunching onions do not store well. They will keep fresh in the refrigerator for a few days, but it is better to pick them for immediate use.

PESTS AND DISEASES

Spring and bunching onions are vulnerable to the same problems that affect larger varieties of onions (see pp.316–7). Downy mildew and onion white rot are the most common diseases; remove infected plants and destroy, as there is no effective cure. To reduce the risk and spread of disease, practise good garden hygiene and keep plants well ventilated.

You may also need to cover your seedlings with fleece to protect them from onion fly. Spring or bunching onions grown from sets are less at risk.

'Crimson Forest'

This very striking spring onion produces conventional green foliage, but a deep red shaft. The colouration can penetrate for several layers, making this a very attractive variety to use in salads, especially as the flavour is mild.

- suitable for containers
- early spring to midsummer
- poor resistance
- fairly hardy
- late spring to autumn

'Deep Purple'

These vigorous spring onions have bright, medium-green leaves and attractive deep red-purple bases. The bulbous, torpedo-shaped base colours up whatever the age of the plant or the temperature. Overall this is a good-looking variety with a pleasant flavour.

- suitable for containers
- early spring to midsummer
- poor resistance
- fairly hardy
- late spring to autumn

'Lilia' ♀

This Italian spring onion has a strong, pungent flavour. It has a very attractive appearance with dark green leaves and shiny, deep purple-red stems. It does tend to be bulbous and, if planted at wider spacing or thinned, it can be left to form full-sized onions.

- suitable for containers
- early spring to midsummer
- poor resistance
- fairly hardy
- late spring to autumn

'Performer'

This is an upright spring onion with dark green leaves. The stems have a mild flavour and do not become bulbous with age. If provided with cloche protection, this variety will continue to crop through into winter.

- suitable for containers
- early spring to midsummer
- poor resistance
- fairly hardy
- late spring to early winter

'White Lisbon Winter Hardy'

A particularly tough selection of 'White Lisbon', this spring onion can be grown virtually all year round to provide a fresh, tasty crop. It's a good choice for colder, more exposed areas as it has improved frost tolerance.

- suitable for containers
- late summer to mid-autumn
- poor resistance
- hardy
- early to late spring

'North Holland Blood Red'

This attractive and versatile variety can be used young, as a spring onion, or allowed to grow on and develop into a bulb. The red colour deepens with age, and it has a mild flavour and crisp flesh. It is good for containers.

- suitable for containers
- early spring to midsummer
- poor resistance
- fairly hardy
- late spring to autumn

'Eiffel'

A very upright grower, with improved disease resistance, this spring onion variety produces mid-green leaves and long, white shafts that stay narrow through the summer, and show high resistance to developing bulbs at the base.

- suitable for containers
- late summer to mid-autumn
- some resistance
- hardy
- early to late spring

'Ramrod' ♛

This very upright-growing spring onion variety produces stiff, medium-green leaves and a good length of white shaft. It has a mild flavour and makes a good choice for overwintering to produce an early contribution to the salad bowl.

- suitable for containers
- late summer to mid-autumn
- some resistance
- hardy
- early to late spring

'Guardsman' ♀

This very vigorous, F1 bunching variety produces medium to dark green leaves. The lower part is well-blanched, with some tendency to form bulbs. It stands well, remaining in good condition for longer than older varieties, and can be harvested over several weeks from one sowing.

- suitable for containers
- early spring to midsummer
- some resistance
- fairly hardy
- late spring to autumn

'Parade' ♀

This bunching variety is notable for its very straight, strong-growing, uniform stems. There is a good length of blanched white base, and the variety stands well once mature, so can be harvested over a long period without forming bulbs or running to seed.

- suitable for containers
- early spring to midsummer
- some resistance
- fairly hardy
- late spring to autumn

'Ishikura' ♀

This strong-growing, bunching type can be picked when they are pencil-thin, or left to become as thick as a baby leek. It remains straight and does not form bulbs at the base. There is a good proportion of white stem to green, so little is wasted.

- suitable for containers
- early spring to midsummer
- some resistance
- fairly hardy
- late spring to autumn

'Emerald Star' ♀

This F1 hybrid, bunching variety produces medium-green leaves with a good contrast between the leafy tops and the lower, blanched, white stems. It is slow to bolt, meaning that you can continue to harvest it over a longer period.

- suitable for containers
- early spring to midsummer
- some resistance
- fairly hardy
- late spring to autumn

'White Lisbon' ♀

The best-known spring onion of all, this variety is quick and easy to grow. It has dark green leaves, a mild flavour, and a tendency to become bulbous at the base as it matures. It is a good choice for growing in containers.

- suitable for containers
- late summer to mid-autumn
- some resistance
- hardy
- early to late spring

'White Spear' ♀

A vigorous, bunching hybrid with dark, blue-green leaves and long, straight, slender stems. The crop is uniform in appearance and is quick growing, making it a good choice for sowing early or late in the season.

- suitable for containers
- early spring to midsummer
- some resistance
- fairly hardy
- late spring to autumn

'Beltsville Bunching' ♀

This tall, bunching variety produces a good length of blanched white stem. It has a crisp texture and mild flavour, and tolerates hot, dry weather conditions well. A good choice for late summer and autumn cropping.

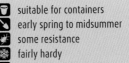

- suitable for containers
- early spring to midsummer
- some resistance
- fairly hardy
- late spring to autumn

'Emerald Isle' ♀

This bunching variety produces a very uniform crop, which could make it a good choice for gardeners interested in showing their produce at exhibition. It develops medium, strong stems, with straight tops, and an average balance between green and white.

- suitable for containers
- early spring to late summer
- some resistance
- fairly hardy
- late spring to autumn

'Shimonita'

A hardy bunching variety that can stand through the winter, this variety has very thick foliage. The blanched shaft is sweet at the base and pungent near the leaves. If thinned out to wider than normal spacing the plants can grow on to become as thick as leeks.

- suitable for containers
- early spring to late summer
- poor resistance
- hardy
- mid-spring to late autumn

'Long White Koshigaya' ♀

Named after a Japanese city, this bunching variety produces uniform plants with medium to dark green, slender leaves that are carried erect. There is a good length of blanched white stem, and it is slow to bolt.

- suitable for containers
- early spring to midsummer
- some resistance
- fairly hardy
- late spring to autumn

'Photon' ♀

This bunching variety produces neat plants, so would make a good choice for growing in containers. It is also attractive-looking, with uniform growth, dark green leaves, and a long portion of blanched white stem.

- suitable for containers
- early spring to midsummer
- some resistance
- fairly hardy
- late spring to autumn

'Summer Isle' ♀

This relatively late-cropping, bunching variety is vigorous and uniform. It produces strong, bright green tops with plenty of blanched white shaft below. It has a sweet flavour, with low pungency, so makes a good choice for eating raw.

- suitable for containers
- early spring to midsummer
- some resistance
- fairly hardy
- late spring to autumn

'Savel' ♀

This good-flavoured, bunching variety has tall, upright stems with a good length of blanched white base. Try sowing seed close, then use the thinnings as baby vegetables and leave the remaining plants to grow on. These will hold well once mature without producing bulbs.

- suitable for containers
- early spring to midsummer
- some resistance
- fairly hardy
- late spring to autumn

'Ishiko' ♀

This is a strong-growing, bunching variety that produces high yields suitable for using fresh in salads or cooking in stir fries. The leaves are mid- to dark green and contrast attractively with the white part of the stem.

- suitable for containers
- early spring to midsummer
- some resistance
- fairly hardy
- late spring to autumn

'Feast' ♀

This F1 hybrid, bunching variety has medium to dark green, upright leaves. The bases are a good pure white, and are long and slender. It copes well with hot weather, stands well, and is slow to bolt. 'Feast' is resistant to downy mildew.

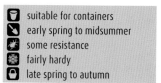

- suitable for containers
- early spring to midsummer
- some resistance
- fairly hardy
- late spring to autumn

Stem Vegetables

- Asparagus
- Rhubarb
- Celery
- Celeriac
- Florence fennel

ASPARAGUS *Asparagus officinalis*

Asparagus is a valuable crop, yielding succulent stems that are costly to buy, at a time of year when little else is available. It has a reputation for being difficult to grow, but modern high-yielding, high-quality cultivars are available and make success much easier; all-male varieties now dominate as they produce a greater number of thicker spears. Although you must wait two years before the first crop, it's well worth it.

	SPRING	SUMMER	AUTUMN	WINTER
SOW/PLANT				
HARVEST				

SOWING AND PLANTING

Any fertile, well-drained garden soil in full sun will suit asparagus. Dig in plenty of well-rotted manure or compost shortly before planting. Asparagus does best with a pH between 6.3–7.5, so plant it in a raised bed if your soil is alkaline.

If you are raising asparagus from seed, sow it indoors in late winter. Sow singly in module trays and keep warm using a heated propagator. The seedlings can be planted out in late spring.

However, most gardeners buy dormant asparagus crowns and plant them directly into the ground in early spring. Dig trenches 20cm (8in) deep and incorporate fertilizer into the base. Set the plants in the soil

Spread the roots on the trench base.

in the bottom of the trench. Although close planting is possible, allowing 40cm (16in) between crowns and 1.2m (4ft) between trenches will give a longer lasting plantation.

CROP CARE

Asparagus plants should be well watered, and fed with general purpose fertilizer every spring. Once established, no further

watering is needed but fertilizer should be applied each year in midsummer, after stems have been harvested. In autumn the ferny foliage will become straw-like and should be cut down.

HARVESTING

After two years, asparagus will be ready to harvest. In the third year a light crop is taken in mid-spring, and subsequently full cropping can begin. Use a knife to slice stems free, taking care not to harm emerging spears nearby. Cut the stems 2.5cm (1in) below the soil surface when they reach about 13–18cm (5–7in) tall.

PESTS AND DISEASES

Asparagus beetle is the only serious pest. Treat infected plants with an appropriate insecticide or by picking off the beetles and larvae. Root diseases sometimes occur; fresh crowns must be planted on a new site. Slugs may also damage emerging spears.

Asparagus beetles strip plant foliage.

'Jersey Knight'

This high-quality, robust, all-male hybrid is reliable and produces good yields of thick but tender spears. The green stems are succulent and numerous, with attractive purple tips. Best suited to warmer regions, it has good resistance to root diseases.

- unsuitable for containers
- early spring
- good resistance
- hardy
- mid-spring to midsummer

'Grolim'

This all-male hybrid produces many stems of exceptional thickness and succulence, with fewer thin stems than other varieties. Cropping peaks early in the season; stems are produced even when closely spaced, making it good for small gardens.

- unsuitable for containers
- early spring
- poor resistance
- hardy
- mid-spring to early summer

'Ariane'

This vigorous and reliable all-male hybrid bears purple tips on deep green stems; the shoots are thick and succulent. It crops early in the picking season, when asparagus is most appreciated, and the overall yields are heavy throughout the season.

- unsuitable for containers
- early spring
- poor resistance
- hardy
- mid-sping to midsummer

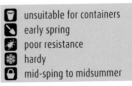

'Connover's Colossal'

Although old-fashioned, and consisting of both male and female plants, this variety can give fair yields, especially if you seek out the better strains. Seed is much cheaper than for hybrid types, so this variety is useful where resources are limited.

 unsuitable for containers

early spring

poor resistance

hardy

mid-spring to midsummer

'Dariana'

This all-male hybrid bears good yields of especially thick, straight stems; the spears are succulent and numerous and overall yields are high. Its ferny leaves are healthy and vigorous with good weed-suppressing properties, but will need to be supported.

unsuitable for containers

early spring

poor resistance

hardy

mid-spring to midsummer

'Martha Washington'

This old-fashioned, non-hybrid variety has both male and female plants. Its yields and quality are fair, and it has more poor-quality spears than hybrid plants, but despite this there are reasons to grow it: seed is cheap, and it has a reputation for longevity.

unsuitable for containers

early spring

some resistance

hardy

mid-spring to midsummer

'Backlim'

This long-established, all-male hybrid has stood the test of time, giving good yields year after year, in a wide range of conditions. Its stems are thick, succulent, and numerous. Most of the stems are ready to harvest later in the season but yields are high overall.

- unsuitable for containers
- early spring
- some resistance
- hardy
- mid-spring to early summer

'Mondeo'

This all-male hybrid produces exceptional yields of high-quality, thick stems; spears have notably tight tips. Cropping is heaviest early in the season, when asparagus is most appreciated. A vigorous grower, it has abundant and healthy, ferny leaves.

- unsuitable for containers
- early spring
- poor resistance
- hardy
- mid-spring to midsummer

'Purple Pacific'

This non-hybrid variety produces purple stems of good flavour. Colour is lost with prolonged cooking but can be retained by careful steaming or microwave cooking. The tender stems are especially suited to eating raw, and are often especially sweet.

- unsuitable for containers
- early spring
- poor resistance
- hardy
- mid-spring to midsummer

'Gijnlim' ♀

This long-established, all-male hybrid has proved reliable and will crop well over many years. The mid-green stems are thick, succulent, and numerous, and have pronounced purple tips. Production peaks early in the season with high yields overall.

 unsuitable for containers

early spring

some resistance

hardy

mid-spring to early summer

'Lucullus' ♀

This all-male hybrid has proved reliable over many years in a wide range of gardens. It bears high yields of good-quality spears, which peak later in the season. Arguably however, it is not in the same class as more modern asparagus cultivars.

unsuitable for containers

early spring

some resistance

hardy

mid-sping to midsummer

'Guelph Millennium'

This robust, all-male hybrid has proved reliable, producing good yields even in cold regions. The green stems are of excellent quality and are thick, succulent, and numerous. Production peaks later in the season with high yields overall.

unsuitable for containers

early spring

poor resistance

hardy

mid-spring to early summer

RHUBARB *Rheum x hybridum*

Rhubarb is an anomaly; it is a vegetable that is eaten as a fruit, and one that produces plenty of tasty stalks at a time of year when little else is available, especially if "forced". Although it can get by with little care and attention, it repays generous treatment with greater yields of better produce. Unlike most vegetable crops, it is perennial, and can give several years of productive growth before it needs to be replaced.

	SPRING	SUMMER	AUTUMN	WINTER
PLANT				
HARVEST				

PLANTING

Rhubarb prefers an open site and should be planted in soil that has been improved with plenty of manure or other bulky organic matter – it needs soil that will drain well, but not become waterlogged. Additional general purpose fertilizer is helpful, and should be applied annually in late winter.

It is possible to raise your own rhubarb from seed, but buying a plant, or separating a piece of long root, complete with at least one bud, from the outside of the parent clump in winter or early spring is better. Plant out immediately; make sure that the bud is at the same depth as when it was dug out. Allow 90cm (36in) space between plants.

Pull stems gently to protect the clump.

CROP CARE

Newly planted rhubarb should be watered during dry spells for the first year. Mulch it with a 7cm (3in) layer of organic matter.

FORCING

Forcing your rhubarb results in earlier, sweeter, and more tender stems. Pile organic matter around the forcing container to ensure that no

light can reach the plant. Forced rhubarb should be left for a year or two to recover.

HARVESTING

Do not harvest any rhubarb stems in the first year, and only remove a light crop in the second. Full harvests can be taken thereafter for many years. When stems reach a sufficient size, harvest them by grasping the base and pulling the sticks away from the clump, taking care not to snap them. Light crops can be harvested until early summer; heavy crops until late summer.

PESTS AND DISEASES

Rhubarb suffers from few pests, but fungal diseases such as honey fungus and crown rot can damage the crowns, particularly if the soil is poorly drained. Both can cause the plant to rot and die, but may not be fatal if you act promptly to remove any diseased parts of the plant. Destroy rather than compost infected material, to reduce the risk of infection spreading.

Viruses are common and any rhubarb that fails to thrive should be replaced. Buy healthy, new plants mail order or from garden centres.

'Grandad's Favorite' ♛

One of the few rhubarb varieties bred in recent times, this mid-season variety has an excellent flavour. It is highly productive, bearing large yields of bright red stems, and is especially well-suited to producing later crops, rather than being forced.

- unsuitable for containers
- winter to early spring
- some resistance
- hardy
- spring to early summer

'Early Champagne'

This long established and widely grown variety is sold as plants, rather than seed. It produces pink stalks with redder bases. The early stems have good flavour and texture and can be readily forced; they are well suited to any good garden soil.

- unsuitable for containers
- winter to early spring
- some resistance
- hardy
- spring to early summer

'Hawke's Champagne' ♛

This long established and very widely grown, early rhubarb produces bright red stems of good flavour and texture. It is especially well suited to forcing, although it is a good performer later in the season as well. It will grow in any good garden soil.

- unsuitable for containers
- winter to early spring
- some resistance
- hardy
- spring to early summer

'Stein's Champagne' ♛

This long established variety is suited to all good garden soils. It has the typical 'champagne rhubarb' attributes of good, deep red colour and sweet tender flavour. It is an early variety, so is suitable for both forced and unforced cultivation.

- unsuitable for containers
- winter to early spring
- some resistance
- hardy
- spring to early summer

'Early Champagne'

'Glaskins Perpetual'

This vigorous rhubarb variety is long established and has stood the test of time – it is widely grown and sold. It produces long red stems of fair texture and flavour, which are borne over a long cropping period, from spring into summer. It is available as plants but seldom as seed.

- unsuitable for containers
- winter to early spring
- some resistance
- hardy
- spring to early summer

'Timperley Early'

This very early rhubarb is ideally suited for the first forced crops, although it is also satisfactory in the open garden too. It is long established and reliable, with red-based stems that have a good pink-green colour. The sticks are rather thin but their flavour and texture are satisfactory.

- unsuitable for containers
- winter to early spring
- some resistance
- hardy
- spring to early summer

'Victoria'

This long established and widely grown rhubarb is sold as both plants and seed. It produces high yields of late-growing stalks with fair texture and flavour. The stems have a greenish tint and are produced for a long period from spring into summer.

- unsuitable for containers
- winter to early spring
- some resistance
- hardy
- spring to early summer

'Crimson Red'

This vigorous, strong-growing, US-only rhubarb produces thick, succulent, deep red stems of very good flavour, texture, and appearance. It is well suited to all climatic zones with cold winters, including areas with very harsh winter weather.

- unsuitable for containers
- winter to early spring
- some resistance
- hardy
- spring to early summer

'Reed's Early Superb' ♀

This strong-growing, vigorous, long established rhubarb is well suited to any garden soil and position. It is moderately early and very suitable for forcing. It is also very attractive, with long red stems of good texture and flavour.

- 🪣 unsuitable for containers
- 🗡 winter to early spring
- 🕷 some resistance
- ❄ hardy
- 🔒 spring to early summer

'Valentine'

Reliable and robust, this very vigorous US-only variety will grow well in any good garden soil in all climatic zones with sufficiently cold winters. Stalks are dark red, thick, and succulent, with good flavour. It seldom produces seed stalks.

- 🪣 unsuitable for containers
- 🗡 winter to early spring
- 🕷 some resistance
- ❄ hardy
- 🔒 spring to early summer

'Paragon'

This 19th-century, heirloom, US-only variety produces mild-flavoured, bright red stems and vigorous foliage. It is not especially recommended for forcing, but is very hardy, and likely to thrive in the coldest continental climates.

- 🪣 unsuitable for containers
- 🗡 winter to early spring
- 🕷 some resistance
- ❄ hardy
- 🔒 spring to early summer

'Fulton's Strawberry Surprise' ♀

This long established, strong-growing cultivar is best suited for outdoor production and will grow in any good garden soil. When unforced, its bright red stems are especially attractive, and are tender and well-flavoured.

- 🪣 unsuitable for containers
- 🗡 winter to early spring
- 🕷 some resistance
- ❄ hardy
- 🔒 spring to early summer

CELERY *Apium graveolens* var. *dulce*

Celery comes in four kinds: self-blanching celery is most common and should be closely planted in blocks, where the plants shade each other enough to blanch their stems. Trench celery is grown in trenches and earthed up as it grows, to give blanched, tender stems that are free from bitterness. Green celery is bred to be succulent without blanching, while some celery is grown as a leafy herb, in the same way as parsley.

	SPRING	SUMMER	AUTUMN	WINTER
SOW				
HARVEST				

SOWING

Celery plants flower prematurely if planted out too early. To avoid this, planting should be done in early summer from sowings made indoors in mid-spring, as the seed takes a long time to germinate.

Sow seed thinly, barely covering it with soil, in shallow pots or module trays. Seedlings should be grown under cover until they develop a few leaves, and their roots fill their pots. Keep them in a moderately warm environment, such as a greenhouse, with plenty of light.

Celery does best in soil that has been enriched with plenty of organic matter and has been supplemented with a dose of general fertilizer before planting. Space trench celery seedlings

Dig up the plants from midsummer.

30–45cm (12–18in) apart in a prepared trench; self-blanching and green types in blocks, spaced 25cm (10in) apart. Allow leaf celery 13cm (5in) between plants.

CROP CARE

Water seedlings after planting and keep them free of weeds. Water frequently, as tender stems will not form if the plants dry out. Add extra fertilizer if

growth slows. Trench celery may require tying together as it forms, to keep the plants free from mud.

HARVESTING

Harvest when the heads are big enough. Water before harvesting for longer storage.

STORING

Trench celery can be left in the ground in mild regions if heads are protected with soil and boards, to exclude rain and frost. Other celery must be harvested when it matures. Kept in the fridge it will store in usable condition for several weeks.

PESTS AND DISEASES

Foliage may be "mined" by celery fly, which cause brown patches on leaves and slows the overall growth. Picking affected leaves before the problem spreads is usually sufficient control.

Celery leaf spot causes small brown rings to appear on leaves – destroy infected plants immediately as fungicides are seldom available for later control. Plants may also be at risk from foot and root rots, violet root rot, and sclerotina. These diseases have no treatments, so remove and destroy any infected plants.

'Celebrity' ♀

This non-hybrid, self-blanching celery produces pale, slender sticks; it is well-ribbed and succulent, and has exceptional flavour and texture. It resists premature flowering, making it suitable for summer crops and for growing indoors for winter crops.

🪣	unsuitable for containers
🌱	spring
🐛	some resistance
❄	hardy
🔒	summer

'Loret' ♀

This non-hybrid, self-blanching variety has good vigour, and although the stems are not especially long, the heads are dense. The pale stems have a slightly green tinge and are of very good quality. It has good resistance to bolting.

🪣	unsuitable for containers
🌱	spring
🐛	some resistance
❄	hardy
🔒	summer to autumn

'Victoria' ♀

This green hybrid celery produces tall stems with dense, heavy heads. It is vigorous and tolerates a wide range of conditions, maturing early to produce succulent, fleshy stems. It resists bolting and will store in good condition for long periods.

🪣	unsuitable for containers
🌱	spring
🐛	some resistance
❄	hardy
🔒	summer to autumn

'Golden Self Blanching'

This traditional, non-hybrid, self-blanching variety produces medium-quality stalks of good texture and flavour. They are thick and wide, but not as long as more modern varieties, and are more variable. It requires no exclusion of light to blanch its stems.

- 🪣 unsuitable for containers
- 🌱 spring
- 🕷 poor resistance
- ❄ hardy
- 🔒 summer to autumn

'Giant Pink' ♀

This traditional trench celery has long, crisp stems that can grow up to 60cm (24in) high and 5cm (2in) thick. Stems require blanching and take on an attractive pink tinge afterwards. For optimum crispness and mild flavour grow in rich soil.

- 🪣 unsuitable for containers
- 🌱 spring
- 🕷 some resistance
- ❄ hardy
- 🔒 summer to early winter

'Ivory Tower' ♀

This non-hybrid, self-blanching variety has long, succulent, pale stems that are slow to become stringy if grown in fertile, moist conditions. Stems have a refined, delicate, true celery flavour, and blanching is not required.

- 🪣 unsuitable for containers
- 🌱 spring
- 🕷 some resistance
- ❄ hardy
- 🔒 summer

'Tango' ♀

This non-hybrid, self-blanching celery produces long, bright, succulent stems of very good flavour. It resists premature flowering and remains in good condition for long periods, even in hot weather. It is relatively slow-growing however, and is not best suited to early crops.

🪣	unsuitable for containers
🌱	spring
🌿	some resistance
❄	hardy
🔒	summer to autumn

'Octavius' ♀

This hybrid green celery produces medium-green stems that are especially suited to autumn cropping. The plant is tall and vigorous and the heads are large and dense – the total yield is very high. 'Octavius' has good flavour and texture.

🪣	unsuitable for containers
🌱	spring
🌿	some resistance
❄	hardy
🔒	summer to autumn

'Moonbeam' ♀

This non-hybrid, self-blanching celery grows well where the soil is moist and enriched with plenty of organic matter. In summer and autumn 'Moonbeam' produces large, dense heads of long, pale stems that are especially smooth and attractive.

🪣	unsuitable for containers
🌱	spring
🌿	some resistance
❄	hardy
🔒	summer

'Green Utah'

This long-established, tall, green-stemmed variety bears crisp, succulent, well-flavoured stems in tight hearts, that keep well in cool storage. Although more variable and less reliable than modern varieties it is still valuable. No blanching is required.

 unsuitable for containers

🍃 spring

✳ poor resistance

❄ hardy

🔒 summer to autumn

'Loretta' ♥

An outstanding self-blanching, hybrid celery with very good vigour, 'Loretta' produces very heavy crops of excellent quality, upright heads. Stalks are smooth, succulent, and of very good flavour. It will grow in all conditions and resists bolting.

🪣 unsuitable for containers

🍃 spring

✳ some resistance

❄ hardy

🔒 summer to autumn

'Giant Red'

This traditional trench celery produces long, crisp stems that can grow up to 60cm (24in) high and 5cm (2in) thick. The stems are red in colour but pale after blanching; some people prefer to use the unblanched red stems despite their stronger flavour.

🪣 unsuitable for containers

🍃 spring

✳ poor resistance

❄ hardy

🔒 summer to winter

CELERIAC   *Apium graveolens* var. *rapaceum*

Celeriac is, botanically speaking, very similar to celery but with
a swollen lower stem that can be eaten cooked, or grated and
eaten raw. The texture of celeriac is similar to that of turnips and
its flavour is mild and celery-like. Unlike celery however, it is lifted
in late autumn and will store well in frost-free sheds and cellars.
It is popular in cooler regions, where celery is easily damaged.

	SPRING	SUMMER	AUTUMN	WINTER
SOW				
HARVEST				

SOWING

Celeriac is tolerant of most
conditions and should be treated
in the same way as celery: enrich
the soil with plenty of compost
or organic matter, adding general
fertilizer shortly before planting.
Add lime too, if the soil is acidic.

Sow seed thinly in shallow
pots and barely cover with a
layer of compost. Move seedlings
into small, individual pots when
they have developed three leaves,
and place them in moderate
warmth in a bright greenhouse
or similar environment until
the roots have grown to fill the
pot. Feed plants regularly to
encourage strong growth.

Like celery, celeriac bolts if
planted out too early, reducing
the crop. To avoid this, plant out

Allow seedlings plenty of space to grow.

greenhouse-grown, mid-spring
sowings in early summer.

CROP CARE

Water plants frequently,
especially in dry periods,
as they must not be allowed
to dry out; celeriac is a little
more tolerant of dry soil than
celery. Apply additional general
fertilizer if growth is slow. Any
sideshoots or fallen foliage should

be removed, to allow the roots to become smooth and large.

HARVESTING

Roots can be lifted when they are the size of tennis balls, but will go on swelling until early winter.

STORING

Celeriac can be left in the ground over winter in mild regions; pull a layer of soil up over the roots to protect them. In cold areas, dig up the roots, remove the foliage, and store in boxes of damp sand or soil to prevent the roots drying out. Roots will remain sound until early spring.

PESTS AND DISEASES

Celeriac is vulnerable to several pests and diseases. The maggots of celery leaf fly mine holes in foliage, creating brown, dry patches, and causing the stem to become stringy. Remove and destroy infected leaves before the problem spreads. Carrot fly is also attracted to celeriac – cover crops with fine, insect-proof mesh or horticultural fleece to prevent the flies reaching and attacking the roots (see pp.174–5).

Celery leaf spot disease causes brown patches on leaves. Remove and destroy any infected plant material.

'Brilliant'

This excellent celeriac variety produces bold white roots. It responds well to generous feeding and to soils that have been enriched with organic matter, producing a fine texture and flavour. It has good resistance to bolting, and stores well.

🪣	unsuitable for containers
🌱	spring
🕷	poor resistance
❄	hardy
🔒	summer

'Diamant' ♀

This high-quality celeriac has medium-sized, slightly flattened, white roots. It responds to generous feeding, producing bulbs with a fine texture and flavour. It has good resistance to bolting, and stores well.

	unsuitable for containers
🌱	spring
🕷	some resistance
❄	hardy
🔒	summer

'Giant Prague'

This traditional celeriac has smaller than average white roots. It requires generous feeding and a soil that is enriched with ample organic matter to produce a fine texture and flavour. 'Giant Prague' has fair storage potential.

	unsuitable for containers
🌱	spring
🕷	poor resistance
❄	hardy
🔒	summer

'Prinz'

This very high-quality variety has excellent early vigour, abundant healthy foliage, and high resistance to bolting. The medium-sized, slightly flattened roots have good storage potential, and an outstanding texture and flavour. It responds well to generous feeding and watering.

- unsuitable for containers
- spring
- some resistance
- hardy
- summer

'Monarch' ♀

This high-quality celeriac variety has refined, well-finished, bold, white roots, and upright deep green foliage. Although remarkable for quality, it is also heavy-yielding and has good storage potential. It is resistant to bolting.

- unsuitable for containers
- spring
- some resistance
- hardy
- summer

'Kojak' ♀

This is a good celeriac variety with very attractive and appetizing, whiter than usual roots, that store well. Given generous feeding with compost or manure, its texture and flavour will be outstanding. 'Kojak' has good resistance to bolting.

- unsuitable for containers
- spring
- some resistance
- hardy
- summer

FLORENCE FENNEL
Foeniculum vulgare var. *azoricum*

If you can provide Florence fennel with the conditions it needs, it makes a wonderful garden plant. The crisp, swollen stems have a mild aniseed flavour and are good cooked or shredded raw, while the attractive feathery foliage can also be used as a herb. It grows best, and is less likely to bolt, where the weather is cool and nights are mild and short.

	SPRING	SUMMER	AUTUMN	WINTER
SOW				
HARVEST				

SOWING
Before sowing or planting out, prepare the site by digging in well-rotted manure or compost and adding general fertilizer. Florence fennel prefers well-drained, sandy soil, which may need liming if its pH is too acidic.

It is best to sow seed directly into the ground in early summer, but seed can be sown in spring, under cover or in a greenhouse, or outside if you choose a bolt-resistant variety and protect it with a cloche or cold frame.

If you are sowing under cover, place three seeds into each small pot or module, and thin as soon as the seedlings are strong enough to be handled. Plant them out when large enough, and frosts have finished. Plants will need

Harvest once the bulbs are fully formed.

to be spaced about 30cm (12in) apart. If sowing directly into the ground, sow several seeds where each plant is to grow and then thin out the weakest as seedlings develop.

CROP CARE
If plants are subjected to too much heat or too little water they are prone to bolting, so it is essential to give them plenty of

water during dry spells. Their foliage casts little shade to smother weeds, so careful weeding is often needed. Earth up around the bulbs as they mature, to whiten them and provide early frost protection.

HARVESTING AND STORING

The foliage can be cut as a herb, in moderation, at any time. Stems will be big enough to harvest from midsummer to late autumn; lift them and discard unwanted foliage. Stems will stand in good condition for some weeks if earthed-up outdoors, or kept in the salad drawer of the fridge.

PESTS AND DISEASES

Generally, fennel has no significant pests or diseases and bolting is the most likely problem. Discourage this by sowing in summer when days are long and nights are mild, and by ensuring that the soil does not dry out. Bolt-resistant varieties are available.

One fungus that sometimes affects fennel is rhizoctonia, which stunts plant growth and causes colourful sores on the swollen stem. This disease has no cure, so dig up and destroy any infected plants, and practise crop rotation in future years.

'Perfection'

This selected, non-hybrid cultivar has larger bulbs and better resistance to bolting than older types. It is potentially suitable for sowing from spring until autumn but it may need protection in cooler regions with cold springs and short summers.

- suitable for containers
- spring to summer
- some resistance
- hardy
- late summer to early winter

'Atos' ♛

This quick-growing, non-hybrid fennel produces medium to large, white, rounded bulbs with ample robust foliage. It is well-suited to cooler, rainy regions, but is lacking in bolt resistance so is best sown in midsummer for a reliable crop.

- suitable for containers
- spring to summer
- some resistance
- hardy
- late summer to early winter

'Pronto' ♛

This non-hybrid fennel swells and matures early, producing medium-sized bulbs that are slighter flatter than usual, but of very good quality. It is best suited for midsummer sowing in regions with cold springs and cool summers.

- suitable for containers
- spring to summer
- some resistance
- hardy
- late summer to early winter

'Zefa Fino'

This long-established, Swiss non-hybrid variety matures fast, producing quick-swelling, large, white bulbs that are a uniform, rounded shape and of excellent quality. It is especially well-suited to summer sowing in areas with cooler conditions, and has some resistance to bolting.

 suitable for containers
spring to summer
some resistance
hardy
late summer to early winter

'Victorio' ♛

This excellent hybrid fennel has strong vigour, producing robust foliage and a heavy crop of large, dense, quick-maturing fennel. The bulbs are of good quality, and have a slight green tinge. It is especially well-suited to cooler regions for summer sowing.

 suitable for containers
spring to summer
some resistance
hardy
late summer to early winter

'Dover' ♛

This non-hybrid fennel has excellent vigour and will grow in a range of conditions. It produces large, white, rounded bulbs of good quality, with strong, robust foliage. It suits cooler regions, where, lacking bolt resistance, it is best sown in midsummer.

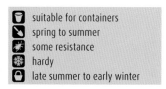 suitable for containers
spring to summer
some resistance
hardy
late summer to early winter

Peas and Beans

- Peas
- Runner beans
- Climbing and dwarf French beans
- Broad beans
- Beans for drying

PEAS *Pisum sativum*

Harvested and eaten fresh, peas are a real sweet treat. Most peas will need shelling, but some, such as snow peas, sugar (or snap) peas, and mangetout, are edible-podded, and can be eaten whole. All are delicious eaten raw or cooked, and many varieties are also grown for their edible pea shoots, which are good in salads. Peas are classified as early, second early, maincrop, or late, depending on when they are ready to harvest.

	SPRING	SUMMER	AUTUMN	WINTER
SOW/PLANT				
HARVEST				

SOWING

Dig in well-rotted manure or compost the autumn before sowing. Pea roots are nitrogen-fixing; they convert nitrogen from the air and store it in nodules on their roots. For this reason they don't need any extra nitrogenous fertilizer. Peas prefer a sunny, moist site that will not get too hot or become waterlogged. A slightly alkaline pH is ideal.

Sow seed any time from late winter onwards. Seedlings can be raised in modules or pots and transplanted when the soil warms up, or sown directly in the ground, although seedlings will need protection from frost with a cloche or cold frame. Seed can be sown successively through spring until midsummer. Sow at

Plant out strong seedlings in springtime.

a depth of 4–5cm (1½–2in) and leave at least 5cm (2in) space between plants. Sow in single or double rows.

CROP CARE

Most peas require some support, so construct a framework for them using canes or netting. This will keep them upright, and make the best use of the space available. Peas are

attractive to birds, so use netting to keep them at bay. Keep the plants well watered, ensuring they get plenty of water when in flower, and when the pods are swelling.

HARVESTING

Peas should be ready to harvest from early summer, within about three months of sowing. Once the first pods are ready, pinch out the top growing shoots of each plant to encourage more pods to develop. Shoots can also be harvested and eaten. Peas can be stored for a short while, but taste sweetest when fresh.

PESTS AND DISEASES

Slugs and snails are troublesome on young plants, and birds on older plants. Protect with netting. To prevent a build-up of diseases, such as pea leaf and pod spot or downy mildew, ensure that you practise crop rotation.

Downy mildew (left) shrivels leaves. Pea moths (right) devour young peas.

'Sugar Snap'

This variety bears a large crop of delicious pods on vigorous growth, so needs good support. Pick pods early for a crisp, succulent mangetout that can be added to salads and stir-fries. The young shoots and new leaves at the tip ends are also very tasty.

- unsuitable for containers
- mid- to late spring
- poor resistance
- not hardy
- late summer to early autumn

'Canoe'

A second early, this variety is grown because it bears more peas per pod than most; a maximum of 12. It also produces a heavy crop of pods, each slightly curved and pointed like a canoe. When grown in blocks the plants are almost self-supporting.

- unsuitable for containers
- early to mid-spring
- poor resistance
- not hardy
- early to late summer

'Oregon Sugar Pod' ♀

This first-rate variety is a widely sold mangetout pea. It is popular for its heavy crop of medium length, broad, flat, very tasty pods, which keep appearing over a long period. Although they can become larger, pick at 7.5cm (3in), before they become stringy.

- unsuitable for containers
- mid- to late spring
- some resistance
- not hardy
- late summer to early autumn

'Ambassador' ♀

A maincrop pea, grown for its medium-sized pods and sweet, tender peas. Also use the shoots and sideshoots in salads. Keep picking from the bottom of the plant, working up, and use promptly for the maximum flavour.

🯄 unsuitable for containers

🍃 early to mid-spring

✷ some resistance

❄ not hardy

🔒 mid- to late summer

'Delikata' ♀

This tall mangetout bears a heavy yield of tasty pods, similar to 'Oregon Sugar Pod' but earlier. Pick pods when young and crisp, before they become stringy, and use as soon as possible, cooking them quickly and gently. This variety is mildew-resistant.

🯄 unsuitable for containers

🍃 mid- to late spring

✷ good resistance

❄ not hardy

🔒 mid- to late summer

'Feltham First'

This popular, traditional, first early variety gives a heavy crop of large, 10cm (4in) long pods packed with sweet, tasty peas. For two crops, sow one batch in autumn to harvest in summer, and another the following spring to harvest in autumn.

🯄 unsuitable for containers

🍃 autumn and spring

✷ poor resistance

❄ hardy

🔒 early summer

'Waverex'

This first-rate petit pois produces tiny, sweet-tasting peas that appear on 60cm (24in) tall plants. Cook them quickly and gently to preserve their texture and flavour, and use them in risottos, salads, and stews. They also make a delicious pea soup, with stock, garlic, and butter.

- suitable for containers
- mid- to late spring
- poor resistance
- not hardy
- late summer to early autumn

'Kelvedon Wonder' ♀

This top-quality, first early variety produces long, dark green pods, each containing about eight peas. This versatile variety is well worth growing as you can plant a second crop in early summer for extra peas in autumn. It has good pea wilt and mildew resistance.

- unsuitable for containers
- early spring to early summer
- good resistance
- hardy
- early summer to early autumn

'Rondo' ♀

This very productive maincrop variety bears a substantial yield of paired pods that are rich green and straight, each containing about 10 plump, sweet-tasting peas. The peas have a good flavour and are suitable for freezing.

- unsuitable for containers
- early to mid-spring
- good resistance
- not hardy
- mid- to late summer

'Douce Provence'

This French first early variety grows to around 75cm (30in) high, producing a large crop of particularly sweet, tender peas. Being hardy, it can be sown outside in late autumn for an early summer crop, or the following spring when the soil has warmed up.

- unsuitable for containers
- mid-autumn and spring
- poor resistance
- hardy
- early summer to early autumn

'Sugar Ann' ♀

This very popular sugar variety produces a large crop of pale green, delicious, sweet pods. The strong vines and medium height means that plants don't need supporting. The peas can be eaten raw or can be used in stir-fries or risottos.

- unsuitable for containers
- mid- to late spring
- some resistance
- not hardy
- late summer to early autumn

'Hurst Greenshaft' ♀

This reliable, popular maincrop gives a heavy yield over a long period. The dark green pods, each containing about nine peas, appear in pairs on the tall plants. Impressive on the showbench and in the kitchen, it is good for freezing, and resists mildew.

- unsuitable for containers
- early to mid-spring
- good resistance
- not hardy
- mid- to late summer

RUNNER BEANS *Phaseolus coccineus*

Attractive and easy to grow, runner beans are a delicious garden staple. They are a real asset, since most varieties grow very tall and add structure and interest to the garden. They will also produce an abundance of beautiful red, white, or bi-coloured flowers. Runner beans can be found in a range of colours, and dwarf varieties are available, which are ideal for container cultivation if space is limited.

	SPRING	SUMMER	AUTUMN	WINTER
SOW/PLANT				
HARVEST				

SOWING

Site your runner beans carefully; most will grow fairly tall and can become top-heavy, so give them plenty of support and a sheltered location to protect them from strong winds. They thrive in deep fertile soil, so dig in some well-rotted manure or compost the autumn, before planting the following spring. Also, ensure not to plant them where peas or beans have grown in the last two years.

Sow seed in mid-spring for a midsummer crop, or sow in midsummer for an autumn crop. If the weather is cold, warm up the soil with a cold frame or cloche. Construct the supports for your beans, using bamboo canes in rows or wigwams, and sow seed at a depth of 5cm (2in)

Train bean seedlings up bamboo supports.

at the base of each cane. Seed can be sown under cover before planting out, but bear in mind that roots will grow deep, so use deeper plastic pots, or long paper "tube pots", which can be planted straight into the ground.

CROP CARE

Train the young seedlings around the canes, tying them in with string if necessary. Once plants

reach the top of the supports, pinch out the growing tips. In order to produce pods it is crucial that beans are not allowed to dry out, so mulch around the bases of the plants, and water frequently.

HARVESTING

If beans are left too long they will become tough and stringy, so harvest when they are still young and tender, this may be up to two or three times a week. This will also encourage the plants to produce more pods. Beans do not store long, but freeze well, and seeds can be stored for future crops.

PESTS AND DISEASES

Discourage the diseases that affect runner beans, such as halo blight and foot and root rot, by practising careful crop rotation – plant where root crops have grown the previous year. Halo blight causes dark spots ringed with yellow "haloes" on leaves. Remove and destroy any infected plants.

Blackfly are strongly attracted to the growing tips, so pinch these out when plants have reached full height. Bad infestations may need treating with an appropriate insecticide. Mice may eat seed sown directly in the soil.

'Painted Lady'

An old variety, 'Painted Lady' produces a beautiful display of red and white flowers and makes a striking feature in ornamental beds and borders. The flowers are followed by large, medium length pods with a fine flavour and tender texture.

- unsuitable for containers
- late spring to early summer
- poor resistance
- not hardy
- midsummer to mid-autumn

'Titan'

This variety is very reliable, giving strong, vigorous growth, a good show of flowers, and a crop of long, tasty pods. Keep the plants well-watered during dry periods, and pick runner beans regularly to encourage more pods to develop.

- unsuitable for containers
- late spring to early summer
- some resistance
- not hardy
- midsummer to mid-autumn

'Wisley Magic' ♀

Although its bright red flowers are very attractive to birds, 'Wisley Magic' still produces a huge, flavourful crop of 38cm (15in) long, straight, smooth pods from the end of summer through into autumn. It was awarded its AGM for its heavy yields.

- unsuitable for containers
- late spring to early summer
- some resistance
- not hardy
- midsummer to mid-autumn

'Polestar'

This attractive red-flowering
variety produces a good show of
attractive summer flowers, which
are eye-catching in beds and
borders. It then produces a
good yield of 25cm (10in) long,
flavourful pods. it is vigorous,
and will easily reach the top
of a 1.7m (5½ft) high support.

- unsuitable for containers
- late spring to early summer
- poor resistance
- not hardy
- midsummer to mid-autumn

'Flare' ♀

This red-flowering variety was
awarded an AGM for its high
yields of straight, narrow,
virtually stringless pods that can
reach up to 30cm (12in) in length.
It is an attractive plant, making
an good addition to the
ornamental garden.

- unsuitable for containers
- late spring to early summer
- some resistance
- not hardy
- midsummer to mid-autumn

'Achievement' ♀

This improved, very popular
variety bears an abundance of
red flowers that are followed by
tasty beans in long, straight pods.
It produces excellent results for
the kitchen and show bench.
Pick regularly, before the pods
mature, for continuous flowering.

- unsuitable for containers
- late spring to early summer
- some resistance
- not hardy
- midsummer to mid-autumn

'White Lady'

This top-of-the-range runner bean produces vigorous growth and a multitude of white summer flowers that are largely ignored by birds; it will need a sturdy support. The heavy crop develops over a long period, well into autumn, and the long pods are smooth, fleshy, and stringless.

- unsuitable for containers
- late spring to early summer
- some resistance
- not hardy
- midsummer to mid-autumn

'White Apollo'

This vigorous, prolific variety produces long, straight, stringless pods, up to 35cm (14in) in length, which emerge over a long cropping season. The beans are flavourful and excellent for cooking. Its attractive white flowers are largely ignored by birds.

- unsuitable for containers
- late spring to early summer
- some resistance
- not hardy
- midsummer to mid-autumn

'Aintree'

This red-flowering variety produces long, very slender, smooth, flavourful pods, which are stringless if picked young. It is a good choice in regions with high summer temperatures, and looks striking when grown beside a white-flowering variety.

- unsuitable for containers
- late spring to early summer
- some resistance
- not hardy
- midsummer to mid-autumn

'Red Rum' ♀

This very reliable variety is highly rated because the plants generate showy red flowers and a large crop of stringless, flavourful pods, even in adverse weather. The pods are straight, fleshy, and should be harvested when they grow to about 23cm (9in).

- unsuitable for containers
- late spring to early summer
- some resistance
- not hardy
- midsummer to mid-autumn

'Desiree' ♀

This outstanding bean has many attributes: its vigorous growth generates about 40 flavourful, 30cm (12in) long, broad, stringless pods per plant; its white flowers are largely untouched by birds; and it's also very productive, even through long, dryish summers.

- unsuitable for containers
- late spring to early summer
- some resistance
- not hardy
- midsummer to mid-autumn

'Red Flame' ♀

This trouble-free variety produces a good yield of long, smooth, straight pods, which will grow to about 28cm (11in) long. It bears an abundance of bright red flowers, and will provide striking, colourful architecture in the kitchen garden.

- unsuitable for containers
- late spring to early summer
- some resistance
- not hardy
- midsummer to mid-autumn

'Enorma' ♀

This aptly-named, heavy-cropping variety produces runner beans that reach up to 45cm (18in) in length. They are highly flavourful, and remain crisp and tender even when mature. The plants have good vigour and need a strong support system.

- unsuitable for containers
- late spring to early summer
- some resistance
- not hardy
- midsummer to mid-autumn

'Celebration' ♀

This early-cropping variety is highly prized for its abundance of delicate, highly ornamental, pale salmon-pink flowers. These are followed by high yields of straight, smooth, fleshy pods, containing numerous highly flavourful beans.

- unsuitable for containers
- late spring to early summer
- some resistance
- not hardy
- midsummer to mid-autumn

'Lady Di' ♀

This variety will regularly produce a good crop of showy, red flowers, followed by 30cm (12in) long, dark green, stringless pods, which are borne over a prolonged season. The beans have a good flavour and are excellent for exhibitions.

- unsuitable for containers
- late spring to early summer
- some resistance
- not hardy
- midsummer to mid-autumn

'St George'

This early-cropping variety
bears numerous bi-coloured red
and white flowers, followed by
a large crop of juicy, crisp pods;
it is prized for its heavy yields.
It makes a flamboyant feature
in beds or borders when grown
up strong supports.

 unsuitable for containers
late spring to early summer
poor resistance
not hardy
midsummer to mid-autumn

'Scarlet Empire'

This improved version of 'Scarlet
Emperor' has higher levels of
disease resistance, and is grown
for its high yields of narrow,
stringless pods, which grow to
about 30cm (12in) long, with good
flavour. Plants are vigorous and
will do well from early sowings.

unsuitable for containers
late spring to early summer
poor resistance
not hardy
midsummer to mid-autumn

'Summer Medley'

This variety puts on a colourful
show with a lively mix of red,
white, and pink flowers. The
mid-green runner beans are
borne over a long cropping
season, and have a good flavour
and texture. The plants are
often grown as an ornamentals.

unsuitable for containers
late spring to early summer
poor resistance
not hardy
midsummer to mid-autumn

FRENCH BEANS *Phaseolus vulgaris*

Call them what you like, snap, string, kidney, haricot, borlotti, or flageolet, French beans are delicious eaten when pods are young and fresh, or podded like peas, and eaten fresh or dried. Choose your favourite from a range of options – French beans are generally either dwarf or climbing, and are available in a wide variety of colours, from yellow and purple, to multicoloured or traditional green.

	SPRING	SUMMER	AUTUMN	WINTER
SOW/PLANT				
HARVEST				

SOWING

French beans like a sheltered, warm site; frost will kill them, and climbing varieties will need protection from the wind. Dig in well-rotted manure or compost the autumn before sowing. They need a moisture-retentive, fertile soil, but do not usually need nitrogenous fertilizer as their roots fix and store nitrogen in the soil.

Sow French beans from spring to early summer. If sowing under cover, sow seed in modules, deep plastic pots, or paper "tube pots", at a depth of 5cm (2in). Harden off, and then plant out when seedlings have reached 8cm (3in) in height, and the soil has warmed up. Alternatively, wait until the last frosts have passed,

Sow three seeds to a pot in early spring.

and sow seed directly into the ground at a depth of 5cm (2in). Construct bamboo cane supports for climbing varieties, and sow or plant at the bottom of each cane.

CROP CARE

Mulch well around seedlings and water regularly; ensure that plants do not dry out once their flowers appear. Dwarf varieties will become quite top-heavy, so

support them with twigs or short canes, and earth them up to give stability. Guide climbers up their supports and pinch out growing tips when they reach the top.

HARVESTING

Harvest once pods are large enough for use and eat while they are still young and tender. The more pods you pick, the more are produced, so check plants every few days for new growth. If beans are grown for drying, leave them on the plant until they dry out and the seed pods rattle. French beans can also be frozen for later use.

PESTS AND DISEASES

Protect seedlings against slugs and snails, and be wary of bean seed fly, blackfly, and black bean aphids, which will target young pods. Discourage diseases such as halo blight and foot and rot root by practising crop rotation.

Bean seed fly may attack germinating seeds – protect by sowing under cover.

'Golddukat'

The long, slightly curved, pale yellow pods of this attractive, early variety are borne in very high yields, over a long harvesting season. The pods are stringless and tender, with a good flavour. The plants look striking when grown next to a dark green variety.

	suitable for containers
	late spring to midsummer
	some resistance
	not hardy
	early summer to mid-autumn

'Purple Queen'

This variety is worthy of a prominent position in the kitchen or flower garden because of its attractive purple flowers, followed by deep purple pods. The beans lose their colour and revert to green when cooked; once blanched, pods can be frozen.

	suitable for containers
	late spring to midsummer
	poor resistance
	not hardy
	midsummer to mid-autumn

'Delinel'

Ever popular, 'Delinel' scores high points for its strong growth and heavy crops of 15cm (6in) long, stringless beans; they appear over a long harvesting season if regularly picked. The plants are resistant to bean common mosaic virus.

	suitable for containers
	late spring to midsummer
	good resistance
	not hardy
	midsummer to mid-autumn

'Sonesta' ♀

This easy-to-grow variety produces 13cm (5in) long, slim, pale yellow pods. The plants are resistant to common bean mosaic virus and crop over a long period; start picking before the beans start bulging inside the pod. They make an attractive addition to salad dishes.

- suitable for containers
- late spring to midsummer
- good resistance
- not hardy
- midsummer to mid-autumn

'Ferrari' ♀

One of the best dwarf French varieties, 'Ferrari' produces high yields of 15cm (6in) long, straight, slender, stringless, flavourful pods. The beans are borne early on the highly decorative plants, which are resistant to halo blight and bean common mosaic virus.

- suitable for containers
- late spring to midsummer
- excellent resistance
- not hardy
- midsummer to mid-autumn

'Irago' ♀

Ideal if you need an early crop, this dwarf French variety produces a high yield of long, straight, mid-green pods. The beans have a good flavour. The compact plants are attractive, and look good grown in containers on a patio.

- suitable for containers
- late spring to midsummer
- some resistance
- not hardy
- early summer to mid-autumn

'Annabel' ♀

This high quality, stringless, dwarf French variety is guaranteed to produce a very large number of early, pencil-thin pods. It is fast-growing, and its compact size makes it ideal for small gardens, where it should be located for easy picking.

- suitable for containers
- late spring to midsummer
- some resistance
- not hardy
- midsummer to mid-autumn

'Safari'

The 45cm (18in) high, upright growth of this variety makes for easy picking. The fairly short, stringless pods have a good flavour and texture, although yields can be slightly variable. For the best results, cook quickly to preserve the flavour.

- suitable for containers
- late spring to midsummer
- some resistance
- not hardy
- midsummer to mid-autumn

'The Prince' ♀

Good in both the kitchen garden and on the showbench, 'The Prince' reliably produces slim, straight pods about 15cm (6in) long. The pods have a delicious flavour and are good for eating fresh or for freezing. Keep picking for a lengthy crop.

- suitable for containers
- late spring to midsummer
- some resistance
- not hardy
- early summer to mid-autumn

'Maradonna' ♀

This compact, bushy variety bears a very good crop, whether grown in containers or in the open ground. It produces medium-length, mid-green, moderately flat pods, which have a delicious flavour and suit a variety of recipes.

- suitable for containers
- late spring to midsummer
- some resistance
- not hardy
- midsummer to mid-autumn

'Speedy'

As the name implies, everything about this variety is a little quicker than the average, with early growth and quick emergence of the sweet, small pods, sometimes in as little as just seven weeks. Either pick for flavourful young beans or dry them as haricots.

 suitable for containers
late spring to midsummer
poor resistance
not hardy
early summer to mid-autumn

'Slenderette'

This compact variety produces a good crop of dark green, 13cm (5in) long pods. The beans are stringless, tender, and tasty – delicious raw or cooked. At only 45cm (18in) high, the bushy plants are ideal for a container or sown in the front of a border.

 suitable for containers
late spring to midsummer
poor resistance
not hardy
midsummer to mid-autumn

'Berggold' ♀

This attractive dwarf variety produces a large crop of golden-yellow, stringless, pencil-thin pods that grow to about 13cm (5in) long. It has a bushy, compact habit and looks especially attractive grown next to contrasting dark green varieties.

suitable for containers
late spring to midsummer
some resistance
not hardy
midsummer to mid-autumn

'Goldfield'

This climbing French variety puts on an attractive show with its dangling array of yellow pods, and is worth growing in the flower border as it makes a strong focal point. The tasty pods are flat, stringless, and flavourful and are borne over a long cropping period.

	unsuitable for containers
	late spring to midsummer
	poor resistance
	not hardy
	midsummer to mid-autumn

'Sultana' ♀

The long, thin, straight, pencil-thin pods of this variety keep developing from early summer; it bears an above-average yield of stringless, flavourful beans. Alternatively, let the pods mature and shell them, drying the beans like haricots.

	unsuitable for containers
	late spring to midsummer
	some resistance
	not hardy
	midsummer to mid-autumn

'Cobra' ♀

A reliable choice, 'Cobra' bears a prolific, very early yield of 18cm (7in) long beans, which follow on from eye-catching violet flowers. The pods are stringless and tender, with an excellent flavour. Give this ornamental variety a prominent position.

	unsuitable for containers
	late spring to midsummer
	some resistance
	not hardy
	early summer to mid-autumn

'Kingston Gold' ♀

Aptly named, this variety produces attractive yellow pods that are slow to mature. The pods are borne in abundance from near the bottom of the plant, right to the top of the supporting frame. This variety looks striking grown beside a dark green variety.

- unsuitable for containers
- late spring to midsummer
- some resistance
- not hardy
- midsummer to mid-autumn

'Hunter' ♀

Heavy crops of stringless, flat pods, growing up to 25cm (10in) long, containing eight peas each, are borne by this early variety. Give the plants a sheltered warm position, protected from cold winds, and they should crop quicker than other varieties.

- unsuitable for containers
- late spring to midsummer
- some resistance
- not hardy
- midsummer to mid-autumn

'Kwintus' ♀

This variety produces an excellent crop of 28cm (11in) long, flat pods that are thin and tender when young. All French beans are frost-sensitive, but this variety copes better than most with cool conditions, giving a moderately quick harvest.

- unsuitable for containers
- late spring to midsummer
- some resistance
- not hardy
- midsummer to mid-autumn

'Musica' ♀

This green, flat-podded variety is capable of producing a hefty crop of well over 1kg (2.2lb) per plant. The beans are flavourful and excellent for eating raw or for use in cooking. The plants make a striking focal point in the kitchen garden or border.

- unsuitable for containers
- late spring to midsummer
- some resistance
- not hardy
- midsummer to mid-autumn

BROAD BEANS *Vicia faba*

Eat home-grown broad beans as soon as possible after harvesting, as this is when they are at their sweetest and most delicious, beating shop-bought versions hands down. Or, try picking while pods are very young and tender, cook them whole or eat them in salads. Dwarf varieties can be grown in containers on a patio or in small gardens, and their beautifully-scented flowers will attract bees.

	SPRING	SUMMER	AUTUMN	WINTER
SOW/PLANT				
HARVEST				

SOWING

Dig in plenty of well-rotted manure or compost in the autumn before sowing. Broad beans will probably not need any extra fertilizer, as nodules on their roots fix and store nitrogen in the soil. They prefer well-drained, fertile soil, and taller varieties will appreciate some shelter. Plant where root crops have previously grown.

Seed can be sown directly in the ground and protected from frost if necessary, or it can be sown in pots or modules and transplanted later. Sow at a depth of 5cm (2in), leaving about 15cm (6in) between plants, and 60cm (24in) between rows. Sow in spring or autumn and harvest throughout the summer.

Create deep planting holes with a dibber.

CROP CARE

Construct supports for taller varieties using bamboo canes. Dwarf varieties may need some support or earthing up as they develop and become top-heavy. Use sticks or canes to prevent dwarf varieties from trailing on the ground, where they will be at greater risk from pests. Mulch well around plants and ensure that they are kept well-watered.

As soon as a good number of seed pods have started to form, pinch out the plants' growing tips. This encourages the plant to channel its energy into developing pods, and will also help to discourage attack from black bean aphid.

HARVESTING

Young pods can be cooked and eaten whole, but the broad beans themselves are ready to harvest in about three to four months, once they can be felt through the pods. Harvest from the bottom of the plant first. Do not leave them on the plant too long or they will become tough.

PESTS AND DISEASES

Use netting if attacks from birds and mice are bad. Pinching out the growing tips will help to deter black bean aphids. Bean seed beetle may nibble leaves. There is no cure for chocolate spot; remove and destroy plants.

Black bean aphids will swarm leaves.

'The Sutton' ♔

This is a dwarf broad bean that can be repeat-sown outdoors in spring, and under cloches during autumn and winter, to give a sustained harvest. It is a good choice for smaller gardens and exposed sites. Pick frequently; this variety is good for freezing.

🪣	suitable for containers
🌱	spring or autumn
✳	some resistance
❄	hardy
🔒	late spring to autumn

'Express' ♔

This is one of the quickest varieties to mature and a good choice for a second sowing in spring. It produces a heavy crop of greenish-white beans that are ready in time for summer. They can be frozen, and will still be tender when defrosted.

🪣	unsuitable for containers
🌱	mid- to late autumn
✳	some resistance
❄	hardy
🔒	late spring

'Super Aquadulce'

This popular broad bean is an extremely hardy, if not the hardiest, variety. It can be sown in autumn or early in spring, giving large crops of tasty pods, each with five to eight white beans. The plant are compact, reaching about 75cm (30in) tall.

🪣	unsuitable for containers
🌱	autumn and spring
✳	poor resistance
❄	hardy
🔒	late spring

'Bunyard's Exhibition'

This traditional variety gives a
reliable crop of large, tasty beans,
producing up to nine per pod. It
is a tall plant, growing to 1.4m
(4¹/₂ft), and needs support as it
grows. Pinch out the tips to
restrict their height on smaller
plots or in exposed regions.

🪣	unsuitable for containers
🌱	spring or autumn
🕷	some resistance
❄	hardy
🔒	late spring to autumn

'Jubilee Hysor' ♀

This early variety gives an
excellent crop of pods filled with
six to eight tasty, light green
beans. It is quick to mature from
a spring sowing, or if raised
earlier under a cloche, which
gives ample time for further
sowings and late summer crops.

🪣	unsuitable for containers
🌱	late winter to late spring
🕷	some resistance
❄	fairly hardy
🔒	early to late summer

'Stereo'

This upright, high-yielding
variety produces broad bean
pods that are very similar to
mangetout – the whole tender,
sweet pod can be eaten raw. The
pods can also be lightly steamed
and are excellent in a variety of
recipes, from stir-fries to salads.

🪣	suitable for containers
🌱	late winter to late spring
🕷	some resistance
❄	fairly hardy
🔒	early to late summer

BEANS FOR DRYING *various*

Growing beans for drying means that you can enjoy these nutritious vegetables long after the summer crops of fresh beans are over. There is no special technique, you simply leave the beans to dry on the plant until the end of their growing season. Once harvested, they take up little storage space and will keep for several months. Easily grown varieties suitable for drying include lima, borlotti, and kidney beans.

	SPRING	SUMMER	AUTUMN	WINTER
SOW/PLANT				
HARVEST				

SOWING

Beans need full sun and warmth, so delay spring sowing outside until the minimum temperature is around 12°C (54°F). Otherwise start the seeds off indoors and plant out seedlings only when there is no danger of late frosts. Work plenty of well-rotted compost into the soil before sowing or planting out.

Beans suitable for drying come in both dwarf or climbing varieties. If you are growing dwarf beans, sow the seeds approximately 5cm (2in) apart in staggered rows.

For climbers, make a row of canes or poles, or a wigwam, for the plants to scramble up; sow a couple of seeds at the base of each cane, allowing about 30cm (12in) space between each plant.

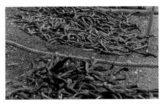
Construct netting for drying beans outside.

CROP CARE

Unless conditions are very dry, there is no need to water your beans until the first flowers appear. Then water generously and regularly, never allowing the soil to dry out completely.

Dwarf beans may need short supporting canes as they grow. Climbing beans usually twine round their supports without needing to be tied in.

HARVESTING

Beans will be ready to harvest once the pods have dried and the plants are starting to shed their leaves. If the pods are completely dry, you can shell the beans as soon as you pick them. In a particularly wet season, leave the pods to dry in a well-aired, rodent-free place before removing the beans.

STORING

Place the shelled beans in an airtight container and use as required. If stored in a cool, dry place they should keep for several months.

PESTS AND DISEASES

Slugs and snails are among the enemies of emerging bean seedlings because they eat the tender tips. To deter them, use pellets, set up beer traps around your plot to attract them away from plants, or use crushed shells, grit, or a line of copper tape as a barrier. Pick them off by hand as you spot them. Birds may target pods, so construct netting to deter them.

In summer, blackfly may attack plants, withering the leaves; spray with an appropriate pesticide if severe, or wash and rub off by hand.

'Borlotto Lingua di Fuoco'

The borlotti, Italian "tongue of fire" takes on a spectacular red-splashed appearance as the pale green pods ripen, although it disappears on cooking. The young pods can be eaten as flageolets or the seeds can be left to fully mature for use as haricot beans.

- 🪣 unsuitable for containers
- 🍃 late spring to early summer
- 🕷 good resistance
- ❄ not hardy
- 🔒 midsummer to early autumn

Cannellini Beans

A popular Italian bean that has a kidney shape with slightly squared-off ends and a creamy white colour. When cooked they have a fluffy texture and a nutty, mild flavour. Harvest when the pods turn pale yellow.

- 🪣 unsuitable for containers
- 🍃 late spring to midsummer
- 🕷 good resistance
- ❄ not hardy
- 🔒 early autumn

Kidney Beans

As the name suggests, these beans have a distinct kidney shape. The most popularly used variety are a dark red colour with a soft, creamy flesh. They need to be cooked well before eating to destroy the toxins in their skins.

- 🪣 unsuitable for containers
- 🍃 late spring
- 🕷 good resistance
- ❄ not hardy
- 🔒 midsummer

'Blue Lake'

This traditional, dual-purpose variety is a climbing bean, bearing long, round, stringless, green pods that are tender and have a characteristic French bean flavour when eaten young. When left until the end of the season the white seeds can be dried and used as haricots.

- unsuitable for containers
- late spring to early summer
- good resistance
- not hardy
- midsummer to early autumn

'Supremo'

A dual-purpose French variety that bears kidney-shaped borlotti beans. Although only a dwarf bush, it produces heavy yields of good-quality pods and beans, both of which are a cream colour, flecked with red.

- suitable for containers
- late spring to early summer
- good resistance
- not hardy
- midsummer to early autumn

Lima Beans

Part of the kidney bean family, these are available as large or baby types (and include "butter beans"). All have a buttery texture and delicate flavour. Harvest in late summer or autumn to eat fresh or for drying.

- unsuitable for containers
- late spring
- good resistance
- not hardy
- late summer to early autumn

'Fasold'

This modern climbing French bean bears huge crops early in the season. The long, fleshy, round, mid-green, stringless pods have a superb flavour and are quick to mature but slow to seed. The black beans are ready for harvest in autumn.

- unsuitable for containers
- late spring to early summer
- good resistance
- not hardy
- autumn

'Algarve' ♀

This excellent, high-yielding variety is grown for its very good flavour. The straight, flat pods will grow to about 27cm (11in) long, and are stringless. The young pods can be frozen, and the mature beans dried. It has good disease resistance.

- unsuitable for containers
- late spring to midsummer
- good resistance
- not hardy
- late spring to midsummer

Lablab Beans

A dual-purpose plant, this ornamental climber also produces edible pods. Known as the hyacinth bean, in warm temperatures it bears fragrant, bi-coloured pink flowers that precede brown seed pods. Boil harvested beans before eating.

- suitable for containers
- early summer
- good resistance
- not hardy
- late summer to early autumn

'Yin Yang'

This dwarf plant produces high yields of dual-purpose kidney beans. The green pods can be eaten when young and tender or left to mature for drying. The mild beans have a black and white pattern reminiscent of the Chinese Yin Yang symbol.

- suitable for containers
- late spring to midsummer
- good resistance
- not hardy
- midsummer to mid-autumn

Soya Beans

Hailed as a new "super food", this highly nutritious bean can be eaten hot or cold. The short pods contain two or three beans each, and are ready for harvesting when the leaves have fallen and the pods are dried up.

 suitable for containers

late spring to midsummer

good resistance

not hardy

late summer to early autumn

'Solista'

This borlotti, climbing French bean bears heavy yields of pods right the way up the plant. The kidney-shaped, maroon-speckled, white beans have a creamy texture and sweet flavour, and can be eaten fresh or left to mature for drying.

 unsuitable for containers

late spring to early summer

good resistance

not hardy

mid- to late summer

Southern Peas

A popular cooking ingredient in the USA, these are also known as cowpeas or field peas because they can be fed to livestock or used as green manure. There are several varieties available, the best-known being the black-eyed pea.

suitable for containers

late spring

good resistance

not hardy

midsummer

Salad Vegetables

- Lettuces
- Salad leaves
- Chicory
- Endives

LETTUCE *Lactuca sativa*

Freshly picked, home-grown lettuce tastes so much better than
supermarket salad leaves. There are two main types of lettuce, "loose-
leaf" and "hearted", distinguished by whether or not they form heads.
With the correct care and conditions, it is possible to have a continuous
crop of lettuce all year round. Getting seeds to germinate can be tricky,
but once they have started, lettuces are among the easiest crops to grow.

	SPRING	SUMMER	AUTUMN	WINTER
SOW				
HARVEST				

SOWING

Lettuces will grow well in most
moisture-retentive soils, and as
long as you give them enough
water, and enough compost to
grow in, they are suited to
container cultivation, too.
Site them next to taller crops to
provide shade in high summer as
full sun may cause them to bolt.

Shallow-rooted lettuce will thrive in pots.

The best time to plant lettuces
is soon after the soil has warmed
up in the spring, but if you want
a harvest earlier in the summer,
sow the seeds under cover then
transplant outside. For winter
harvests, a heated greenhouse
is essential unless you are using
a particularly hardy cultivar.

Make shallow drills and
sow at a depth of 1cm (¹/₂in).
Small and medium lettuces
will need around 15–25cm
(6–10in), and larger lettuces
about 35cm (14in), as they will
need more space to expand.

Sow seed in the afternoon,
once the heat of the day has
passed, as the cooler temperature
increases the chance of seeds
germinating. If necessary, thin
out the seedlings as they grow,
leaving only the strongest ones
to develop to full size.

PLANTING

Seedlings that have been planted indoors, whether in modules or in small pots, will be ready to plant out when they have grown four or five mature leaves. Keep them moist and lift them out carefully, trying not to disturb the roots too much, as this can damage later growth.

Plant into a moist bed of soil that has some shade, to help prevent crops wilting. If the weather turns cold, or you are worried about pests and diseases, protect vulnerable seedlings with a cloche or cold frame.

CROP CARE

Once lettuces have been planted out, keep them free from weeds and well-watered at all times.

Harvest as cut-and-come-again crops.

This is especially important in the one or two weeks before harvesting, because too much heat or a lack of water can cause the lettuces to bolt. It can also cause them to become bitter.

Most lettuces will not need any extra feeding, but if growth seems slow, feed them with a high-nitrogen fertilizer.

TIP   PREVENTING A GLUT

Lettuce can be grown in every season with managed planting, especially if you can provide winter protection. Plant carefully to avoid gluts because lettuce doesn't keep well once picked. To ensure a steady harvest, sow seed frequently and in small batches – a handful of seeds every few weeks. Intercrop lettuces to harvest as early season "catch crops" to maximize space.

Seed sown in batches will provide you with a continual supply of lettuce.

HARVESTING

Hearted lettuces take longer to mature than the loose-leaf varieties, but all lettuces are fairly quick to grow and can be ready for eating in as little as eight or nine weeks. When harvesting, make sure to cut the hearted lettuces out as soon as they are mature, otherwise you risk them rotting in wet conditions or bolting in hot or dry conditions.

You can harvest loose-leaf lettuces to use whole, or use them as cut-and-come-again crops. Remove the outer leaves as you need them and leave the inner ones to continue growing. Or, if cutting the entire lettuce, use scissors and cut away the leaves, leaving around 2.5cm (1in) of the plant in the ground.

Lettuce stumps regrow and may provide you with a second crop of leaves – continue to care for them as usual and in a couple of weeks the new leaves will sprout.

STORING

Lettuce can be kept for a little while in a sealed plastic bag in the fridge, but it is best eaten as fresh as possible. Try to only harvest as much as you need at any given time, to prevent spoilage and waste.

PESTS AND DISEASES

Lettuces are susceptible to these pests and diseases, so guard against them wherever possible.

- Slugs and snails love tender young leaves and may munch their way into the hearts of larger lettuces. Use pellets, or create a barrier to crops using a cloche.
- Cutworms, leatherjackets, and wireworms attack the roots of lettuces, causing them to wilt.
- Lettuce root aphids can be a big problem. They feed on lettuce roots, causing the plant to wilt. Apply an appropriate insecticide, and grow resistant varieties in the future.
- Botrytis – or grey mould, might strike lettuces if weather is wet. Fluffy grey mould will appear on the leaves and can destroy the entire plant.

Slugs (left) can devastate an entire row of vulnerable lettuce seedlings. Use a line of grit or sand (right) to keep slugs or snails away from plants.

'Little Gem' ♔

One of the best-known cos varieties, this dwarf, compact lettuce produces crisp, medium-sized hearts with an outstanding sweet flavour. This fast-growing mid-green lettuce is perfect for smaller gardens and grows well under cloches.

- suitable for containers
- early spring to midsummer
- good resistance
- fairly hardy
- late spring to late autumn

'Valamaine'

This reliable cos variety is ideal for growing in small spaces. It is relatively quick-growing and produces tall, upright heads of bright green, crisp leaves. The leaves can be harvested young, too, as they have no bitterness.

- suitable for containers
- early spring to late summer
- good resistance
- not hardy
- late spring to early autumn

'Little Leprechaun' ♔

Also known as 'Cimaron Red Romaine', this heirloom variety produces tall, tender, crisp heads of red leaves with creamy green and red hearts. It tastes as good as it looks and bears reliable crops, having good tolerance to heat and being slow to bolt.

- suitable for containers
- early spring to midsummer
- good resistance
- fairly hardy
- late spring to early winter

'Freckles'

This unusual, heirloom, cos lettuce bears bright green leaves splattered with crimson. It is a hardy variety that can be successively sown from early spring to autumn, producing crisp, upright heads with a buttery texture and sweet flavour.

- suitable for containers
- early spring to early autumn
- good resistance
- fairly hardy
- late spring to early winter

'Parris Island'

This cos lettuce is popular with both commercial and home growers. The large, uniform, upright heads have deep green leaves, with white midribs and hearts, with a crisp texture and sweet flavour. It is heat-tolerant with good disease resistance.

- suitable for containers
- early spring to late summer
- good resistance
- not hardy
- late spring to early autumn

'Marshall' ♀

This vigorous, quick-growing cos provides a real splash of colour. The tall lettuces have dark, burgundy-coloured, shiny leaves with a very sweet flavour, and can be used as baby leaves or left to develop crisp, tender hearts.

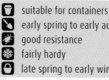

- suitable for containers
- early spring to early autumn
- good resistance
- fairly hardy
- late spring to early winter

'Tintin' ♀

An attractive, improved 'Little Gem', this variety has a similar sweet flavour but a unique appearance, with slightly bubbled, bright, lime-green leaves and golden hearts. It has outstanding disease resistance, which makes it ideal for growing organically year round.

- suitable for containers
- early spring to early autumn
- good resistance
- hardy
- late spring to early winter

'Rouge d'Hiver'

A popular winter variety, as its name suggests, it is also good for autumn and spring crops. A French cos type, the red-tinted leaves turn deeper red in cold weather, and can be harvested as baby leaves or as compact heads when mature.

- suitable for containers
- mid-autumn to early spring
- good resistance
- hardy
- late spring to midwinter

'Claremont' ♀

A neat mini-cos lettuce, this variety produces large, upright hearts. The dark green leaves have crispy ribs that add a crunchy texture to their sweet flavour. It is vigorous but slow to bolt, and is resistant to mildew and lettuce mosaic virus.

- suitable for containers
- early spring to early autumn
- good resistance
- not hardy
- late spring to early winter

'Dazzle'

This attractive lettuce is similar to 'Little Gem' in size, flavour, and texture, but the big difference is in its deep red outer leaves and crisp yellow interior. It is a quick grower and will produce good crops early in the season.

- suitable for containers
- early spring to late summer
- good resistance
- fairly hardy
- early summer to late autumn

'Rouge d'Hiver'

'Winter Density'

This hardy, semi-cos lettuce is sown in autumn to overwinter for a spring harvest. Upright, densely packed heads have crisp leaves with a sweet flavour to rival that of 'Little Gem'. It is slow to bolt and tolerant of heat.

🪴	suitable for containers
🌱	late summer to early autumn
🦋	good resistance
❄️	hardy
🔒	early spring

'Black-Seeded Simpson Improved' ♀

An early maturing, large, crisphead variety that has frilly, light yellow-green leaves with a sweet and juicy flavour. The lettuce can be grown and harvested as baby leaves or left to develop large, crunchy hearts.

🪴	suitable for containers
🌱	early spring to late summer
🦋	good resistance
❄️	hardy
🔒	early summer to early autumn

'Webbs Wonderful'

Sold as "Icebergs" these are the most popular crisphead lettuces amongst commercial and home growers. It reliably produces large, green-leaved crops with solid, crunchy hearts and an excellent flavour. It is slow to bolt, even in hot weather.

🪴	suitable for containers
🌱	early spring to midsummer
🦋	good resistance
❄️	not hardy
🔒	late spring to mid-autumn

'Yugoslavian Red'

This name of this butterhead variety says it all. A Yugoslavian discovery, it produces large, loose heads of puckered green leaves tinged with red, which when cut in half reveal a solid bright greeny yellow centre. It has an excellent mild, buttery flavour.

- suitable for containers
- early spring to late summer
- good resistance
- not hardy
- late spring to early autumn

'Cassandra' ♀

This butterhead variety produces very good-quality, pale green leaves, around a dense heart that have an excellent flavour. It can be grown all year round with protection from frost, and is resistant to downy mildew and lettuce mosaic virus.

- suitable for containers
- early spring to late summer
- good resistance
- fairly hardy
- late spring to early winter

'Tom Thumb'

An old, popular variety, 'Tom thumb' produces solid, butterhead lettuces, about the size of tennis balls, with soft, sweet leaves. Easy to grow and quick to mature, it is good as a summer crop, or for sowing under cover and harvesting year round.

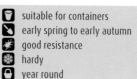

- suitable for containers
- early spring to early autumn
- good resistance
- hardy
- year round

'Marvel of Four Seasons'

Also known as 'Merveille de Quatre Saisons', this large, round, butterhead variety is a traditional favourite. It is a very hardy, semi-hearting lettuce that can be grown almost all year round to produce dark green leaves with an attractive brownish-red tinge.

- suitable for containers
- early spring to late summer
- good resistance
- hardy
- mid-spring to early winter

'Mottistone' ♀

This reliable, new butterhead variety produces upright, wavy, green leaves with red speckling, set around a blanched centre. The pretty leaves are excellent for decoration or eating, and have a crisp texture. It is slow to bolt and resistant to mildew.

- suitable for containers
- late spring to mid-summer
- good resistance
- not hardy
- early to late summer

'Buttercrunch'

The small, compact heads of these butterhead lettuces have open but tightly bunched rosettes. This variety is slow to bolt and stands well, producing leaves that are dark green with a crisp, crunchy, sweet flavour, and a buttery heart.

- suitable for containers
- early spring to midsummer
- good resistance
- fairly hardy
- late spring to late autumn

'May Queen'

This heirloom lettuce is a fast-growing butterhead variety, and produces small, round heads with loosely packed leaves that are pale green, tinged with red. The tender leaves have a buttery flavour, while the yellow, red-blushed hearts have a sweet taste.

- suitable for containers
- early spring to late summer
- good resistance
- not hardy
- late spring to early winter

'Green Salad Bowl' ♀

A reliable, popular variety, this loose-leaf lettuce produces rosettes of large, light green, deeply cut leaves very quickly. It is slow to bolt and heat tolerant, and if only the most tender leaves are selected for picking, it will continue to replace them.

- suitable for containers
- early spring to late summer
- good resistance
- fairly hardy
- late spring to early winter

'Red Salad Bowl' ♀

The red form of the loose-leaf, green, oak-leaf variety 'Salad Bowl', it produces large heads of green leaves with burgundy-flushed edges. It is very productive over a long period; pick leaves as required or cut full heads.

- suitable for containers
- early spring to midsummer
- good resistance
- fairly hardy
- late spring to late autumn

'Lollo Rossa'

A very popular, beautiful Italian lettuce, with frilled pale green leaves that have a crimson edge, and a crisp texture and excellent flavour. The plants are compact and non-hearting, and are very easy to grow anywhere in the garden.

- suitable for containers
- early spring to late summer
- good resistance
- not hardy
- late spring to early autumn

'Forellenschluss'

The name of this Austrian heirloom variety means "speckled like a trout", which reflects the attractive red spots that appear all over the large, flavoursome green leaves. It is cold tolerant and also withstands hotter temperatures very well.

- suitable for containers
- early spring to late summer
- good resistance
- fairly hardy
- late spring to early winter

'Green Lollo Bionda'

A classic green lettuce, this is an attractive partner to 'Lolla Rossa'. The mid-sized, open heads form mounds of pale green, ruffled leaves with a good flavour. Excellent for intercropping, you can harvest the whole plant or pick leaves as required.

- suitable for containers
- early spring to mid-autumn
- good resistance
- not hardy
- late spring to early winter

'Multy'

A new, fast-growing, Dutch variety, 'Multy' produces attractive, uniform lettuces. The identical leaves are dark green and shiny, with crisp, finely serrated leaves. It is very resistant to downy mildew and has an excellent shelf life.

- suitable for containers
- early spring to late summer
- good resistance
- not hardy
- late spring to early autumn

'Bergamo'

A green 'Lollo Rossa' type with frilly, loose-leaf heads of glossy, finely curled, bright green leaves. It is slow to bolt, which makes it good for growing over a long season, from late spring to mid-autumn. Harvest them whole or pick the leaves as required.

- suitable for containers
- early spring to midsummer
- good resistance
- not hardy
- late spring to mid-autumn

'Revolution'

This variety is a sensational, loose-leaf, 'Lollo Rosso'-type lettuce. The compact heads of deep red, almost black, frizzy-edged leaves have a good flavour. This variety has good vigour and is slow to bolt, and can be sown under cover in winter.

- suitable for containers
- early spring to late summer
- good resistance
- fairly hardy
- late spring to early winter

'New Red Fire'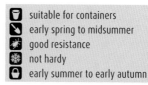

A dramatic oak-leaf variety with an attractive appearance and good flavour. The large, tight, compact heads of lettuce have deep red, fringed leaves above a bright green base, and are crisp and sweet. It has good resistance to disease and bolting.

- suitable for containers
- early spring to midsummer
- good resistance
- not hardy
- early summer to early autumn

SALAD LEAVES *various*

Salad doesn't have to mean small and expensive supermarket portions – there is a huge range of distinctive leaf crops that you can grow at home. Sow seed in batches throughout the year and enjoy an almost perpetual harvest. Red orache and texsel greens may sound exotic but they are just as easy to grow as the more familiar cress or rocket. Or try Oriental cut-and-come-again leaves, such as mibuna or mizuna.

	SPRING	SUMMER	AUTUMN	WINTER
SOW				
HARVEST				

SOWING

Leafy salad plants all share a preference for fertile soil that is moisture-retentive but not prone to waterlogging. Some varieties, such as corn salad, thrive in full sun; others, including rocket and purslane, are happier if grown in partial shade. Salad leaves sown in late spring will be ready to harvest in summer. For autumn and early winter crops, and for most oriental leaves, start sowing in late summer and early autumn.

If you are sowing directly into the ground, wait until the soil has warmed up in spring. For successional crops, sow the seeds a few at a time in short rows. Repeat every two to three weeks, or as soon as the previously sown batch of seeds begin to shoot.

Seedlings will need thinning as they grow.

PLANTING OUT

Salad leaves can also be sown in successive batches under cover, either for planting outside later or as an indoor winter crop.

Seedlings should be ready to transplant about four weeks after sowing. To minimize disturbance of fragile roots, sow them in modules, one or two seeds per cell, or in coir pots. Thin to about 10cm (4in) as seedlings develop.

CROP CARE

Hoe regularly between the planted rows to control weeds; this also reduces the risk of pests and diseases (see opposite), and promotes good air circulation.

Keep your plants well watered and do not let the soil dry out – salad crops have a very shallow root system, so require frequent watering. Lack of moisture will spoil the flavour and texture of salad leaves and encourages the plant to bolt. In hot weather, water either in the early morning or evening to avoid scorching the delicate leaves.

Many salad crops appreciate top-dressing with a nitrogen-rich fertilizer, which can be applied around the base of the plants. Apply fertilizer when growth

Harvest your leaves using scissors.

appears to be slowing down; check the fertilizer application rates before using.

Plants sown outside in early spring may need protection if there is a exceptionally cold spell. Keep an eye on the weather and be prepared to cover your crops with fleece or cloches if the temperature drops.

TIP GROWING IN CONTAINERS

In a small garden, salad leaves can be container-grown successfully on the patio or beside the kitchen door.

- Water plants regularly and take care not to let containers either dry out or become waterlogged.
- Make sure you choose the best position for your containers. Once filled, large pots are heavy to move.
- Raise containers on blocks or feet to improve drainage.

With their shallow roots, most salad leaves will happily grow in a container.

HARVESTING

Pick young leaves as soon as they are large enough to use. Leaves should be ready within six to eight weeks. Salad plants reach maturity quickly, after which they become coarse and bitter, with tough stems.

If you are growing your crops for cut-and-come-again salads, keep harvesting the leaves a few at a time, working your way through the successive sowings. Picking encourages the plants to produce more leaves and just one small batch could supply you with harvests over several weeks.

You can also cut a whole plant while it is still young. The stump left behind will rapidly grow another crop of leaves. Once a plant has bolted, its leaves will no longer be useful, so pull it up.

STORING

Once harvested, salad leaves are best used almost immediately, as they soon lose freshness. The leaves do not freeze well, because they become mushy when thawed. However, repeated cropping means that storing salad leaves will not be necessary. If you happen to pick more leaves than you need, they will keep for a short while if wetted and kept in a plastic bag in the refrigerator.

PESTS AND DISEASES

Pest damage and infections can destroy tender salad crops. Stay vigilant for signs of trouble.

- Slugs and snails can rapidly demolish a row of seedlings. Deter them with barriers and traps, use pellets or nematodes, or hunt for them at night and pick them off by hand.
- Rocket in particular is susceptible to attack by flea beetles, which chew holes in leaves. Cover plants with fleece or fine mesh to help deter these and other pests, such as cabbage root fly and caterpillars, which target oriental brassicas.
- Downy mildew is a disease that causes a fluffy white mould to develop on leaves. It is common in plants grown under cover. Pull off the leaves and improve air circulation.

Snails can rapidly demolish leafy salad crops so use defences to keep them at bay. Ensure that you wash leaves thoroughly before use.

Land Cress

Also known as American Cress, these spicy leaves are often used as a substitute for watercress. This salad leaf is easy to grow and can be harvested as a cut-and-come-again crop. It can be picked throughout winter, given frost protection.

suitable for containers
early spring to late summer
some resistance
hardy
year round

Watercress

Despite its name, this crop doesn't need to be grown in water; sow into pots stood in deep saucers, or in polythene-lined trenches, keeping the soil permanently wet. Harvest the young shoots regularly to encourage regrowth.

suitable for containers
late spring and summer
some
hardy
summer

Sorrel

This salad leaf is used in French cuisine, particularly in soups and sauces. The bright green leaves are produced in abundance and have a sharp, refreshing taste that becomes bitter with age. Although it is a perennial it can be grown as an annual.

suitable for containers
mid- to late spring
some resistance
hardy
early to late summer

Purslane

This sprawling plant produces juicy, succulent stalks and rosettes of bright green, oval leaves that taste a little like mangetout. The leaves are quick to mature and can be harvested as a cut-and-come-again crop, for use in salads or stir-fries.

 suitable for containers
late spring to midsummer
some resistance
fairly hardy
early to late summer

Mibuna

A vigorous Japanese plant with long, narrow leaves possessing a peppery flavour, mibuna can regrow after cutting up to five times in a season; successional sowing will give a long-lasting crop. The leaves are good in salads or lightly cooked.

 unsuitable for containers
mid-spring to early autumn
poor resistance
hardy
late spring to late autumn

Wild Rocket

This salad crop is closely related to garden rocket but has a much stronger peppery taste. It is a perennial, often grown as an annual. The leaves should be cropped when young and tender, although the flowers of more mature plants can also be eaten.

suitable for containers
early spring to late summer
some resistance
hardy
late spring to early winter

Rocket

The deep green, oval, often serrated leaves have a distinctive peppery flavour and are ideal as a salad on their own or with other leaves. Pick regularly as a cut-and-come-again crop, as it has a tendency to bolt in hot summers.

- suitable for containers
- early spring to late summer
- some resistance
- fairly hardy
- late spring to early winter

Par-cel

An easy-to-grow variety of celery, developed for its pretty curled leaves rather than its stalks. The finely cut, dark green, glossy leaves have a strong celery taste, and are used as a garnish or in soups, stocks, and stews.

- suitable for containers
- early spring to midsummer
- some resistance
- hardy
- early summer to late autumn

Perilla

This is grown for its crinkled red or green leaves, which are widely used in Japanese cuisine, and have a distinctive cinnamon scent and taste. It is an attractive plant that doubles as an ornamental, making it a good choice for smaller gardens.

- suitable for containers
- late spring and summer
- some resistance
- not hardy
- summer and autumn

Greek Cress

These quick-growing microgreens are best eaten as young seedlings. The curled, bright green leaves add a spicy, peppery flavour to salads, sandwiches, and stir-fries. They can be grown year round indoors, and also outdoors if protected from frost.

- suitable for containers
- year round
- some resistance
- fairly hardy
- year round

Par-cel

Red Orache

This easy-to-grow plant is as ornamental as it is productive. The dark red leaves are good in salads when young, or can be cooked as spinach when mature. It has a tendency to bolt, so is best grown from successional sowings.

🪴	suitable for containers
🌱	early spring to late summer
🌸	some resistance
❄	not hardy
🔒	early summer to mid-autumn

Chop Suey Greens

This new variety of Japanese chrysanthemum lacks the bitterness of other types and is very easy to grow. The fine, deeply cut, bright green leaves have a sweet, peppery, and slightly fragrant flavour, and are ideal for salads or stir-fries.

🪴	suitable for containers
🌱	mid-spring to late summer
🌸	some resistance
❄	not hardy
🔒	midsummer to late autumn

Heuristic

Texsel Greens

Also known as Ethiopian Greens, this quick-growing salad leaf has a mild, mustard-like flavour. Mature leaves can be cooked as a vegetable, or pick them young for salads or stir-fries. Grow it under cover for a year-round crop.

 suitable for containers
early spring to late summer
some resistance
hardy
year round

Celtuce

This dual-purpose crop get its name from its celery-like stems, which can be harvested by cutting off mature plants; and its lettuce-like leaves, which can be cut young and used in salads. Crop leaves as needed and cut the stem at 20cm (8in) long.

suitable for containers
early spring and summer
some resistance
not hardy
early to late summer

Corn Salad

Also known as Lamb's Lettuce, this popular salad variety grows slowly to produce rosettes of small, green leaves that can be picked during the winter months. It can be sown successionally year round, and the hardy leaves can withstand frost.

suitable for containers
early spring to mid-autumn
some resistance
hardy
year round

Tatsoi

A type of pak choi, this rosette-shaped salad leaf is hardy and prolific. The dark green, spoon-shaped leaves grow on short, sturdy, greenish-white stems and can be used at any stage of growth; they are mild-flavoured and good for salads or winter dishes.

- suitable for containers
- early spring to mid-autumn
- poor resistance
- hardy
- late spring to midwinter

New Zealand Spinach

Unrelated to traditional spinach, this plant can be cropped in the same way, and has small, green fuzzy leaves. It has a spreading habit and grows well in hot, dry conditions, but keep it well watered to encourage plenty of growth. Harvest it regularly.

- unsuitable for containers
- mid-spring to early summer
- some resistance
- not hardy
- midsummer to autumn

Mustard Greens

This group of vegetables have good nutritional values and tangy flavours that intensify to hot as the plants mature. According to variety, the leaves may be large and crinkled or pretty fronds, several possessing attractive colours, from purple to red or gold.

- suitable for containers
- late spring to early autumn
- poor resistance
- fairly hardy
- late summer to late autumn

Mizuna

Related to mibuna, but with a milder taste and slower to bolt, mizuna has slender white stalks and dark green serrated leaves that can be harvested young for salads or later for cooking. It grows prolifically after cutting and is easy to look after.

- suitable for containers
- mid-spring to early autumn
- poor resistance
- hardy
- late spring to late autumn

Buckler Leaf Sorrel

This type of sorrel has small, soft, slightly succulent leaves, with a sharp, lemony flavour. Although perennial, it can be sown each year as an annual, and can be used raw in salads, or cooked in soups and fish dishes. It self-seeds freely if allowed.

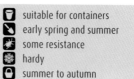

- suitable for containers
- early spring and summer
- some resistance
- hardy
- summer to autumn

Chinese Broccoli

Chinese Broccoli

Also known as Chinese kale, this is quite similar to European purple sprouting broccoli in appearance and flavour but is more refined and tender. The leaves, stems, and flowers are all edible, and the leaves can be used raw in salads when young.

- suitable for containers
- late spring to early autumn
- poor resistance
- fairly hardy
- midsummer to late autumn

Komatsuna

A fast-growing Japanese vegetable, komatsuma can be harvested at about 30 days after sowing for baby leaves or when it reaches the size of kale at around 70 days. The flavour of the leaves, flowers and stems is mild and fresh, excellent in salads and stir-fries.

- suitable for containers
- early spring to early autumn
- poor resistance
- hardy
- mid-spring to late autumn

Oriental Saladini

This seed mix provides a range of oriental leaf vegetables, such as pak choi, mibuna, mizuna, mustard, and komatsuma, which will provide salad leaves over a long period. Sow successionally and treat them as a cut-and-come-again crop.

- suitable for containers
- mid-spring to late summer
- poor resistance
- fairly hardy
- late spring to mid-autumn

Choy Sum

This vegetable is grown for its broad, crisp leaf stalks, which can be green, white or purple, and are harvested just before flowering. The stalks can be eaten raw in salads or stir-fried. It is a quick growing crop that does best in milder regions.

- suitable for containers
- early summer to early autumn
- some
- not hardy
- summer to autumn

CHICORY *Cichorium intybus*

A highly ornamental plant, there are three distinct, attractive types of chicory: Witloof or Belgian, which has elongated heads of tight, white leaves, and is forced and blanched; radicchio or red chicory, which has tight heads of crisp, red leaves, similar in appearance to a small lettuce; and sugarloaf, which has looser, green leaves. All types have a decidedly bitter taste, but can be eaten raw in salad, or cooked.

	SPRING	SUMMER	AUTUMN	WINTER
SOW				
HARVEST				

SOWING

Chicory is a very tolerant crop, and will grow well even in poor soils and partial shade. It is best not to sow seed too early or plants might bolt, so begin in late spring and sow through to midsummer.

Sow seed directly into the ground at a depth of 1cm (¹/₂in). Once seedlings develop, thin Witloof chicory to leave about 23cm (9in) space between plants, and about 30cm (12in) between radicchio or sugarloaf types, as these will develop larger heads.

CROP CARE

Ensure that chicory crops are kept weeded and well-watered to discourage them from bolting. Protect with cold frames or cloches if late frosts are forecast.

A large box is ideal for forcing chicory.

HARVESTING

Chicory is usually ready for harvesting in about a month, once heads are firm. Raddichio or sugarloaf types will store once lifted, or they can be left in the ground for longer if not immediately needed. Dig up Witloof types and force (see opposite). Once chicons have been cut, re-cover the stumps – you may get a second crop.

FORCING AND BLANCHING

Forcing Witloof chicory will produce a crop of blanched leaf shoots that are less bitter in taste than the green leaves. Dig up mature plants in late autumn to early winter. Cut the leaves off the plant to within 2.5cm (1in) above the root collar, and trim the bottom of the root so that it measures 20cm (8in) in length. Plant these trimmed roots in boxes of moist potting compost, so that their tops are just showing above the soil surface. Then cover with 23cm (9in) of compost. Move the box to a warm, dark place for three to four weeks.

PESTS AND DISEASES

Chicory may be at risk from slugs and snails, which will happily munch their way through leaves. To deter them, create a protective barrier using a cloche or cold frame; set up beer traps to draw them away from crops; and lay a ring of coarse material such as sand or crushed shells around the planting area. Alternatively, use slug pellets, as these are the most effective control. Keep a close eye out for aphids too. If infestations are severe, spray with an appropriate insecticide.

'Red Rib'

Also known as Italian Dandelion, this variety bears serrated, dandelion-like leaves on long stems. The dark green leaves have distinctive, bright red stems and mid-veins. Eaten raw or cooked, the leaves have a pleasant, bitter flavour with a little sweetness.

- 🪣 suitable for containers
- 🌱 late spring to late summer
- 🐛 good resistance
- ❄️ fairly hardy
- 🔒 midsummer to autumn

'Palla Rossa Verona'

This Italian variety produces round, compact, firm heads with heart-shaped, deep red leaves with white ribs. The excellent quality of the leaves and their sharp flavour makes them popular with chefs. It is a good variety for forcing.

- 🪣 suitable for containers
- 🌱 midsummer to early autumn
- 🐛 good resistance
- ❄️ hardy
- 🔒 autumn to early winter

'Apollo'

This witloof variety produces compact, well-flavoured chicons when grown and forced. The green, unforced leaves have a good, slightly bitter flavour when eaten raw in salads, or steamed or braised as a vegetable.

- 🪣 suitable for containers
- 🌱 early to midsummer
- 🐛 good resistance
- ❄️ fairly hardy
- 🔒 winter

'Indigo' ♀

A reliable radicchio, this variety produces dense, round heads of green outer leaves with white midribs, red hearts, and a good flavour. The heads are ready for harvesting early in the season and are resistant to bolting, tipburn, and bottom rot.

- suitable for containers
- early to mid-spring
- good resistance
- hardy
- midsummer to late autumn

'Lightning'

This very productive Witloof chicory variety is excellent for forcing in mid- to late season. It will reliably produce long, smooth chicons with a good, mild flavour. They will keep well after harvesting.

- suitable for containers
- mid-spring to early summer
- good resistance
- fairly hardy
- winter

'Pan di Zucchero' ♀

Also known as 'Sugar Loaf', this popular variety produces upright, tight heads with dark green outer leaves. The crunchy hearts are ideal for shredding into salads. It can also be grown as an under cover cut-and-come-again crop through winter.

- suitable for containers
- mid- to late summer
- good resistance
- hardy
- late autumn to midwinter

'Palla Rossa' ♀

This round, red, ball-type originates from Chioggia in Italy. The green leaves of the medium to large, firm, well-filled heads have white midribs, and turn red as temperatures drop. The crisp leaves have a sweet flavour with a touch of bitterness.

- 🪣 suitable for containers
- 🌙 mid- to late summer
- 🌼 good resistance
- ❄️ hardy
- 🔒 midwinter

'Leonardo' ♀

This vigorous variety produces large, round, dense heads of red leaves. The hearts are well-developed with a red colour that deepens as the weather becomes colder. The flavour of the leaves is enhanced by cooler temperatures and frost.

- 🪣 suitable for containers
- 🌙 mid- to late summer
- 🌼 good resistance
- ❄️ hardy
- 🔒 autumn to midwinter

'Castelfranco'

In summer, this variety produces creamy-green leaves with a red mottling, which deepens as winter approaches. The round, closed heads are good for forcing. It is a late-maturing variety with a crunchy texture; the fresh leaves are good in salads.

- 🪣 suitable for containers
- 🌙 mid- to late summer
- 🌼 good resistance
- ❄️ hardy
- 🔒 midwinter

'Rossa Di Treviso'

This classic Italian variety bears slender, tall, upright radicchio leaves, which have white midribs and need cold temperatures to take on their distinctive red colour. Good raw or grilled, the leaves have a pleasant bitter taste – remove outer leaves before eating.

- suitable for containers
- mid- to late summer
- good resistance
- hardy
- mid-autumn to midwinter

'Orchidea Rossa'

This early-maturing variety produces attractive, rosette-shaped heads. The small to medium-sized heads are round, and the leaves red with white midribs. The crisp leaves can be cooked to remove their bitterness or used raw in salads.

- suitable for containers
- late spring to late summer
- good resistance
- hardy
- autumn to midwinter

'Treviso Precoce Mesola'

This Italian chicory produces firm, long heads with red leaves and white midribs. The leaves have a distinctive flavour and texture and are ideal for use in autumn or winter, raw or cooked. The baby leaves are excellent in salads.

- suitable for containers
- mid-spring to late summer
- good resistance
- hardy
- autumn to midwinter

ENDIVE *Cichorium endivia*

Endive is closely related to chicory and forms sprawling rosettes of bitter-tasting, lettuce-like leaves. There are two main types of endive – those with flat, broad leaves that are known as "escarole" or "Batavian", and those with frilly, finely-serrated leaves known in the UK as "frisée", or as "chicory" in North America. Endive can be blanched to reduce the bitterness of its taste, and can be used in salads like lettuce.

	SPRING	SUMMER	AUTUMN	WINTER
SOW/PLANT				
HARVEST				

SOWING

Endives like a fertile, well-drained soil and a pH of around 5.5–7.5. They are generally quite tolerant plants and are not too fussy about position – they will grow happily in full sun and will tolerate partial shade too.

Exposure to cold weather may encourage plants to bolt, so don't plant them out too early. Instead, sow under cover in spring and plant seedlings out once the soil has warmed up in early or midsummer. Alternatively, sow seed directly into the ground in early summer. Sow seed at a depth of 1cm (¹/₂in), and later thin seedlings out depending on type: allow compact varieties about 23cm (9in) between plants, and give spreading varieties

Clay pots can be used to blanch leaves.

about 38cm (15in). Space rows of plants 25–38cm (10–15in) apart.

CROP CARE

Keep plants weeded and well-watered at all stages of their growth. Protect crops with cloches or cold frames if the weather turns cold – this will discourage them from bolting and will also extend the length of the harvesting season.

HARVESTING

Harvest endives as required; either cut the whole head off and wait for new leaves to re-sprout, or harvest individual leaves as a cut-and-come-again crop.

BLANCHING

Preventing light from reaching the leaves will blanch them and reduce their bitter flavour. Cover frisée types with a plate, or gather up and tie together the leaves of Batavian types shortly before crops are harvested. Block the light for about ten days. After this time the leaves will have whitened and be ready to eat.

PESTS AND DISEASES

Be vigilant against slugs as they will probably be the biggest threat to your crop. Use slug pellets, or if you prefer, protect plants with cloches or set up beer traps. Also consider laying grit, crushed shells, or copper tape as a barrier. Aphids and caterpillars may also target your crops. Pick off any caterpillars that you find, and spray infested plants with an appropriate insecticide. Lettuce root aphid, which feed on plant roots, and tip burn, which shrivels the edges of leaves, might pose a problem. Treat as required.

'Natacha' ♀

An attractive and vigorous escarole type that produces big, heavy heads of bright green, strong-flavoured leaves around a central creamy heart. It is the best performing variety, and has excellent resistance to bolting, tip burn, and bottom rot.

- suitable for containers
- early spring to midsummer
- excellent resistance
- hardy
- late spring to early autumn

'Tres Fine Maraichere'

This classic, US-only variety requires cool temperatures to grow well. Its finely cut inner leaves are mild and delicious, and add interesting texture to salads. It is sensitive to tip burn, particularly if grown in soils that lack calcium.

- suitable for containers
- late spring to midsummer
- poor resistance
- hardy
- midsummer to late autumn

'Kentucky' ♀

This variety is a very productive, robust, easy-to-grow, frisée type. Plants produce large heads of very fine, deep green leaves around a yellow heart that has a distinctive, sharp taste. This variety is ideal for blanching.

- suitable for containers
- late spring to midsummer
- good resistance
- hardy
- midsummer to late autumn

'Batavian Full Heart'

An escarole type, this variety has large, thick, dark green leaves around a creamy-coloured centre. The outer leaves have a sharp flavour, while the heart is milder in taste. It can be harvested into winter as it is very hardy.

- suitable for containers
- early spring to late summer
- good resistance
- hardy
- late spring to early winter

'Frenzy'

This compact, uniform variety is a 'Tres Fine' type. The dense heads produce finely curled, deeply cut leaves around a centre that self-blanches to a creamy yellow colour. The leaves can be picked when young or left to mature. A popular choice among chefs.

- 🪣 suitable for containers
- 🌱 early spring to midsummer
- ✳️ good resistance
- ❄️ hardy
- 🔒 midsummer to autumn

'Glory'

A frisée endive with uniform, deeply, yet finely cut, lacy leaves that have a distinctive, slightly bitter flavour. The tender young leaves are a traditional ingredient of Mesclun, the classic French salad. Harvest as whole heads or as baby leaves.

- 🪣 suitable for containers
- 🌱 early spring to midsummer
- ✳️ good resistance
- ❄️ hardy
- 🔒 late spring to late autumn

'Rhodos'

This US-only, frisée-type endive has a naturally self-blanching heart with mild-flavoured, tender white leaves that are a salad delicacy. Maturing in 42 days, it is sensitive to tip burn and bottom rot, and should be cut before signs of either appear.

- 🪣 suitable for containers
- 🌱 early spring to midsummer
- ✳️ poor resistance
- ❄️ not hardy
- 🔒 late spring to early autumn

Fruiting Vegetables

- Globe artichokes
- Tomatoes
- Sweet and Chilli peppers
- Aubergines
- Sweetcorn

GLOBE ARTICHOKES *Cynara scolymus*

The succulent petal bases and centres of tender, immature globe artichoke flowers are delicious boiled, while young shoots can be blanched for use in salads. When grown from seed, globe artichokes can be variable in quality, so if possible purchase named offsets that have been propagated. It is also possible to select from the best of your seed-raised plants to produce a good quality offset.

	SPRING	SUMMER	AUTUMN	WINTER
SOW				
HARVEST				

SOWING

Give globe artichokes a sheltered but sunny position. They do best in well-drained, fertile, moisture-retentive soil, so dig in plenty of well-rotted manure or compost and apply some general purpose fertilizer before planting.

In spring, sow seed in pots indoors, or in outdoor seedbeds, at a depth of 5cm (2in). The young seedlings should be transplanted to their final positions in early summer. However, offsets taken in spring from the sides of mature plants are a better way of raising artichokes if good quality mother plants are available. Offsets are also sold by specialist nurseries.

Ensure that plants have enough space, allowing 75cm (30in)

Apply a compost mulch every spring.

between plants and 90cm (36in) between rows. Push offsets deep enough into the soil that they can stand upright, then water in well.

CROP CARE

Keep plants well weeded and apply plenty of water in dry spells. Apply fertilizer and an organic mulch every spring. In autumn, plants die back and the dead material should be removed.

In cold regions, protect the crown of the plant with a layer of straw or other insulating material. Plants should be replaced every three years as clumps become less productive with age.

HARVESTING

Abundant flowerbuds are borne from late spring to early summer, and if the stem is cut back may fruit again in early autumn. Cut the heads from about golf ball size; they can become appetizingly woolly when larger than a tennis ball. They should be cut with a slight amount of edible stalk; long stalks tend to be woody.

PESTS AND DISEASES

Globe artichokes are largely problem free, but blackfly and root aphids may target plants. As blackfly affect stalks, wash off by hand or treat with an appropriate insecticide. Little can be done about root aphids, but water and feed to help plants overcome the effect.

Aphids are a food source for ladybirds.

'Purple Globe'

The rather unruly, thistle-like plants of this highly ornamental variety produce variable artichokes in early summer. The smallish globes tend to lack firmness and are on the spiny side, but they have good flavour and are best gathered when small.

- unsuitable for containers
- spring to summer
- some resistance
- hardy
- early summer to autumn

'Green Globe Improved'

This hybrid artichoke variety is more reliable than its parent plant, and more vigorous, producing larger, firmer artichokes on more uniform plants. The globes are suitable for harvesting when they are both small and large in size.

- unsuitable for containers
- spring to summer
- some resistance
- hardy
- early summer to autumn

'Violetto di Chioggia'

This handsome, seed-raised variety originated in Italy. The spiky and variable artichokes are carried on thistle-like foliage. Fairly hardy and productive, the plants are not very uniform but this is outweighed by the fact that cropping is good.

- unsuitable for containers
- spring to summer
- some resistance
- hardy
- early summer to autumn

'Gros Vert de Lâon'

This hardy, high-quality variety
will survive winters in cooler
regions. The artichokes are
round, green, and can be
gathered when small or large.
The best forms are propagated
by offsets and are of superior
quality to seed-raised cultivars.

🪣 unsuitable for containers
🌱 spring to summer
🐜 some resistance
❄️ hardy
🔒 early summer to autumn

'Romanesco'

This productive variety produces
rounded, purple-tinted artichokes
that are relatively tight and firm,
which is unusual for a seed-
raised variety. Tall, vigorous,
and variable, the plants are very
ornamental even without their
coloured flower buds.

🪣 unsuitable for containers
🌱 spring to summer
🐜 some resistance
❄️ hardy
🔒 early summer to autumn

'Imperial Star'

This selection of 'Green Globe' is
less variable than other cultivars
and is raised from seed. As it
matures quickly and can produce
artichokes in its first year, it can
be grown in regions with winters
that are more severe than
artichokes normally tolerate.

🪣 unsuitable for containers
🌱 spring to summer
🐜 some resistance
❄️ hardy
🔒 early summer to autumn

TOMATOES *Lycopersicon esculentum*

With flavourful, attractive fruits that range from tiny currant-like types to huge, fleshy, beefsteak varieties, in colours as diverse as, pink, red, yellow, maroon, and even purple, it is no wonder that the easy-to-grow tomato is loved by gardeners. A wide range of varieties are available as seed, but young plants are also widely sold. These are valuable for gardeners without the warm conditions needed to raise seedlings.

	SPRING	SUMMER	AUTUMN	WINTER
SOW/PLANT				
HARVEST				

SOWING

Sow seed in early spring, ensuring a temperature of between 18–25°C (64–77°F). Good, sturdy growth depends on ample warmth and light; crowded plants become elongated and hard to handle later. As soon as they are large enough, seedlings should be set out into individual containers and grown on either in a greenhouse or outdoors. Containers filled with fertile potting media will support good crops.

For outdoor tomatoes, plant out only once the danger of frost has passed, after hardening off. Mix a 5cm (2in) layer of rotted organic manure or compost and general-purpose fertilizer into the soil. A warm, sunny, sheltered site is essential outdoors.

Support vine tomatoes with canes.

CROP CARE

Water plants during dry periods. Tomatoes are self-fertile but may need shaking to effect pollination.

Bush tomatoes need no special treatment – each shoot ends with flowers and therefore will not grow very long. With many such shoots, bush tomatoes require minimal staking. Vine tomato flowers grow out from the stem.

The stem also has growing points that give rise to many trailing sideshoots. These should be cut out, and the main stem tied to a stake. When the plant reaches the top of the stake, remove its growing tip. A few varieties have aspects of both bush and vine, and requiring minimal trimming; merely tie them to a stake. Plants will need regular feeding with tomato fertilizer.

HARVESTING

Gather fruits once they have attained their full colour and have begun to soften. They will not keep long in storage.

PESTS AND DISEASES

In greenhouses, caterpillars, whitefly and red spider mite may be a problem. Tomatoes also share several problems with potatoes, such as potato cyst eelworm and potato blight. Outdoor crops are prone to blight in cool damp weather; its effects can be devastating.

Tomato blight causes fruits to rot.

'Chocolate Cherry'

Recently introduced, this heavy-cropping vine variety bears small, purple-brown fruits with excellent flavour. Perfect for use in salads, these tomatoes are especially rich in beneficial antioxidants. Plants will need support with sticks or string.

- 🪣 suitable for containers
- 🌱 late spring to early summer
- 🐛 some resistance
- ❄ not hardy
- 🔒 summer to early autumn

'Sweet Million'

This hybrid cherry tomato can be grown in greenhouses or outdoors, and has a vine habit so should be trained up sticks or string. The trusses are very long and carry large numbers of small, bright red, very sweet, round fruits.

- 🪣 suitable for containers
- 🌱 late spring to early summer
- 🐛 some resistance
- ❄ not hardy
- 🔒 summer to early autumn

'Sun Baby' ♀

This high-yielding, vine variety bears numerous bright red fruits, borne on large trusses, which ripen to a sweet flavour. Plants need support with sticks or string, and are suitable for either greenhouse or outdoor cultivation.

- 🪣 suitable for containers
- 🏷 late spring to early summer
- 🕷 some resistance
- ❄ not hardy
- 🔒 summer to early autumn

'Chadwick'

A juicy cherry variety, this tomato is named after its originator and is sometimes called 'Camp Joy'. Its fruits are on the large side for cherry types, and are borne on plants with a vine habit, in greenhouses or outdoors.

- 🪣 suitable for containers
- 🏷 late spring to early summer
- 🕷 some resistance
- ❄ not hardy
- 🔒 summer to early autumn

'Gardener's Delight' ♀

This long-established cherry tomato has a vine habit and should be supported with sticks or string. Famed for its flavour, this variety bears medium yields of larger than usual fruits on long trusses. The fruits mature early, even in cooler regions.

- 🪣 suitable for containers
- 🏷 late spring to early summer
- 🕷 some resistance
- ❄ not hardy
- 🔒 summer to early autumn

'Matt's Wild Cherry'

A tomato of Mexican origin, this variety produces cherry-sized, round, red fruits of good flavour. Plants have good cropping potential and should be supported with sticks or string. Give them a warm, sunny site.

- suitable for containers
- late spring to early summer
- some resistance
- not hardy
- summer to early autumn

'Gold Nugget'

This heavy-cropping bush variety bears round, cherry-sized, yellow fruits, whose succulent, firm flesh is ideal for slicing or stuffing. 'Gold Nugget' was bred in the USA and is therefore suitable for other regions with a maritime climate.

- suitable for containers
- late spring to early summer
- some resistance
- not hardy
- summer to early autumn

'Golden Cherry'

This hybrid cherry tomato produces heavy crops of bright orange, sweet, succulent fruits ideal for salads. Plants have a vine habit and will grow in greenhouses or outdoors, even in cooler regions, in a warm, sunny site.

- suitable for containers
- late spring to early summer
- some resistance
- not hardy
- summer to early autumn

'Sungold' ♀

This heavy-cropping cherry variety bears sweet, round, attractive, golden-orange fruits. Plants can be cultivated in a greenhouse or grown outdoors, and have a vine habit, so will need support from sticks or string.

- suitable for containers
- late spring to early summer
- some resistance
- not hardy
- summer to early autumn

'Glacier'

This early-cropping variety bears numerous, small, bright red fruits, even in cool weather. It grows with aspects of both bush and vine habit so is best trained roughly to a stick or string. Plants have potato-leafed foliage; and are best grown outdoors.

- suitable for containers
- late spring to early summer
- some resistance
- not hardy
- summer to early autumn

'Tumbling Tom Red'

The prolific, bright red fruits of this variety are attractive and delicious, and hang for a long time. The plants grow fast, crop early, and are very robust. Their trailing bush habit is ideally suited for hanging baskets and other ornamental containers.

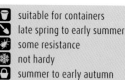

- suitable for containers
- late spring to early summer
- some resistance
- not hardy
- summer to early autumn

'Totem'

This dwarf, bush tomato is attractive and quick-growing. The well-flavoured crimson fruits are produced abundantly and hang on the plant, enhancing its ornamental value. It is ideal for growing in patio containers, and support is often needed.

- suitable for containers
- late spring to early summer
- some resistance
- not hardy
- summer to early autumn

'Legend'

This hybrid bush variety produces early crops of large, bright red fruits that have some tolerance to late blight. Plants are best grown outdoors, but may need protection under cloches or horticultural fleece.

- suitable for containers
- late spring to early summer
- good resistance
- not hardy
- summer to early autumn

'Balconi Red'

This variety has a trailing, bush habit and is ideally suited for hanging baskets and ornamental containers. The plants grow fast, crop early, and are unusually prolific. The bright red fruits are attractive and delicious and will hang for a long time.

- suitable for containers
- late spring to early summer
- some resistance
- not hardy
- summer to early autumn

'Tumbler'

This bush tomato has a compact, trailing habit so is ideal for hanging baskets and containers. The small fruits are well-flavoured and abundant, and plants are very robust and reliable, even when grown in hanging baskets.

🪣	suitable for containers
🌱	late spring to early summer
✹	some resistance
❄	not hardy
🔒	summer to early autumn

'Tornado' ♉

This reliable bush variety produces heavy crops of small, bright red, juicy, thin-skinned fruits of fair flavour. The plants grow fast, crop early, and have been bred to perform well in cool, rainy regions.

🪣	suitable for containers
🌱	late spring to early summer
✹	some resistance
❄	not hardy
🔒	summer to early autumn

'Minibel'

This variety has a trailing, bush habit so is ideally suited for hanging baskets. Plants are very compact and produce prolific, bright red, cherry-size fruits that hang for a long time. It is suitable for outdoor cultivation, even in cooler regions.

🪣	suitable for containers
🌱	late spring to early summer
✹	some resistance
❄	not hardy
🔒	summer to early autumn

'Juliet'

This hybrid vine variety needs supporting with string or sticks for cultivation outdoors or in a greenhouse. Fruits are small, elongated, and bright red, with a rich flavour. They hold well on the vine and are especially delicious in salads and sauces.

- suitable for containers
- late spring to early summer
- some resistance
- not hardy
- summer to early autumn

'Verde'

Closely related to tomatoes and grown in the same way, these bushy tomatillo plants are trouble-free and crop heavily. The green, sharply-flavoured fruits are used in Mexican cuisine and are also suited to relishes when used in the same way as green tomatoes.

- suitable for containers
- late spring to early summer
- some resistance
- not hardy
- summer to early autumn

'Ailsa Craig'

This long-established variety bears medium-sized, round, red fruits with fair flavour. Plants have a vine habit and are best for greenhouse cultivation. They are reliable even under difficult growing conditions.

- suitable for containers
- late spring to early summer
- some resistance
- not hardy
- summer to early autumn

'Black Russian'

Originally from Russia, this compact, beefsteak variety produces heavy crops of fairly large, deep maroon fruits, which are succulent, with a hint of salt. Plant have a vine habit and will need support with sticks or string. Protect against blight in cool, wet regions.

 suitable for containers
late spring to early summer
some resistance
not hardy
summer to early autumn

'Tigerella' ♀

Although flavour is fair and crops only reasonable, this vine variety is grown for its small, red- and green-striped, attractive fruits.Best suited to greenhouse growing, it will also crop outdoors in warm regions. Support plants with sticks or string.

 suitable for containers
late spring to early summer
some resistance
not hardy
summer to early autumn

'Stupice'

This heavy-cropping vine tomato was originally bred in the Czech Republic. It bears heavy crops of bright red, round fruits of good flavour, which ripen early, even in cool regions. Plants should be supported with sticks or string, and can be grown indoors or out.

suitable for containers
late spring to early summer
some resistance
not hardy
summer to early autumn

'Sweet Olive' ♀

This vigorous, easy-to-grow, vine variety bears heavy crops of small, bright red, round- to plum-shaped tomatoes. Plants should be supported with sticks or string, and are suitable for both greenhouse growing and for growing outdoors.

- suitable for containers
- late spring to early summer
- some resistance
- not hardy
- summer to early autumn

'Golden Sunrise' ♀

This high-yielding, vine variety bears small-sized, round, golden-yellow fruits with excellent flavour. They are capable of good outdoor crops in warm, sunny situations, and are reliable even in cooler regions. Support plants with sticks or string.

- suitable for containers
- late spring to early summer
- some resistance
- not hardy
- summer to early autumn

'Fantasio'

This hybrid, vine variety has good cropping potential, producing medium-sized, round, red fruits with good flavour. Plants should be supported with sticks or string, and will grow indoors, or outdoors in a warm, sunny site. It is tolerant of late blight.

- suitable for containers
- late spring to early summer
- some resistance
- not hardy
- summer to early autumn

'Tomatoberry Garden'

This cascading vine variety
produces long trusses of small,
bright red fruits with pointed
ends and a good flavour. Plants
should be supported with sticks
or string and are suitable for
growing indoors or outdoors.
It is tolerant of late blight.

 suitable for containers
late spring to early summer
some resistance
not hardy
summer to early autumn

'Moneymaker'

This vine variety is long
established for greenhouse use
and needs support with sticks
or string. It produces moderate
yields of bright red, round fruits
of fair flavour. Plants tolerate
poor soil, and seed is inexpensive
and widely available.

suitable for containers
late spring to early summer
some resistance
not hardy
summer to early autumn

'Ferline'

Reliable, even outdoors, this
medium-sized, beefsteak variety
produces a heavy crop of well-
flavoured, bright red fruits that
ripen slowly on the vine, and are
ideal for cooking. Plants need
support with sticks or string,
and have good blight tolerance.

suitable for containers
late spring to early summer
some resistance
not hardy
summer to early autumn

'Green Zebra'

The large, richly-flavoured fruits of this variety are green- and yellow-striped, becoming deeper yellow as they ripen. Plants have a vine habit, and are best grown outdoors. Originally bred in the USA, they suit a maritime climate.

- suitable for containers
- late spring to early summer
- some resistance
- not hardy
- summer to early autumn

'Alicante' ♀

A long-established, vine variety, 'Alicante' bears heavy crops of medium-sized, round, red fruits with fair flavour. Capable of good outdoor crops in warm sunny situations, it is reliable even under difficult conditions. Support with sticks or string.

- suitable for containers
- late spring to early summer
- some resistance
- not hardy
- summer to early autumn

'Outdoor Girl' ♀

An early-maturing, high-yielding vine variety, it bears medium-sized, round, red fruits with excellent flavour. Suitable for greenhouse or outdoor crops, it is reliable even in cooler regions. Support with sticks or string.

- suitable for containers
- late spring to early summer
- some resistance
- not hardy
- summer to early autumn

'Yellow Perfection'

This long-established, high-yielding variety produces medium-sized, mild-flavoured, pale yellow fruits. Plants have a vine habit and should be supported with sticks or string. They are suitable for greenhouses or for growing outdoors in cooler regions.

 suitable for containers
late spring to early summer
some resistance
not hardy
summer to early autumn

'Shirley' ♀

This reliable, well-established variety bears medium-sized, round, red fruits with fair flavour. Plants have excellent cropping potential and grow best in a greenhouse, although they are also capable of fair outdoor crops in warm, sunny situations.

 suitable for containers
late spring to early summer
some resistance
not hardy
summer to early autumn

'Tiger Tom'

This long-established variety produces yellow-striped tomatoes with orange flesh and good flavour. Originally from the United States, it is suitable for outdoor crops in warm regions, but may need greenhouse conditions in cooler areas.

 suitable for containers
late spring to early summer
some resistance
not hardy
summer to early autumn

'San Marzano Lungo'

A traditional, Italian plum tomato, this variety bears heavy crops of bright red fruits with good flavour, which are ideal for cooking. Plants have a vine habit so should be supported with sticks or string, and need protection from late blight in cool, wet regions.

- suitable for containers
- late spring to early summer
- some resistance
- not hardy
- summer to early autumn

'Summer Sweet' ♀

This early-maturing plum type bears high yields of bright red, well-flavoured, small- to medium-sized fruits. Plants have a vine habit so should be supported with sticks or string. They are suitable for growing in a greenhouse or for outdoors in warmer areas.

- suitable for containers
- late spring to early summer
- some resistance
- not hardy
- summer to early autumn

'Principe Borghese'

This heavy-cropping, Italian plum variety produces bright red, solid fruits that last well on the vine; the succulent, firm flesh is ideal for sauces. Plants should be supported with sticks or string, and need protection from late blight in cool, wet regions.

- suitable for containers
- late spring to early summer
- some resistance
- not hardy
- summer to early autumn

'Roma'

This traditional, bush, plum tomato is originally from Italy. It produces heavy crops of bright red, solid fruits. Plants must be protected from late blight in cool, wet regions, although 'Roma VF' is also available, which is resistant to fungal wilt diseases.

- suitable for containers
- late spring to early summer
- some resistance
- not hardy
- summer to early autumn

'Summer Sweet'

'Black Krim'

This traditional, beefsteak tomato originated in Russia. It bears heavy crops of large, dark brown-red fruits, with succulent, firm flesh, ideal for stuffing. Support the vine plants with sticks or string, and protect in cool, wet regions to prevent late blight.

- suitable for containers
- late spring to early summer
- some resistance
- not hardy
- summer to early autumn

'Costoluto Genovese'

This heavy-cropping, beefsteak variety was originally bred in Italy. It produces very large, ribbed, bright red fruits, which are succulent and sweet. Plants have a vine habit and should be protected from late blight in cool, wet regions.

- suitable for containers
- late spring to early summer
- some resistance
- not hardy
- summer to early autumn

'Brandywine'

Originally from the USA, this beefsteak variety bears moderate crops of large, flat, red fruits with succulent, pink flesh and potato-type foliage. Plants have a vine habit and need support with sticks or string; they suit growing indoors or out.

- suitable for containers
- late spring to early summer
- some resistance
- not hardy
- summer to early autumn

'Country Taste'

This beefsteak type has a vine habit so should be grown up sticks or string, either indoors or out. It bears heavy, early-maturing crops of bright red, flattened, ribbed fruits with succulent, firm flesh. Plants are more robust and heavier yielding than similar heirloom varieties.

- suitable for containers
- late spring to early summer
- some resistance
- not hardy
- summer to early autumn

'Costoluto Fiorentino' ♀

This traditional, Italian beefsteak variety bears heavy crops of bright red, flattened, ribbed fruits. The tomatoes have succulent, firm flesh. Plants have a vine habit and should be protected from late blight in cool, wet regions.

- suitable for containers
- late spring to early summer
- some resistance
- not hardy
- summer to early autumn

'Marmande' ♀

This heavy-cropping, beefsteak variety originated in Italy and produces bright red, flattened, ribbed fruits with succulent, solid flesh. Plants have a vine habit so should be supported with sticks or string, and protected from late blight in cool, wet regions.

- suitable for containers
- late spring to early summer
- some resistance
- not hardy
- summer to early autumn

SWEET AND CHILLI PEPPERS

Capsicum anuum Longum Group and *C. anuum* Grossum Group

Amazingly diverse, peppers are available in a range of vivid shades, from green to red, purple, yellow, black, and orange. They can also be round, barrel-shaped, pointed, and flat. As well as being good to eat – either sweet or intensely fiery – they are often highly ornamental, and are easy to grow as long as they have enough warmth.

	SPRING	SUMMER	AUTUMN	WINTER
SOW/PLANT				
HARVEST				

SOWING

Peppers will thrive in containers, as long as these contain fertile soil and are large enough to sustain them. Before planting, dig in plenty of well-rotted manure or compost, and apply some general fertilizer.

Sow seed in early spring. Scatter it thinly and cover with a thin layer of soil; it will need a minimum temperature of around 18–25°C (64–77°F). Transfer the seedlings into individual pots as soon as they are large enough to be handled. They need warmth and light, must not get crowded, and will need liquid fertilizer when roots appear at the bottom of the container.

When the seedlings have filled their pots with roots, plant them

Plant peppers out after hardening off.

in a greenhouse, or move them outside and protect with cloches or fleece if necessary. Allow 38–45cm (15–18in) between plants.

CROP CARE

Water to keep the root zone moist. Plants usually branch naturally but it will be necessary to pinch out the growing tips to induce bushy growth. Support plants with canes and string,

as otherwise plants can topple under the weight of their fruits.

HARVESTING

Peppers change colour as they ripen, from green to a range of colours. Harvest when green and unripe, or leave to ripen fully. Ripe fruits have a richer, sweeter flavour but the overall yield can be reduced by leaving them.

STORING

Less fleshy forms of peppers, especially hot chillies, can be dried for long term storage. Otherwise, use sweet peppers as soon as possible after picking.

PESTS AND DISEASES

Peppers can be attacked by sap-sucking insects such as capsid bugs or aphids, or by caterpillars. Biological controls are effective in greenhouses but insecticides might be required outdoors. Pick off any caterpillars that you find and apply an appropriate insecticide if necessary. Few diseases affect peppers but fungal rots might require control. To ensure healthy plants, practise good garden hygiene and ensure that plants are kept well ventilated, especially if you are growing them in a greenhouse.

'Friggitello' ♀

This excellent sweet pepper bears numerous, long, thin, horn-shaped fruits, which ripen from green to red. The yield is moderate, but fruits have a very sweet flavour and pickle well. Plants may need greenhouse protection in cool regions.

🪴 suitable for containers
🌱 spring to summer
✳️ some resistance
❄️ not hardy
🔒 late summer to early autumn

'Gourmet' ♀

This sweet variety bears good yields of blocky fruits that are fleshy and sweetly flavoured, ripening from green to bright orange. The plants are compact and suit container cultivation. They are best for warmer regions or for cultivation in a greenhouse.

🪴 suitable for containers
🌱 spring to summer
✳️ some resistance
❄️ not hardy
🔒 late summer to early autumn

'Corno di Toro Rosso' ♀

This non-hybrid, sweet pepper bears long, horn-shaped fruits, which ripen from pale green to strong red. The fruits are fleshy and well-flavoured; quality is excellent but yield is often moderate. Slow to mature, plants are best suited to a greenhouse.

🪴 suitable for containers
🌱 spring to summer
✳️ some resistance
❄️ not hardy
🔒 late summer to early autumn

'Mohawk'

Abundant, medium-sized fruits are borne on compact plants, which are ideally suited to a container or windowsill. The peppers ripen from green to yellow with fair flavour, but tend to be thin-walled. The plants are, reliable even in cooler regions.

 suitable for containers
spring to summer
some resistance
not hardy
late summer to early autumn

'Marconi'

Also known as 'Red Marconi' or 'Marconi Rosso', this long-established, Italian sweet pepper bears long, thin, rather thin-walled fruits that ripen from green to red. It is a good variety for hot regions but will need protection in cooler areas.

suitable for containers
spring to summer
some resistance
not hardy
late summer to early autumn

'Giallo d'Asti'

Also known as 'Quadrato Giallo d'Asti', this long-established Italian variety bears large, sweet, blocky fruits that ripen yellow from green. In cooler regions, the fruits are best grown in a greenhouse in order to develop the richest yellow colour.

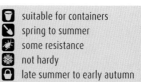 suitable for containers
spring to summer
some resistance
not hardy
late summer to early autumn

'Gypsy' ♀

This hybrid sweet pepper bears long, green, fleshy fruits that ripen to bright red. Quality and flavour are excellent and, in greenhouses or hot areas, yields are very good. The plants are compact and are well suited to greenhouses or containers.

🪣	suitable for containers
🟥	spring to summer
✳	some resistance
❄	not hardy
🔒	late summer to early autumn

'Sweet Orange Baby'

This highly ornamental, sweet variety bears many small, conical fruits on compact plants. The fruits ripen from green to bright orange, with good flavour. It suits pot cultivation and will thrive in any warm site, but protection is advisable in cooler areas.

🪣	suitable for containers
🟥	spring to summer
✳	some resistance
❄	not hardy
🔒	late summer to early autumn

'California Wonder'

This non-hybrid sweet pepper produces large, blocky, fleshy fruits that ripen from green to red. The plants will do best in warm regions and may require protection in cooler areas in order to produce a good yield.

🪣	suitable for containers
🟥	spring to summer
✳	some resistance
❄	not hardy
🔒	late summer to early autumn

'Bell Boy' ♀

This conventional sweet pepper bears very heavy crops of blocky, fleshy fruits, which ripen from bright green to glistening red. Early, and with unusually good tolerance of cool conditions, this variety has very good cropping potential both indoors and out.

- suitable for containers
- spring to summer
- some resistance
- not hardy
- late summer to early autumn

'Ariane' ♀

This hybrid sweet pepper produces heavy, early crops of sweet, fleshy, blocky fruits, which ripen from green to orange. Plants grow to 75cm (30in) tall, and have an open, easy-to-manage habit. They are well adapted to cooler regions.

- suitable for containers
- spring to summer
- some resistance
- not hardy
- late summer to early autumn

'Alma Paprika'

This non-hybrid, paprika pepper is not sweet, but neither is it burning hot. The delightful, round fruits have thick walls and ripen from creamy-white through orange to a deep red. Plants are best suited to warmer regions.

- suitable for containers
- spring to summer
- some resistance
- not hardy
- late summer to early autumn

'Ferrari'

This hybrid sweet pepper bears good yields of medium-sized, blocky fruits that ripen red from green. The plants are tall and will require staking. This robust variety tolerates cool climates, but prefers warmer regions or greenhouse cultivation.

- suitable for containers
- spring to summer
- some resistance
- not hardy
- late summer to early autumn

'Sweet Chocolate'

This early, non-hybrid sweet pepper produces large, blocky, fleshy fruits that ripen from green to brown; their flavour is sweet. The plants are well adapted to regions with short summers, but perform best in greenhouses in cooler areas.

- suitable for containers
- spring to summer
- some resistance
- not hardy
- late summer to early autumn

'Big Banana'

This hybrid sweet pepper bears long, fleshy fruits that ripen from green to red. Peppers can be up to 25cm (10in) in length, making them excellent for stuffing. Plants are likely to do best in warmer regions and will require protection in cooler areas.

- suitable for containers
- spring to summer
- some resistance
- not hardy
- late summer to early autumn

'Purple Beauty'

This non-hybrid sweet pepper
produces medium-sized, blocky
fruits that ripen early through
purple to red. The plants are
compact and bushy and the
fruits fleshy and well-flavoured.
As it is early maturing, this
pepper can be grown in cool
as well as hot regions.

🪣 suitable for containers

🌱 spring to summer

🕷 some resistance

❄ not hardy

🔒 late summer to early autumn

'Ace'

An early, hybrid sweet pepper,
'Ace' forms many blocky fruits,
which ripen from green to red;
quality and flavour are excellent.
The plants are very tolerant
of cooler growing conditions
although greenhouse protection
may sometimes be needed.

🪣 suitable for containers

🌱 spring to summer

🕷 some resistance

❄ not hardy

🔒 late summer to early autumn

'Red Knight'

This early, hybrid sweet pepper
bears very large, blocky fruits,
which ripen from dark green to
strong red. Plants are a moderate
size and have a higher than usual
disease resistance. Best for hot
regions, they may require a
greenhouse in cooler areas.

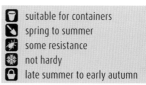

🪣 suitable for containers

🌱 spring to summer

🕷 some resistance

❄ not hardy

🔒 late summer to early autumn

'Cherry bomb'

This fast-growing variety bears large, 7cm (2½in) long, rounded fruits, which ripen to red with a moderately hot taste. The peppers are good for stuffing or using in cooking. The plants crop heavily and produce fruits early, even in cooler regions.

- suitable for containers
- spring to summer
- some resistance
- not hardy
- late summer to early autumn

'Aji Amarillo'

This non-hybrid chilli is more a type than a variety, originating in Peru. The plants are medium size and carry long, thin, very hot peppers ripening from green through yellow to red. It is best suited to hot regions or to greenhouses in cooler areas.

- suitable for containers
- spring to summer
- some resistance
- not hardy
- late summer to early autumn

'Long Thin Cayenne'

This tall, non-hybrid chilli produces long, thin, very hot fruits that ripen from green to glistening red. Peppers are attractive and excellent for drying. This variety does best in regions with hot summers, but is also reliable in cooler areas.

- suitable for containers
- spring to summer
- some resistance
- not hardy
- late summer to early autumn

'Ring O' Fire'

The fiery, long, thin chillis of this variety ripen from green to bright red on tall, bushy plants. Quick-growing, prolific, and tolerant of cooler conditions, the plants respond well to sun and warmth. Fruits dry well and have great ornamental value.

 suitable for containers
spring to summer
some resistance
not hardy
late summer to early autumn

'Meek and Mild'

This non-hybrid chilli produces large, deep green fruits ripening to deep red. Fruits have very little heat and some sweetness, so are good for stuffing or eating raw. Plants are reliable even in cooler climates, and suit container cultivation.

suitable for containers
spring to summer
some resistance
not hardy
late summer to early autumn

'Firecracker'

This very hot chilli produces many upright peppers that ripen from white to purple, through orange then finally red. The tall plants will need staking and are well suited to container growing, even in cooler regions.

suitable for containers
spring to summer
some resistance
not hardy
late summer to early autumn

'Fiesta' ♀

This attractive variety bears abundant, small, conical fruits that ripen from purple, through yellow and orange to intense, glistening red. The compact plants are well suited to container cultivation, and are reliable even in cooler regions.

- 🪣 suitable for containers
- 🌱 spring to summer
- ✻ some resistance
- ❄ not hardy
- 🔒 late summer to early autumn

'Super Chili' ♀

This fiery-hot chilli bears huge numbers of small, very attractive fruits which ripen from pale green to bright red. The fruits are ideal for drying. The compact plant is highly ornamental and is well suited to patio pots, even in regions with cool summers.

- 🪣 suitable for containers
- 🌱 spring to summer
- ✻ some resistance
- ❄ not hardy
- 🔒 late summer to early autumn

'Tricolor Variegatum' ♀

This variegated, non-hybrid chilli bears green leaves splashed with cream and purple. The hot fruits are small and numerous, maturing from purple to orange and finally red. The plants are tall and suited to pots; they are good even in cooler regions.

- 🪣 suitable for containers
- 🌱 spring to summer
- ✻ some resistance
- ❄ not hardy
- 🔒 late summer to early autumn

'Apache' ♀

This ornamental chilli has a bushy habit and bears numerous small, fleshy, hot peppers that ripen from deep green to bright red. The fruits point outwards from the stems and are very decorative. Plants are reliable even in cool regions.

- 🪣 suitable for containers
- 🌱 spring to summer
- ✻ some resistance
- ❄ not hardy
- 🔒 late summer to early autumn

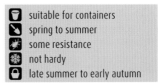

'Super Chili'

'Prairie Fire' ♀

These spreading, dwarf plants thrive even in cooler regions, producing prolific clusters of small and fiery upright fruits, ripening from white through yellow and orange before finally becoming red. The plants are ideal for containers or windowsills.

- suitable for containers
- spring to summer
- some resistance
- not hardy
- late summer to early autumn

'Cayenne'

This non-hybrid, traditional chilli, is more a type than, strictly speaking, a variety. The long, thin, hot fruits may be green, red, or other colours, and are borne abundantly when grown in warm sunny conditions. They are well suited to drying.

- suitable for containers
- spring to summer
- some resistance
- not hardy
- late summer to early autumn

'Tabasco'

This bushy, traditional chilli, bears numerous very small but fiery fruits ripening from pale green to bright red. The plants are best suited to regions with hot summers, or in cooler areas, to greenhouse cultivation.

- suitable for containers
- spring to summer
- some resistance
- not hardy
- late summer to early autumn

'Etna' ♀

This compact, non-hybrid variety bears prolific clusters of upright chillis that mature from green to fiery, glistening red, with corresponding hotness. The robust plants suit container cultivation and will thrive in any reasonably warm environment.

- suitable for containers
- spring to summer
- some resistance
- not hardy
- late summer to early autumn

'Demon Red' ♀

This non-hybrid chilli is bred to grow in pots and on windowsills. It has a very compact habit but is covered in short, thin, pointed fruits that ripen from green to bright red, and are very hot to the taste. The plants are robust and reliable, even in cooler regions.

- suitable for containers
- spring to summer
- some resistance
- not hardy
- late summer to early autumn

'Jalapeno'

This early-cropping chilli is easy to grow and is reliable even in regions with cool, wet summers. The narrowly conical fruits ripen from clear green to fiery red but their flavour is relatively mild; they can even be eaten raw. Yields are relatively modest.

- suitable for containers
- spring to summer
- some resistance
- not hardy
- late summer to early autumn

'Anaheim'

This non-hybrid chilli grows fairly tall and carries heavy crops of very large, bright red fruits that ripen from green. They have mild heat and good flavour. It is best suited to warm regions, or to greenhouse cultivation in cooler areas.

- suitable for containers
- spring to summer
- some resistance
- not hardy
- late summer to early autumn

'Hungarian Hot Wax' ♀

This non-hybrid chilli variety bears long, conical fruits, which ripen from pale yellow to bright red. The peppers have moderate heat and are good for stuffing or using in salads. The plants tolerate cool growing conditions and will perform well in containers.

- suitable for containers
- spring to summer
- some resistance
- not hardy
- late summer to early autumn

'Friar's Hat'

This hot, non-hybrid chilli bears highly unusual, bell-shaped, lobed, medium-sized fruits that ripen from green to red and are exceptionally eye-catching. The tall plants are best suited to hot regions; grow in a greenhouse elsewhere.

- suitable for containers
- spring to summer
- some resistance
- not hardy
- late summer to early autumn

'Habanero' ♀

Strictly speaking, this chilli is a type rather than a variety. It bears rounded, green fruits with pointed ends, which usually ripen to red, but are sometimes orange or yellow. The very hot fruits are borne on medium-sized plants.

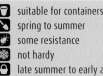

- suitable for containers
- spring to summer
- some resistance
- not hardy
- late summer to early autumn

'Filius Blue' ♀

This fiery, non-hybrid chilli
bears white flowers, followed
by unusual, small, blue fruits
that ripen through pale green to
purple, finally becoming red. The
vigorous plants are medium-sized
and highly ornamental, and are
well suited to cooler regions
and container growing.

 suitable for containers
spring to summer
some resistance
not hardy
late summer to early autumn

'Padron'

Also known as 'Pimiento de
Padron', this traditional, non-
hybrid chilli is originally from
Spain. The small fruits ripen
from green to red; some can be
very hot indeed, although others
are on the mild side. It grows best
in regions with hot summers.

suitable for containers
spring to summer
some resistance
not hardy
late summer to early autumn

'Ciliegia Piccante'

Originating in Italy, this
attractive chilli bears numerous,
cherry-sized fruits of moderate
heat, which reduces on cooking.
Fruits are prominently borne
on bushy plants, and are best in
hot regions but also suit cooler
regions if grown in a greenhouse.

suitable for containers
spring to summer
some resistance
not hardy
late summer to early autumn

AUBERGINES *Solanum melongena*

Also known as "egg plants" or "brinjal", these variable fruits come in
a wide range of shapes, sizes, and colours. They are easy to grow, but
won't do well in cold conditions and will be killed by frost; in cool regions,
they are best in a greenhouse. Although young plants are widely sold and
are a good choice for gardeners without the warm conditions needed to
raise seedlings, a wider range of varieties are offered as seed.

	SPRING	SUMMER	AUTUMN	WINTER
SOW/PLANT				
HARVEST				

SOWING

Sow aubergine seed from early
spring onwards, ensuring a
minimum temperature of
between 18–25°C (64–77°F).
For optimum growth, seedlings
need ample warmth and light,
and must not get crowded.
Plant them out into individual
containers as soon as possible.

Plant out seedlings after hardening off.

Before transplanting, enrich
soil, indoors or out, by digging
in a 5cm (2in) layer of rotted
organic matter and, in poor
soils, apply a generous amount
of general-purpose fertilizer.
A warm, sheltered, sunny site
is essential outdoors, and young
seedlings may need protection
with a cloche or a layer of
horticultural fleece. Aubergine
plants thrive in containers, and
fruit set is often enhanced if
these are not too large.

CROP CARE

During growth, pinch out the
growing tips to induce bushy
growth. Plants can produce large
numbers of fruits, so support
them with string and canes to
prevent damage. The plants
are self-pollinating and do not
require assistance to set fruits.

Greenhouse crops respond to warmer conditions than other tender plants, and benefit from being grown under a fleece tent. They are vulnerable to rotting if conditions are humid and cool. Water plants during dry periods. They will need feeding with liquid fertilizer as they grow. Overripe peppers nearby may suppress the formation of subsequent fruits.

HARVESTING

Gather fruits once they have attained their full colour and stop growing in size. If left too long, they cease to be glossy and lose their colour.

PESTS AND DISEASES

Pests such as whitefly, red spider mite, or caterpillars may be troublesome in greenhouses. Pick off any caterpillars as you see them. Outdoors you may need to apply an appropriate insecticide.

Soil-grown plants are at risk from verticillium wilt. This disease causes wilting and eventual death. Remove and destroy any infected plant material. To reduce the risk of infection, buy plants grafted onto disease-resistant tomato rootstock, and practise good garden hygiene.

'Fairy Tale' ♀

This unusual hybrid aubergine bears long, thin fruits, striped with white and purple and are often carried in clusters. The compact plants are well suited to growing in containers, growing bags, and pots on the patio, and often do well in cooler regions.

	suitable for containers
	spring
	some resistance
	not hardy
	summer

'Bonica' ♀

This tall, hybrid standard-type variety has excellent vigour and is highly productive, even in cooler regions. The lofty plants produce excellent-quality fruits and are suitable for container or soil cultivation, indoors or outdoors, but will need supports.

	suitable for containers
	spring
	some resistance
	not hardy
	summer

'Moneymaker'

This very robust and cold-tolerant hybrid variety bears slightly elongated and rather pointed fruits of good flavour. It is well suited to both cool and warm regions, and can yield well outdoors in hot summers. It is best suited to greenhouse use.

	suitable for containers
	spring
	poor resistance
	not hardy
	summer

'Mini Bambino'

This novelty plant produces numerous glossy, dark, attractive fruits. Although the small size and limited yield make it a poor choice for the kitchen, it is a decorative, highly ornamental vegetable and is especially prized by children. It is suited to both soil and pot growing.

- suitable for containers
- spring
- poor resistance
- not hardy
- summer

'Turkish Orange'

This traditional non-hybrid variety produces highly unusual fruits that are small but numerous and have a sweet flavour. This variety is only suitable for warm conditions, so grow it under plastic or glass in cold regions, or outdoors in hot areas.

- suitable for containers
- spring
- poor resistance
- not hardy
- summer

'Black Enorma'

This hybrid variety produces good yields of fruits that are especially large, with glossy skins and pleasant texture and flavour. The plants are vigorous, making them well-suited to either indoor or outdoor cultivation, in open ground or in borders.

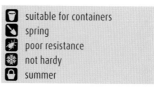

- suitable for containers
- spring
- poor resistance
- not hardy
- summer

'Applegreen'

This novelty, heirloom, non-hybrid variety produces moderate yields of egg-like, apple-green fruits even when conditions are not ideal. The small fruits are tender and of good flavour. It does best in hot regions and should be grown in greenhouses elsewhere.

- suitable for containers
- spring
- poor resistance
- not hardy
- summer

'Prosperosa'

This non-hybrid, traditional variety originates in Italy. The fruits are small and almost spherical. They are of good quality and their pale purple colour is unusual; they are well worth growing for ornamental value. Greenhouse cultivation is best in areas without hot summers.

- suitable for containers
- spring
- poor resistance
- not hardy
- summer

'Galine' ♀

This hybrid standard-type variety bears heavy crops of large, attractively glossy, purple fruits. It is best suited to indoor cultivation in cooler areas. The plants are relatively compact and easily managed, although some staking is required.

- suitable for containers
- spring
- some resistance
- not hardy
- summer

'Long Purple'

This long-established, rather variable, non-hybrid aubergine is widely and inexpensively sold, and has stood the test of time. Although it is not the heaviest cropper, it is reliable, producing long, good-quality violet rather than purple fruits.

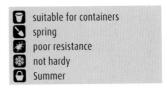

- suitable for containers
- spring
- poor resistance
- not hardy
- Summer

'Rosa Bianca'

This non-hybrid variety bears round, almost ball-shaped fruits that become pink-purple in colour, with a good flavour and texture. It is best grown in warm regions or indoors, and being highly ornamental, it is very good for container cultivation.

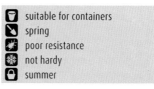

- suitable for containers
- spring
- poor resistance
- not hardy
- summer

'Snowy'

This non-hybrid variety bears medium-sized, white fruits that are highly ornamental but also have good flavour and texture. 'Snowy' can be grown indoors in cool regions or outside in warmer areas. It is highly suited to growing in containers.

- suitable for containers
- spring
- poor resistance
- not hardy
- summer

'Ova'

This variety bears numerous small, white, egg-shaped fruits on compact, robust plants with sturdy stems and foliage. Fruit quality is fair, but plants are more usually grown for their ornamental qualities. Suitable for containers, it needs little staking.

- suitable for containers
- spring
- poor resistance
- not hardy
- summer

'Slim Jim'

This non-hybrid variety produces long, thin, glossy purple fruits of good flavour and texture, which are borne in abundance if grown in warm conditions. 'Slim Jim' is best grown indoors in cool regions but is well-suited to outdoor growing in hot areas.

🪴	suitable for containers
🡖	spring
✳	poor resistance
❄	not hardy
🔒	summer

'Falcon'

This early, hybrid, standard-type variety bears heavy crops of large, smooth, spine-free fruits of an almost black, deep purple colour. It is best suited to indoor cultivation but grows well outdoors in warmer regions. The compact plants require staking.

🪴	suitable for containers
🡖	spring
✳	some resistance
❄	not hardy
🔒	summer

'Listada de Gandia'

This traditional, non-hybrid variety from Italy carries rounded, white- and purple-streaked, well-flavoured fruits on medium-sized plants. The attractive plants are ornamental, and should be grown indoors in areas with cool summers.

🪴	suitable for containers
🡖	spring
✳	poor resistance
❄	not hardy
🔒	summer

'Black Beauty'

This standard-type variety produces good-quality, pear-shaped, dark fruits of good texture and flavour. Being non-hybrid it has modest yields and vigour, and although it will grow in all situations it is best suited for warm regions or indoor cultivation.

- suitable for containers
- spring
- poor resistance
- not hardy
- summer

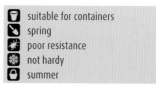

'Violetta Lunga'

This non-hybrid, standard type bears large, glossy, purple fruits and attractive leaves. Plants are robust and medium-sized, and are suitable for indoor cultivation in cool regions, or outdoors in warm areas. It is well suited to growing in containers.

- suitable for containers
- spring
- poor resistance
- not hardy
- summer

'Thai Green'

This non-hybrid variety produces unusual, long, green fruits much used in Thai cuisine. It is suitable for soil or container cultivation but requires warm conditions; it will only grow under glass or plastic in all but the warmest, sunniest regions.

- suitable for containers
- spring
- poor resistance
- not hardy
- summer

SWEETCORN *Zea mays*

Sweetcorn grows easily in warm regions, but good crops are possible in cooler areas if seed is sown under cover. Supersweet corn is the most common type, retaining its very sweet flavour after picking. Extra Tendersweet corn is also very sweet, and widely grown, while hybrid, "synergistic" corn combines the best of both. Baby corn can be grown on closely spaced plants or by using special varieties.

	SPRING	SUMMER	AUTUMN	WINTER
SOW/PLANT				
HARVEST				

SOWING

Any fertile garden soil in full sun is suitable. Dig in plenty of well-rotted manure before planting, and supplement this with an application of general liquid fertilizer. Add lime if soils are acidic. Being wind pollinated, sweetcorn is best raised in squares rather than rows.

Raise early crops by sowing seed under cover, two seeds per small container, at a depth of 2.5–4cm (1–1½in), keeping them at a minimum temperature of 20–20°C (68–81°F). Seedlings can be singled out once they have started to develop. Plant them out in late spring or early summer, and protect them with cloches or fleece if the weather is cold. Ensure that plants have

Plant out seedlings from late spring.

enough space – about 40cm (16in) between plants in the case of full-size corn. Where baby corn is being grown, allow 15cm (6in) between plants, and 30cm (12in) between rows.

If sowing directly into the ground, do so from mid-spring onwards. Sow three seeds for each plant and then thin out later if required. Subsequent crops can be sown every two weeks until

early summer. Bear in mind that cross pollination from nearby agricultural or ornamental corns, or between standard and sweeter types of sweetcorn, will lead to a loss of sweetness.

CROP CARE

Keep plants well weeded, and ensure that they are given plenty of water in dry spells, particularly once flowering begins.

HARVESTING

Gather cobs once the silky parts brown, and the kernels exude a milky juice when split. Once harvested, use as soon as possible.

PESTS AND DISEASES

Exclude birds from cobs using netting, or by covering cobs with plastic bags. Be aware that large mammals may trample plants and eat the cobs, and birds or mice may eat ungerminated seeds, so protect after sowing. Smut disease can cause distorted cobs.

Protect cobs to prevent attack.

'Marshall's Honeydew' ♀

This extra tender variety produces medium-sized, sturdy plants, bearing strong foliage, and medium-sized, well-filled cobs of good texture and flavour. They mature in the mid- to late season period and are suitable for all good garden soils, even in cooler regions.

🪣	unsuitable for containers
🌱	spring
🐞	some resistance
❄️	not hardy
🔒	summer to autumn

'Mirai 302BC' ♀

This hybrid supersweet corn has an unusual mixture of white and yellow kernels, and has good sweetness, tenderness, and flavour. Plants are tall and vigorous, so are not best suited to windy locations.

🪣	unsuitable for containers
🌱	spring
🐞	some resistance
❄️	not hardy
🔒	summer to autumn

'Lapwing' ♀

This heavy-cropping, tendersweet variety bears very sweet and tender, bright yellow kernels in large, elongated, well-filled cobs that mature early to midseason. The plants are robust and will tolerate a wide range of growing conditions.

🪣	unsuitable for containers
🌱	spring
🐞	some resistance
❄️	not hardy
🔒	summer to autumn

'Sundance' ♀

This standard-type variety matures early and is well suited to cooler regions and to areas where the growing season is short. The long cobs have a sweet flavour, good texture, and are filled with cream-coloured kernels. Plants are short but sturdy.

- 🪣 unsuitable for containers
- 🍃 spring
- 🐞 some resistance
- ❄ not hardy
- 🔒 summer

'Northern Extra Sweet' ♀

This exceptionally early-maturing, supersweet type bears long cobs filled with large, flavourful kernels. It is excellent for cooler locations, and for early crops in warm regions. It grows to medium height and is therefore suited to exposed sites.

- 🪣 unsuitable for containers
- 🍃 spring
- 🐞 some resistance
- ❄ not hardy
- 🔒 summer

'Sweet Nugget'

This supersweet variety matures in mid-season, producing large and succulent kernels on medium-sized plants with strong green foliage. This variety grows well in cooler regions and is reliable under a wide range of soil, site, and climatic conditions.

- 🪣 unsuitable for containers
- 🍃 spring
- 🐞 some resistance
- ❄ not hardy
- 🔒 summer to autumn

'Serendipity Hybrid'

This US-only, mid-season hybrid is well suited to cultivation in regions with hot summers. The white and yellow kernels are carried in large cobs and combine the sugary sweetness of supersweets with the succulent texture of sugar-enhanced types.

- unsuitable for containers
- spring
- some resistance
- not hardy
- summer to autumn

'Dynasty' ♀

This tall, supersweet variety produces sturdy growth, strong foliage, and long, large, well-filled cobs of good texture and flavour. 'Dynasty' matures in the mid- to late season period and is suitable for cooler regions.

- unsuitable for containers
- spring
- some resistance
- not hardy
- summer to autumn

'Incredible'

This sugar-enhanced, mid-season variety can produce heavy crops when grown in a wide range of conditions. The cobs are large and sweet, although less so than supersweet types. It is well-suited to sowing in colder regions as it will tolerate cool soils.

- unsuitable for containers
- spring
- poor resistance
- not hardy
- summer to autumn

'Honey Select Hybrid'

This US-only, mid-season hybrid combines the sugary sweetness and full flavour of super sweets with the tender crunchiness of sugar-enhanced corn. The cobs are filled with yellow grains, which are outstandingly sweet and tender.

- unsuitable for containers
- spring
- some resistance
- not hardy
- summer to autumn

'Minipop'

This specialist variety is grown for the sole purpose of producing baby corn and so is unsuitable for other uses. Several cobs are produced on the vigorous, easy-to-grow plants, which often produce more than one stem. Sow the seed closely.

- unsuitable for containers
- spring
- some resistance
- not hardy
- summer to autumn

'Sugar Buns Hybrid'

This early-maturing, US-only hybrid variety produces long ears filled with large, yellow kernels, carried on tall, vigorous plants. The cobs have the excellent, sweet flavour and tender texture typical of this type, and suit regions with warm summers.

- unsuitable for containers
- spring
- some resistance
- not hardy
- summer to autumn

'Prelude' ♀

This medium-sized, supersweet variety has exceptionally vigorous, sturdy growth and produces high yields of large, well-filled cobs of excellent texture and flavour. Maturing in the mid-season period, it suits a wide range of conditions.

- unsuitable for containers
- spring
- some resistance
- not hardy
- summer to autumn

'Country Gentleman'

This US-only, late-maturing, non-hybrid variety has long been grown in warmer regions, where it thrives best. It produces creamy-white kernels of moderate sweetness. In the right climate it will produce more than one shoot, each bearing a cob.

- unsuitable for containers
- spring
- some resistance
- not hardy
- summer to autumn

'Strawberry Popcorn'

This charming ornamental corn bears small, round, attractive cobs of rich, red grains that look similar to strawberries. The dried cobs make good ornaments and the grains can be popped. It should be grown away from other corn or maize.

- unsuitable for containers
- spring
- some resistance
- not hardy
- summer to autumn

'Brocade F1'

This US-only, mid-season, sugar-enhanced variety produces long, heavy cobs full of tender, sweet, and flavourful kernels. Plants are tall and vigorous, and grow best in warmer regions, where their disease tolerance is especially useful.

- unsuitable for containers
- spring
- good resistance
- not hardy
- summer to autumn

'Luscious F1'

This US-only, hybrid, sugar-enhanced corn produces heavy, very sweet and tender heads, filled with yellow and white kernels. The tall, vigorous plants suit regions with hot summers as they tolerate the leaf diseases often found in these areas.

- unsuitable for containers
- spring
- some resistance
- not hardy
- summer to autumn

'Strawberry Popcorn'

'Jubilee'

This excellent-quality variety produces large cobs that are up to 20cm (8in) in length, filled with sweet, tender, vibrant yellow kernels. The delicious cobs freeze well, and are borne on tall, fast-ripening plants.

 unsuitable for containers
spring
some resistance
not hardy
summer to autumn

'Honey Bantam'

This standard, bicoloured type produces yellow and white grains in large cobs. It has excellent texture, and good flavour for its type. The robust plants are well suited for early crops in cooler regions, or where summers are rainy rather than warm.

 unsuitable for containers
spring
some resistance
not hardy
summer to autumn

'Butterscotch'

This is as early-maturing, supersweet-type, F1 hybrid, producing tender kernels that are excellent, even after freezing. Growing to just 1.5m (5ft) tall, it is suitable for cooler, exposed gardens. Grow in good, free-draining soil.

 unsuitable for containers
spring
some resistance
not hardy
summer to autumn

'Earligold'

This early, standard-type, F1 variety is highly reliable for early crops, even in cooler regions. It is medium-sized, with fast growth, strong foliage, and large, well-filled cobs of good texture and flavour. It has the good texture that is typical of standard types.

 unsuitable for containers
spring
some resistance
not hardy
summer to autumn

'Swift'

An extra tender type, this variety produces medium-sized heads filled with succulent, sweet, bright yellow grains. The robust plants mature especially early' reliably bearing heavy crops, even in cooler regions, under a wide range of conditions.

- unsuitable for containers
- spring
- some resistance
- not hardy
- summer to autumn

'Inca Rainbow'

This is an unusual heritage variety that produces distinctive single- or multi-coloured cobs, made up of red, white, yellow, and purple kernels. It reaches 2.5m (8ft) high and needs a long, hot growing season for the best crop. Treat it as a novelty.

- unsuitable for containers
- spring
- some resistance
- not hardy
- summer to autumn

'Bodacious Hybrid'

This US-only, sugar-enhanced variety is early to mature, producing long, good-quality cobs filled with sweet, yellow, tender grains. It has good rust tolerance, and is suitable for cooler regions and where the growing season is short.

- unsuitable for containers
- spring
- some resistance
- not hardy
- summer to autumn

'Sugar Pearl Hybrid'

The white kernels of this "synergistic", US-only hybrid combine the sweet, full flavour of supersweet types with the tender succulence of sugar-enhanced corn. Best suited for regions with hot summers, the tall, vigorous plants mature late in the season.

- unsuitable for containers
- spring
- some resistance
- not hardy
- summer to autumn

'Earlibird' ♀

This tall, supersweet type produces sturdy growth, strong foliage, and even, well-filled cobs of good texture and flavour. Despite its name, 'Earlibird' matures in the mid- to late season period. It is especially suitable for cooler regions.

- unsuitable for containers
- spring
- some resistance
- not hardy
- summer to autumn

'Stowell's'

This US-only, standard-type variety is well suited to regions with hot summers. It matures late, producing sweet, tender, white kernels. The cobs remain milky for a prolonged period, so this variety is also referred to as 'Stowells's Evergreen'.

- unsuitable for containers
- spring
- some resistance
- not hardy
- summer to autumn

'Mirai 421W' ♀

This supersweet type produces long ears filled with white kernels with a high sugar content, and exceptional flavour and tenderness. Plants are early-maturing, vigorous, tall, and leafy. Site in full sun and give them plenty of warmth.

- unsuitable for containers
- spring
- some resistance
- not hardy
- summer to autumn

'Seville' ♀

This tall, supersweet, late-season variety produces vigorous, sturdy growth, strong foliage, and excellent-quality, large, well-filled cobs. The kernels are small and of good texture and flavour. It is suitable for cooler regions, but fertile soils are required for the best cobs.

 unsuitable for containers
spring
some resistance
not hardy
summer to autumn

'Early Sunglow Hybrid'

This early-maturing, US-only hybrid variety produces heads of yellow grains, with moderate sweetness and storage ability, but good tenderness. Satisfactory for cooler regions but best in warm areas, plants are robust with strong green foliage and husks.

unsuitable for containers
spring
some resistance
not hardy
summer to autumn

'Conqueror' ♀

This tall, vigorous, supersweet variety of sweetcorn produces long cobs with sweet and tender kernels. It copes well with a wide range of conditions, and despite being late-maturing, is especially well-adapted to cooler regions.

unsuitable for containers
spring
some resistance
not hardy
summer to autumn

'Avalon Hybrid'

This US-only hybrid bears large cobs and combines the best of supersweet and sugar-enhanced corns, resulting in very sweet, tender kernels. Like supersweets, flavour is retained well after harvest, but like sugar-enhanced, ears need gentle handling.

- unsuitable for containers
- spring
- some resistance
- not hardy
- summer to autumn

'Lark' ♀

This tall, mid-season, tendersweet variety produces sturdy growth, strong foliage, and medium-sized, well-filled cobs. The kernels are bright yellow and of excellent texture and flavour. It is suitable for cooler regions and all good garden soils.

- unsuitable for containers
- spring
- some resistance
- not hardy
- summer to autumn

'Silver Queen Hybrid'

This US-only, standard-type hybrid produces exceptionally long and heavy ears, which mature early and are filled with glistening white kernels. It is well suited to regions with hot summers as it has resistance to diseases common to these areas.

- unsuitable for containers
- spring
- some resistance
- not hardy
- summer to autumn

'Sparrow' ♀

This stocky, mid-season sweetcorn is a tendersweet type. It produces sturdy growth, strong foliage, and medium-sized, well-filled cobs of excellent texture and flavour. Suitable for a wide range of conditions, this variety will thrive in cooler regions.

- unsuitable for containers
- spring
- some resistance
- not hardy
- summer to autumn

'Lark'

Cucumbers and Squashes

- Cucumbers
- Courgettes, Marrows, and Summer squashes
- Pumpkins and Winter squashes

CUCUMBERS *Cucumus sativus*

You can grow a cucumber no matter how small your garden: if you have
limited space, grow a trailing outdoor variety in a container. Outdoor
cucumbers are hardier than their indoor relatives, with a thicker, more
knobbly skin, and are excellent pickled. If you have the luxury of a
greenhouse you can grow indoor varieties too, which are longer,
with thinner skins, and are good for use in salads or sandwiches.

	SPRING	SUMMER	AUTUMN	WINTER
SOW/PLANT				
HARVEST				

SOWING

Most modern greenhouse
varieties are all-female and it is
important that they are grown
where they cannot be pollinated
by male flowers, as this results in
bitter fruits. Site plants carefully,
and pinch out any male flowers
that appear on indoor types.

Be careful not to damage the roots.

Outdoor cucumbers grow best
in a warm, sunny site, and will
thrive in containers or growing
bags, indoors or out. They need
a rich, well-drained soil, so dig in
well-rotted manure or compost
before sowing or planting out.

Seed can be sown indoors from
early spring onwards; it needs a
minimum temperature of 20°C
(68°F) to germinate. Harden off
and plant out seedlings when
they reach about four weeks old,

taking care not to damage the
roots. Space them 45cm (18in)
apart, allowing more room if
plants are to trail.

Alternatively, warm the soil
with a cloche or cold frame and
sow directly into the ground
from early summer, once the
danger of frost has passed. Sow
two or three seeds together
every 45cm (18in), and thin out
the weakest as they develop.

CROP CARE

Trailing types will need support, so construct bamboo cane structures, or use netting. Give them plenty of water during growth, especially while fruits are developing, and feed them every two weeks with a general liquid fertilizer. You will need to hand-pollinate outdoor types yourself (see p.532).

HARVESTING AND STORING

Harvest while young, as leaving cucumbers too long can spoil the flavour of those left on the plant. Cucumbers do not store, but small ones can be pickled.

PESTS AND DISEASES

Discourage the spread of common diseases such as powdery mildew and cucumber mosaic virus by ensuring that plants are well watered and well ventilated. Red spider mite or whitefly may be troublesome under glass. Guard young plants against slugs.

Red spider mite may mottle leaves.

'Bella'

This strong and vigorous F1 cultivar produces healthy foliage that is resistant to both powdery and downy mildew. It produces a heavy yield of long, slightly ribbed, good-quality, dark green fruits.

- suitable for containers
- early to mid-spring
- good resistance
- not hardy
- late summer to mid-autumn

'Emilie'

This all-female cultivar produces fruits with attractive, smooth, dark green skin, crisp white flesh, and a good flavour. They should be grown under cover and produce fruits of a useful size, at around 20cm (8in). It is resistant to a variety of diseases.

- suitable for containers
- early to mid-spring
- some resistance
- not hardy
- late summer to mid-autumn

'Tanja'

A robust cultivar, 'Tanja' produces heavy yields and crops well over a long period. The fruits are 30cm (12in) or more long, with dark green, smooth, shiny skin, and an appetizing flavour. This is a good choice for containers.

- suitable for containers
- early to mid-spring
- poor resistance
- not hardy
- late summer to mid-autumn

'Marketmore' ♀

This very popular cultivar is normally grown outdoors to produce good yields of medium-sized, attractive, dark green fruits with a few white spines. It is reliable, performing well even in a poor season, and is resistant to powdery and downy mildew.

- 🪣 suitable for containers
- 🌱 early to mid-spring
- 🌼 good resistance
- ❄️ not hardy
- 🔒 late summer to mid-autumn

'Eureka Hybrid'

This strong, indeterminate hybrid has extremely good disease resistance, and produces high yields of very dark green 5–18cm (2–7in) long cucumbers. The trouble-free, US-only 'Eureka' plants are, can be grown on a trellis for easy harvesting.

- 🪣 unsuitable for containers
- 🌱 late spring to early summer
- 🌼 excellent resistance
- ❄️ not hardy
- 🔒 midsummer to early autumn

'Palermo'

An F1 hybrid cultivar, 'Palermo' has good resistance to powdery mildew. It makes a good choice for growing in an unheated greenhouse, producing long, juicy, dark green fruits that are equally good in sandwiches or salads.

- 🪣 suitable for containers
- 🌱 early to mid-spring
- 🌼 some resistance
- ❄️ not hardy
- 🔒 late summer to mid-autumn

'Cucino' ♀

This cultivar produces mini-cucumbers 7–10cm (3–4in) long, ideal for snacks and lunch boxes. The fruits are uniform with thin, smooth, dark green skin and tasty, green flesh. It is highly productive, yielding double the fruits of many other cultivars.

- suitable for containers
- early to mid-spring
- some resistance
- not hardy
- late summer to mid-autumn

'Picolino'

This heavy-cropping F1 cultivar produces medium-sized, crisp, juicy cucumbers around 15–18cm (6–7in) long. A relatively healthy variety, it should be grown under cover, and has good resistance to both powdery and downy mildew.

- suitable for containers
- early to mid-spring
- good resistance
- not hardy
- late summer to mid-autumn

'Boothby's Blonde'

This American heirloom cultivar originated in Maine. The fruits have creamy-white skins flushed with yellow or green, and a scattering of black spines. They are short and fat, best picked at 8–10cm (3–4in) long, and may be used fresh or pickled.

- suitable for containers
- early to mid-spring
- poor resistance
- not hardy
- late summer to mid-autumn

'Crystal Apple'

This interesting, easy-to-grow cultivar produces a large crop of pale, yellow-green, spherical cucumbers that turn deeper yellow with age. The unusual fruits are particularly flavourful and juicy, but are quite seedy in the centre.

- suitable for containers
- early to mid-spring
- poor resistance
- not hardy
- late summer to mid-autumn

'Rocky'

This is an unusually compact F1 cultivar, producing clusters of baby cucumbers close to the main stem. It is early-maturing and likes plenty of warmth, so is ideal for cultivation under cover or in a container on a patio.

- suitable for containers
- early to mid-spring
- some resistance
- not hardy
- late summer to mid-autumn

'Naomi' ♀

This F1 cultivar produces long, straight, slightly ribbed fruits with attractive, dark green skin, and a good flavour. It should be grown under cover and has some resistance to a number of fungal diseases that affect foliage, including powdery mildew.

- suitable for containers
- early to mid-spring
- some resistance
- not hardy
- late summer to mid-autumn

'Masterpiece' ♀

This outdoor, ridge-type cucumber produces heavy yields of dark green, slightly spiny, medium-sized fruits with crisp, white flesh. It is a very reliable cropper, with healthy foliage, and would be a good choice for container cultivation.

- suitable for containers
- early to mid-spring
- some resistance
- not hardy
- late summer to mid-autumn

'White Wonder'

This very old, dual-purpose cultivar dates back to the 1800s and was traditionally used for pickling, although it can also be eaten fresh. It starts to crop early in the season, producing creamy-white fruits that are best picked before they exceed 15cm (6in).

- suitable for containers
- early to mid-spring
- poor resistance
- not hardy
- late summer to mid-autumn

'Zeina' ♀

An F1 hybrid, this cultivar is a very strong grower, and produces a good crop of half-size cucumbers that are ideal for harvesting at around 20cm (8in). The fruits have smooth, bright skin, and sweet, juicy flesh.

- suitable for containers
- early to mid-spring
- some resistance
- not hardy
- late summer to mid-autumn

'Green Fingers'

This F1 hybrid cultivar produces masses of mini cucumbers just 8–10cm (3–4in) long. They have very thin skins, green flesh, a firm, crunchy texture, and are very flavourful. The plants are resistant to powdery and downy mildew.

- suitable for containers
- early to mid-spring
- good resistance
- not hardy
- late summer to mid-autumn

'Tasty King'

A Japanese-bred F1 hybrid cultivar, 'Tasty King' can be grown in an unheated greenhouse, or outdoors. It produces a heavy crop of good-looking, tasty fruits that are longer than average, reaching 40cm (16in) or more.

- suitable for containers
- early to mid-spring
- poor resistance
- not hardy
- late summer to mid-autumn

'Byblos' ♀

This F1 cultivar, named after the ancient Lebanese port, produces a heavy crop of long, uniform, smooth-skinned fruits, with a good, dark green colour and good flavour. The plant is resistant to powdery mildew and cucumber mosaic virus.

- suitable for containers
- early to mid-spring
- good resistance
- not hardy
- late summer to mid-autumn

'Tiffany' ♀

This F1 hybrid cultivar produces a uniform crop of long, slightly ribbed fruits. These have an attractive appearance, with dark green skin and a nice, even shape, which could make them a winner on the show bench. It should be grown under cover.

- suitable for containers
- early to mid-spring
- some resistance
- not hardy
- late summer to mid-autumn

'Burpless Tasty Green'

A Japanese cultivar, 'Burpless Tasty Green' was specially bred to be easy to digest, with a tender skin and no bitterness. The medium to long, dark green fruits have crisp, tasty flesh. It is resistant to powdery mildew.

- suitable for containers
- early to mid-spring
- some resistance
- not hardy
- late summer to mid-autumn

'Socrates' ♀

This reliable cultivar produces an early and prolific crop of small, narrow fruits, about 15cm (6in) long. It is a strong and vigorous grower under cover, and the fruits have smooth, shiny skins and a good flavour.

- suitable for containers
- early to mid-spring
- some resistance
- not hardy
- late summer to mid-autumn

'Passandra'

This cultivar bears prolific crops of high-quality, half-size fruits, ideal for picking at around 15–20cm (6–8in). They have smooth, dark skin and crisp, white flesh. The plants show good resistance to powdery and downy mildews, and cucumber mosaic virus.

- suitable for containers
- early to mid-spring
- good resistance
- not hardy
- late summer to mid-autumn

'Carmen' ♈

This F1 hybrid cultivar produces an abundant crop of long, slightly ribbed fruits with a good, dark green colour and full flavour. It should be grown under cover and has good disease resistance to powdery mildew, downy mildew, scab, and leaf spot.

- suitable for containers
- early to mid-spring
- good resistance
- not hardy
- late summer to mid-autumn

'Cool Breeze Hybrid'

This US-only, French cornichon hybrid is disease-resistant and needs no pollination; vines can be protected from insects right up to harvest time. The nearly 100% female flowers mature early, yielding large numbers of dark green, seedless fruits.

- unsuitable for containers
- late spring to early summer
- good resistance
- not hardy
- midsummer to early autumn

'Mini Munch' ♛

A highly-productive cultivar, 'Mini Munch' produces abundant, small fruits, just 10cm (4in) long. They are shiny-skinned, with a crunchy texture, and good flavour. They make a great snack and are an ideal choice for children's lunch boxes.

- suitable for containers
- early to mid-spring
- some resistance
- not hardy
- late summer to mid-autumn

'La Diva'

This cultivar produces a crop of sweet, tender, crisp fruits with a smooth, thin skin. They average about 15cm (6in) long, and have no seeds. With better than average cold tolerance, this is a good variety for growing outdoors in cooler areas.

- suitable for containers
- early to mid-spring
- poor resistance
- not hardy
- late summer to mid-autumn

'Bedfordshire Prize'

This old, traditional, ridge-type cultivar is also known as 'Long Green Ridge'. It produces high yields of light green fruits, with a ridged and bumpy skin. It has a tendency to become bitter with age, so pick while still young for the best flavour.

- suitable for containers
- early to mid-spring
- poor resistance
- not hardy
- late summer to mid-autumn

'Suyo Long'

This US-only, Asian heirloom produces 38cm (15in) long, slim, "burpless" cucumbers with a sweet flavour and crisp texture. Hardy and productive, even under adverse conditions, it is recommended for hot, humid climates.

- unsuitable for containers
- early to mid-spring
- some resistance
- not hardy
- midsummer to early autumn

'La Diva'

COURGETTES, MARROWS, AND SUMMER SQUASHES *Cucurbita pepo* and *C. moschata*

Easy to grow, these reliable vegetables are fast and prolific croppers. Not all types are long and green – they come in a range of colours and unusual shapes, many of which are highly decorative. Although all types will grow to marrow size, harvest courgettes and squashes when small.

	SPRING	SUMMER	AUTUMN	WINTER
SOW/PLANT				
HARVEST				

SOWING

Courgettes, marrows, and summer squashes all do best in a sunny, open site, with rich, well-drained soil. Dig in some well-rotted manure or compost before sowing or planting.

Seed can be sown from mid-spring onwards: if sowing early, do so in a greenhouse or under cover. Later seed can be sown in pots or in the ground, but will need protection with a cloche or cold frame. Sow seed 45cm (18in) apart, and 2.5cm (1in) deep.

CROP CARE

Developing fruits need regular watering and should not be allowed to dry out, especially when they are flowering, or while the fruits are swelling. They may

It may help to pollinate by hand.

benefit from an application of general fertilizer during growth.

If you are growing under glass, your crops may lack insect pollinators, so you may need to pollinate them by hand. Identify a female flower, one that has the thickened stem of the developing fruit, and transfer pollen from a male flower's stamens onto the stigma, by touching the flowers together.

HARVESTING

Courgettes and summer squashes should be harvested when they are small, at about 10cm (4in) long, when they are at their most flavourful. Regular picking will encourage the plant to produce a greater number of fruits.

Marrows can be harvested when they have reached about 15cm (6in). They can be left to grow much larger, and will develop a thick, protective skin.

STORING

Allow marrows to develop a thick skin. Store any undamaged fruits in a warm, dry place.

PESTS AND DISEASES

Ensuring that plants are well watered and well ventilated will help to prevent the most common diseases: powdery mildew, foot and root rot, and cucumber mosaic virus. You may need to support plants carefully to prevent fruits from becoming cramped. Remove and destroy any infected plant material and, if necessary, apply an appropriate insecticide. Seedlings and developing plants are vulnerable to slugs and snails. Use pellets, set up traps, or lay a line of sand or grit, or copper tape, around the base of your plants.

'Custard White'

A patty-pan squash, this American heirloom cultivar produces creamy-white fruits shaped like a flying saucer with scalloped edges. They have firm flesh and can be picked from 5cm (2in) for slicing, or up to 12cm (5in) for stuffing or baking whole.

- suitable for containers
- early to late spring
- poor resistance
- not hardy
- midsummer to early autumn

'Patriot'

This reliable courgette type starts to crop early and continues over a long period. It will produce well in cool or warm summers. The fruits are attractive, with smooth, shiny, dark green skin. The prickle-free plants make picking easier.

- suitable for containers
- early to late spring
- poor resistance
- not hardy
- midsummer to early autumn

'Rugosa Friulana'

This straightneck squash is a traditional Venetian cultivar, producing pale yellow fruits, bulbous at one end, with warty skin. The flesh is firm with a good flavour, making it suitable for dishes that require a long cooking period.

- unsuitable for containers
- early to late spring
- poor resistance
- not hardy
- midsummer to early autumn

'Gold Rush'

This F1 hybrid, standard courgette type produces golden-yellow fruits with green stems, which look good in the garden and on the plate. The colour makes them easy to spot; pick before they get too large.

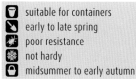

- suitable for containers
- early to late spring
- poor resistance
- not hardy
- midsummer to early autumn

'Peter Pan' ♀

A patty-pan squash, this cultivar produces a uniform crop of light green, flattened fruits with scalloped edges. They are best harvested small, no more than 5cm (2in) across, when they are delicious, raw or cooked. Regular picking encourages fruits to form.

- unsuitable for containers
- early to late spring
- some resistance
- not hardy
- midsummer to early autumn

'Clarion' ♀

A club-shaped courgette type, this F1 hybrid cultivar produces a high yield of light green, mottled fruits on healthy plants. The shape is cylindrical, and fruits are slightly swollen at the flower end. They can be harvested small or large.

- suitable for containers
- early to late spring
- some resistance
- not hardy
- midsummer to early autumn

'One Ball'

A ball-shaped courgette type, this bushy, F1 hybrid cultivar produces a good yield. The fruits are golden yellow, often marked with a green ring or star around the stalk or at the blossom end. They are perfect for roasting whole or stuffing.

- suitable for containers
- early to late spring
- poor resistance
- not hardy
- midsummer to early autumn

'Little Gem Rolet'

This South African, ball-shaped courgette produces dark green, cricket ball-sized fruits. The trailing plants can be trained up a tripod of canes, which also works well for container growing. Once the skin has ripened, they will keep well.

- suitable for containers
- early to late spring
- poor resistance
- not hardy
- midsummer to early autumn

'Yellow Crookneck'

A crookneck squash, this cultivar tends to be late-cropping and needs warm conditions to do well. The fruits are bright yellow when mature, with knobbly, warty skin. Pick young to use like courgettes, or allow them to mature for baking whole.

- unsuitable for containers
- early to late spring
- poor resistance
- not hardy
- midsummer to early autumn

'Jemmer'

This high-yielding, F1 hybrid courgette type produces slim, pale yellow fruits on vigorous, upright, compact plants. The attractive fruits are easy to see for picking, and look equally good in salads or cooked dishes.

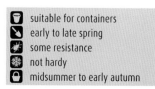

 suitable for containers
early to late spring
poor resistance
not hardy
midsummer to early autumn

'Valiant' ♈

A standard courgette type, this F1 hybrid cultivar produces a good yield of attractive-looking fruits, which have dark green skin speckled with light green. The open habit of the plants makes for easy picking.

 suitable for containers
early to late spring
some resistance
not hardy
midsummer to early autumn

'Acceste' ♈

This standard courgette-type variety is an F1 hybrid, producing a very high yield of heavy, medium to long, lightly speckled, dark green fruits. Pick them small and eat raw, or leave to grow larger for culinary purposes.

suitable for containers
early to late spring
some resistance
not hardy
midsummer to early autumn

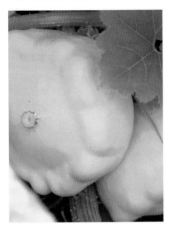

'Sunburst'

A patty-pan squash, this F1 hybrid cultivar produces attractive, glossy, bright yellow fruits with scalloped edges. They are best harvested while still small, at around 5cm (2in), when they are suitable for use raw, or cooked.

🪣	suitable for containers
🌱	early to late spring
🕷	some resistance
❄	not hardy
🔒	midsummer to early autumn

'Striato d'Italia'

A standard courgette type, this productive Italian cultivar starts to crop early in the season. The fruits are unusual in having equal-width stripes of pale and dark green running the length of the fruits. It is a good choice for growing in containers.

🪣	suitable for containers
🌱	early to late spring
🕷	poor resistance
❄	not hardy
🔒	midsummer to early autumn

'Romanesco'

This Italian, heirloom cultivar produces unusual, mid-green courgette type fruits with distinct ribs, giving an attractive, cog-wheel effect when sliced. Pick small while the flower is still attached for frying whole; fruits have a distinct, nutty flavour.

🪣	suitable for containers
🌱	early to late spring
🕷	some resistance
❄	not hardy
🔒	midsummer to early autumn

'Zucchini'

A standard courgette type, this F1 hybrid cultivar starts cropping early in the season and carries on throughout, producing a heavy yield. The fruits are dark green with a tender texture and good flavour.

- suitable for containers
- early to late spring
- poor resistance
- not hardy
- midsummer to early autumn

'Black Beauty'

This standard courgette type is an old but still popular cultivar, producing very dark green, almost black fruits, with little or no flecking. The bushy plants are quite open, making it easier to see the fruits for picking before they get too large.

- suitable for containers
- early to late spring
- poor resistance
- not hardy
- midsummer to early autumn

'Genovese'

This club-shaped courgette type is an early and productive Italian cultivar, producing a generous crop of tapered fruits. The skin is pale green and the flesh smooth and delicate. The fruits are best enjoyed at 7–15cm (3–6in) long.

- suitable for containers
- early to late spring
- poor resistance
- not hardy
- midsummer to early autumn

'Black Forest'

Most courgette type cultivars produce short, bushy plants, but this F1 hybrid is a trailer, so it can be trained up supports to save space and make picking easier. The dark-skinned fruits are of good quality with tender flesh. It is a good choice for containers.

🪣	suitable for containers
🌱	early to late spring
🕷	poor resistance
❄	not hardy
🔒	midsummer to early autumn

'Partenon'

This early-cropping, F1 hybrid courgette type can fruit without the need for pollination, and still crops when there are few insects about, in poor weather or under cover. The fruits are dark green and speckled, and production starts early in the season.

🪣	suitable for containers
🌱	early to late spring
🕷	poor resistance
❄	not hardy
🔒	midsummer to early autumn

'Aristocrat'

This F1 hybrid, standard courgette type produces a high yield of dark green, cylindrical fruits. The plants are bushy and upright, making picking quick and easy. Fruits should be enjoyed at their best when small and tasty.

🪣	suitable for containers
🌱	early to late spring
🕷	poor resistance
❄	not hardy
🔒	midsummer to early autumn

'Defender' ♀

A standard courgette type,
this F1 hybrid cultivar produces
an abundant crop of slender,
very slightly flecked, mid-green
fruits, throughout the season.
The plants show a fair degree
of resistance to cucumber
mosaic virus.

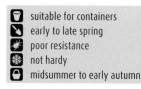

- suitable for containers
- early to late spring
- some resistance
- not hardy
- midsummer to early autumn

'Tromboncino'

This unusual squash produces
curved, slender, yellow-green
fruits with bulbous ends. They
can reach up to 90cm (3ft) in
length, and look spectacular
grown over an archway. For the
best balance of yield and flavour,
pick when about 30cm (12in) long.

- unsuitable for containers
- early to late spring
- poor resistance
- not hardy
- midsummer to early autumn

'Tondo Chiaro di Nizza'

A ball-shaped courgette, this
heirloom cultivar is also known
as 'Ronde de Nice', and produces
round, pale green, mottled fruits.
These can be picked at golf ball
size, or allowed to grow on to
10cm (4in) or so in diameter.

- suitable for containers
- early to late spring
- poor resistance
- not hardy
- midsummer to early autumn

'Parador'

This F1 hybrid, courgette type cultivar starts to crop early, and continues to be productive all season. The fruits are an attractive, shiny, golden-yellow that's hard to overlook, and the flavour is good. It is a good choice for growing in containers.

- suitable for containers
- early to late spring
- poor resistance
- not hardy
- midsummer to early autumn

'Cavili'

A standard courgette type, this F1 hybrid cultivar produces early crops with light green skin and creamy-textured flesh. It can set fruit without pollination, so still crops reliably in poor weather, or when there are no pollinating insects about.

- suitable for containers
- early to late spring
- poor resistance
- not hardy
- midsummer to early autumn

'Eight Ball'

A ball-shaped courgette type, this F1 hybrid cultivar produces a good yield of round, green fruits. The plants are upright and compact, so are a good choice for growing in a container, with fruits that are easily seen and picked.

- suitable for containers
- early to late spring
- some resistance
- not hardy
- midsummer to early autumn

'Tiger Cross' ♀

An F1 hybrid, this prolific cultivar produces long, mid-green, cream-striped marrows. Fruits are uniform in shape and excellent for use in the kitchen. The plants have a bushy habit and are resistant to cucumber mosaic virus.

- unsuitable for containers
- mid-spring to early summer
- some resistance
- not hardy
- midsummer to autumn

'Long Green Trailing'

Producing large, dark green, pale-striped, very flavourful marrows, this cultivar is excellent, but needs a large growing space to accommodate its spreading habit and plentiful yields. Fruits will store well over winter.

- unsuitable for containers
- mid-spring to early summer
- poor resistance
- not hardy
- midsummer to autumn

'Long Green Bush'

This popular variety is an excellent cultivar – good yields of large, dark green, striped fruits are borne on plants with a bush habit. Pick them small and cook them as tender courgettes, or leave them to develop into full-size marrows.

- unsuitable for containers
- mid-spring to early summer
- poor resistance
- not hardy
- midsummer to autumn

PUMPKINS AND WINTER SQUASHES *Cucurbita maxima*, *C. moschata*, and *C. pepo*

Round, orange pumpkins are often used as Jack O'Lanterns at Hallowe'en, but they, and their close relatives winter squashes, are also found in a variety of unusual shapes, colours, and sizes. Delicious cooked, especially baked in pies, they store well, and are an excellent winter crop.

	SPRING	SUMMER	AUTUMN	WINTER
SOW/PLANT				
HARVEST				

SOWING

Pumpkins and winter squashes grow best in fertile, well-drained soil, in a sunny, open site. As plants will spread and become quite large, plan carefully to allow them plenty of space; they will need about 1–1.5m (3–5ft) between plants. Sow seed under cover in mid-spring for planting out later.

Plant seedlings in rich, well-mulched soil.

CROP CARE

Seedlings should be planted out in deep, very fertile soil, once all risk of frost has passed.

Your crops will need slightly different care depending on their growing habit. Trailing types can be trained up supports to keep them well ventilated and off the ground, and to minimize their growing space. Bear in mind that heavy fruits may need support with netting, in the same way as melons do (see p.159). Mulch around the plants, and thin fruits to two or three per plant if you want large specimens.

Pumpkins and winter squashes need watering well, and benefit from regular supplementary feeding with a tomato fertilizer.

HARVESTING

Harvest pumpkins and winter squashes when they have grown to full size and their stems start to crack. It is preferable to leave them growing for as long as possible, to allow their skins to harden well. Cut them from the plant with a sharp knife, with a length of stalk attached.

STORING

Pumpkins and winter squashes will store well over the winter months. Harvest them when they are fully ripe, and prepare them for storage by hardening their skins for a few weeks in the sun.

PESTS AND DISEASES

Guard your crop against slugs and snails, which will target young plants. Use pellets if they attack, or deter them by setting up beer traps, or laying a line of sand, grit, or copper tape around the base of plants.

Ensure that plants are well watered and well ventilated to discourage the spread of diseases, such as powdery mildew and cucumber mosaic virus, which is especially serious as it is incurable and will stunt and kill plants. Remove and destroy infected crops to prevent the spread of disease.

'Sweet Dumpling'

A very pretty squash, the small fruits are cream with green stripes and splashes, and shaped like a green pepper. They have sweet, well-flavoured flesh and are delicious baked whole. The plants are compact trailers, so are good for training up supports.

- unsuitable for containers
- early to late spring
- some resistance
- not hardy
- late summer to mid-autumn

'Honey Bear'

This modern, F1 hybrid, acorn squash cultivar has resistance to powdery mildew. The plants are compact, and the fruits small and ridged, with very dark green skin and tasty orange flesh. Halved and baked, they are ideal for two, with no waste.

- unsuitable for containers
- early to late spring
- some resistance
- not hardy
- late summer to mid-autumn

'Blue Hubbard'

This cultivar produces large, vigorous, trailing plants that need a lot of space. The huge, rugby ball-shaped fruits have yellow-orange flesh, with a good, nutty flavour. They keep well in storage as their steel-grey skin is thick and hard.

- unsuitable for containers
- early to late spring
- poor resistance
- not hardy
- late summer to mid-autumn

'Crown Prince'

This Australian cultivar is one of the finest squashes. The large fruits are a flattened-pumpkin shape, steel-grey in colour, with richly flavoured, dense, orange-yellow flesh. They will store for six months or more.

🪣 unsuitable for containers
🌱 early to late spring
🐛 poor resistance
❄️ not hardy
🔒 late summer to mid-autumn

'Buttercup'

This vigorous, trailing cultivar produces medium-sized fruits with dark green skin. They have a thick layer of solid, bright, yellow-orange flesh, which is dense, sweet, and buttery. They keep for up to three months in storage.

🪣 unsuitable for containers
🌱 early to late spring
🐛 poor resistance
❄️ not hardy
🔒 late summer to mid-autumn

'Butternut'

This is the original butternut cultivar, and bears the buff-skinned, pear-shaped fruits typical of this group. They have rich, dense, orange flesh and only a small seed cavity, so there is little waste. They keep well if fully ripened first.

🪣 unsuitable for containers
🌱 early to late spring
🐛 poor resistance
❄️ not hardy
🔒 late summer to late autumn

'Queensland Blue'

This old Australian cultivar is blocky in shape, narrower at the base, and deeply ribbed. The skin is jade green in colour with some darker mottling. The sweet, golden flesh is useful for roasting, soups, and pumpkin pie, and the very large fruits also keep well.

- unsuitable for containers
- early to late spring
- poor resistance
- not hardy
- late summer to mid-autumn

'Bon Bon'

This is a trailing, buttercup-type cultivar, producing high yields of uniform, medium-sized, blocky fruits with a flattened top and base. The fruits' skin is deep green, and the flesh yellow-orange. They can be stored until midwinter.

- unsuitable for containers
- early to late spring
- poor resistance
- not hardy
- late summer to mid-autumn

'Harrier'

This butternut type produces medium-sized fruits on large, semi-trailing plants. The fruits are pear-shaped, with buff skin and orange flesh. Very early to mature, the fruits develop close to the main stem, so are easy to find and harvest.

- unsuitable for containers
- early to late spring
- poor resistance
- not hardy
- late summer to late autumn

'Burgess'

'Burgess' is a highly-praised, semi-vigorous cultivar, with excellent flavour and sweet, orange flesh. It produces round, dark green fruits, with a light green "button" on the underside. Although the squashes are easy to peel, they also keep well.

- unsuitable for containers
- early to late spring
- poor resistance
- not hardy
- late summer to mid-autumn

'Spaghetti'

This cultivar is a one-off. It is shaped like a fat marrow, and is dull beige in colour, but once baked or boiled and cut open, the flesh pulls away into long, spaghetti-like strands, ideal with cheese, meat, or tomato sauce.

- unsuitable for containers
- early to late spring
- poor resistance
- not hardy
- late summer to mid-autumn

'Uchiki Kuri'

Also known as 'Red Kuri' and 'Onion Squash', this cultivar produces medium-sized, onion-shaped fruits in a stunning, rich red-orange colour. The deep orange flesh is smooth and dry with a rich, sweet, nutty flavour.

- unsuitable for containers
- early to late spring
- poor resistance
- not hardy
- late summer to mid-autumn

'Turk's Turban'

This uniquely decorative squash features a riotous mixture of orange, green, and white fruits. They are medium-sized and resemble a cottage loaf, or a large and small pumpkin stacked together. The orange flesh is moist, and the fruits store well.

- unsuitable for containers
- early to late spring
- poor resistance
- not hardy
- late summer to mid-autumn

'Golden Hubbard'

This American heirloom cultivar produces very large, roughly oval fruits, which store well. The skin is a deep, dull, orange-red, mottled with lighter orange. The golden flesh is dry and fine-textured, with a good flavour.

- unsuitable for containers
- early to late spring
- poor resistance
- not hardy
- late summer to mid-autumn

'Hunter'

This highly productive, F1 hybrid cultivar produces very large crops of medium to large, butternut-type fruits. They are pear-shaped and long, with buff skin and golden-orange flesh. The fruits mature early, and develop close to the main stem, making picking easy.

- unsuitable for containers
- early to late spring
- some resistance
- not hardy
- late summer to late autumn

'Delicata'

This US-only, heirloom cultivar produces small, marrow-shaped fruits that are bright, creamy-white, with fine, green stripes and speckles. The flesh is pale yellow and has a sweet, delicate flavour. Fruits are thin-skinned, so do not keep well.

 unsuitable for containers

early to late spring

poor resistance

not hardy

late summer to mid-autumn

'Cobnut' ♀

This butternut type is a large, semi-trailing plant, which bears a good crop of large, early-ripening fruits. These are pear-shaped with slight ridges and buff-coloured skin. They have orange flesh and a small seed cavity. The flavour is mellow and nutty.

unsuitable for containers

early to late spring

some resistance

not hardy

late summer to late autumn

'Hawk' ♀

This fast-maturing, high-yielding, F1 hybrid cultivar produces small, uniform, very attractive, pear-shaped fruits on a large, semi-trailing plant. The butternut-type fruits have buff skin, orange-gold flesh, and a small seed cavity.

unsuitable for containers

early to late spring

some resistance

not hardy

late summer to late autumn

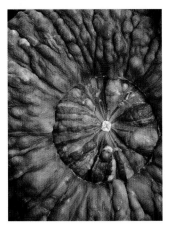

'Marina di Chioggia'

This heirloom cultivar from northern Italy bears very large, pumpkin-shaped fruits, with very warty and knobbly, mid-green skin. The deep yellow flesh is rich and sweet in flavour, and the fruits will store for many months.

- unsuitable for containers
- early to late spring
- poor resistance
- not hardy
- late summer to mid-autumn

'Tennessee Sweet Potato'

This American, heirloom cultivar produces large, pear-shaped fruits with creamy-white skin, faintly lined with green. They have fairly dry flesh and a pleasant flavour. 'Tennessee Sweet Potato' crops well in cool weather, and is also a good keeper.

- unsuitable for containers
- early to late spring
- poor resistance
- not hardy
- late summer to mid-autumn

'Sunshine'

This high-yielding, F1 hybrid cultivar produces attractive, medium-sized fruits on relatively compact, trailing plants. The fruits are smooth, shaped like a slightly flattened ball, with shiny, orange skin, a rich orange flesh, and a sweet and nutty flavour.

- unsuitable for containers
- early to late spring
- poor resistance
- not hardy
- late summer to mid-autumn

'Jack O' Lantern'

This cultivar produces pumpkins of perfect size and shape for carving. They are orange with a slight greenish tinge, smoothly spherical, and about 25cm (10in) across. They also store well, and are suitable for making pies, soups, and stews.

| | unsuitable for containers |
| early to late spring |
| poor resistance |
| not hardy |
| late summer to mid-autumn |

'Long Island Cheese'

Shaped like a buff-coloured 5kg (10lb) wheel of cheese, this US-only, heirloom winter squash is prized by gardeners for its sweet, orange flesh, and is used for making delicious pies. 'Long Island Cheese' fruits ripen in about 100 days, and store well.

| | unsuitable for containers |
| late spring to early summer |
| poor resistance |
| not hardy |
| autumn |

'Baby Bear'

This cultivar produces small, bright orange pumpkins with thick skins and succulent flesh. It is a compact trailer, so is good for smaller spaces. The seeds have no skins, so make a delicious snack, especially when roasted.

| | unsuitable for containers |
| early to late spring |
| poor resistance |
| not hardy |
| late summer to mid-autumn |

'Becky'

This F1 hybrid cultivar produces small, attractive-looking pumpkins that are ideal for decoration. They have smooth, yellow-orange skin and light orange flesh. They are a handy size for cooking whole.

- unsuitable for containers
- early to late spring
- poor resistance
- not hardy
- late summer to mid-autumn

'Atlantic Giant'

This is the cultivar to grow if you want to produce a record beater – it is the current world record holder for the heaviest pumpkin. It can produce vast, oval-shaped specimens without any special treatment, but their flavour is bland.

- unsuitable for containers
- early to late spring
- poor resistance
- not hardy
- late summer to mid-autumn

'Rouge Vif d'Etampes'

This French, heirloom cultivar produces classic, Cinderella's coach-style pumpkins, with rich orange-red skin, a squashed-globe shape, and deep ribs. They store well, and may be used for decoration or for culinary purposes.

 unsuitable for containers
early to late spring
poor resistance
not hardy
late summer to mid-autumn

'Jack Be Little'

This cultivar produces tiny, ribbed pumpkins just 10cm (4in) across, with yellow-orange skin and yellow flesh. They are excellent halved and roasted, stuffed, or just used for decoration.

unsuitable for containers
early to late spring
poor resistance
not hardy
late summer to mid-autumn

'Winter Luxury Pie'

This US-only winter squash has been featured in sweet, velvety pumpkin pies for over 100 years. Typically pumpkin-shaped, but overlaid with a fine-grained "netting", the 20–25cm (8–10in) orange fruits are both prolific and delicious.

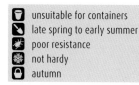 unsuitable for containers
late spring to early summer
poor resistance
not hardy
autumn

SUPPLIER LIST

Bernwode Plants
01844 237415
www.bernwodefruittrees.co.uk
Kingswood Lane
Ludgershall
Buckinghamshire
HP18 9RB

Blackmoor Nurseries
01420 477978
www.blackmoor.co.uk
Blackmoor
Nr Liss
Hampshire
GU33 6BS

Carroll's Heritage Potatoes
01890 883833
www.heritage-potatoes.co.uk
Tiptoe Farm
Cornhill-on-Tweed
Northumberland
TD12 4XD

Chiltern Seeds
01229 581137
www.chilternseeds.co.uk
Chiltern Seeds
Bortree Stile
Ulverston
Cumbria
LA12 7PB

Chris Bowers & Sons
01366 388752
www.chrisbowers.co.uk
Whispering Trees Nurseries
Wimbotsham
Norfolk
PE34 3QB

Dobies of Devon
Customer services: 0844 701 7623
Orderphone: 0844 701 7625
www.dobies.co.uk
Dobies of Devon
Long Road
Paignton
Devon
TQ4 7SX

D.T. Brown
0845 3710532
www.dtbrownseeds.co.uk
D.T. Brown
Bury Road
Newmarket
CB8 7PQ

Edwin Tucker & Sons
01364 652233
www.edwintucker.com
Brewery Meadow
Stonepark
Ashburton
Devon
TQ13 7DG

Garden Organic
01932 253666
www.organiccatalogue.com
The Organic Gardening
Catalogue
Riverdene Business Park
Molesey Road
Hersham
Surrey
KT12 4RG

J. Tweedie Fruit Trees
01387 720880
Maryfield Road Nursery
Nr Terregles
Dumfriesshire
DG2 9TH

Keepers Nursery
01622 726465
www.keepers-nursery.co.uk
Gallants Court
East Farleigh
Maidstone
Kent
ME15 0LE

Ken Muir
01255 830181
www.kenmuir.co.uk
Rectory Road
Weeley Heath
Clacton-on-Sea
Essex
CO16 9BJ

Kings Seeds
01376 570000
www.kingsseeds.com
Monks Farm
Kelvedon
Colchester
Essex
CO5 9PG

Marshalls Seeds
01480 443390
www.marshalls-seeds.co.uk
Alconbury Hill
Huntingdon,
Cambridgeshire
PE28 4HY

Medwyn's
01248 714851
www.medwynsofanglesey.co.uk
Llanor
Old School Lane
Llanfair P.G.
Anglesey
LL61 5RZ

Mr Fothergill's
0845 3710518
www.mr-fothergills.co.uk
Mr Fothergill's
Kentford
Suffolk
CB8 7QB

Nicky's Nursery
01843 600972
www.nickys-nursery.co.uk
Nicky's Nursery Ltd.
Fairfield Road
Broadstairs
Kent
CT10 2JU

Original Touch
01673 866677
www.originaltouch.co.uk
Original Touch
PO Box 1091
Welton
Lincolnshire
LN2 3WB

Peppers by Post
01308 897766
www.peppersbypost.biz
Sea Spring Farm
West Bexington
Dorchester
Dorset
DT2 9DD

Plants of Distinction
01449 721720
www.plantsofdistinction.co.uk
Abacus House
Station Yard
Needham Market
Suffolk
IP6 8AS

Reads Nursery
01508 548 395
www.readsnursery.co.uk
Hales Hall
Loddon
Norfolk
NR14 6QW

Real Seeds
01239 821107
www.realseeds.co.uk
Real Seeds,
PO Box 18
Newport near Fishguard
Pembrokeshire
SA65 0AA

R.V. Roger
01751 472226
www.rvroger.co.uk
The Nurseries
Malton Road
Pickering,
North Yorkshire
YO18 7JW

Seeds of Italy
0208 427 5020
www.seedsofitaly.com
A1 Phoenix Industrial Estate
Rosslyn Crescent
Harrow
Middlesex
HA1 2SP

Simpson's Seeds
01985 845004
www.simpsonsseeds.co.uk
The Walled Garden Nursery
Horningsham
Warminster
BA12 7NQ

Suttons Seeds
Customer services: 0844 922 2899
Orderphone: 0844 922 0606
www.suttons.co.uk
Suttons
Woodview Road
Paignton
Devon
TQ4 7NG

Thompson & Morgan
0844 2485383
www.thompson-morgan.com
Thompson & Morgan
Poplar Lane
Ipswich
IP8 3BU

Thornhayes Nursery
01884 266746
www.thornhayes-nursery.co.uk
St. Andrews Wood
Dulford
Cullompton
EX15 2DF

Tozer Seeds
01932 862059
www.tozerseeds.com
Pyports
Downside Bridge Road
Cobham
Surrey
KT11 3EH

Unwins Seeds
01480 443395
www.unwins.co.uk
Elm House Nurseries
Alconbury Hill
Huntingdon
PE28 4HY

Victoriana Nursery
01233 740529
www.victoriananursery.co.uk
Challock
Ashford
Kent
TN25 4DG

Walcot Organic Nursery
01905 841587
www.walcotnursery.co.uk
Lower Walcot Farm
Walcot Lane
Drakes Broughton
Pershore
Worcestershire
WR10 2AL

ACKNOWLEDGMENTS

The publisher would like to thank the following for their kind permission to reproduce their photographs:
(Key: t-top; b-bottom)

Alamy Images: Eelco Nicodem 163; The Garden Picture Library 58t; **Dorling Kindersley:** Elaine Hewson 5tl, 416, 422t; Mel Shackleton: 238; Rebecca Tennant 118b, 302; **FLPA:** Nigel Cattlin 307b; **GAP Photos:** Maxine Adcock; 323t, 451t, 474t, 549t; Matt Anker 335t; BBC Magazines Ltd 547t; Pernilla Bergdahl 423t; Dave Bevan 319t, 425; Richard Bloom 262t; Christina Bollen 56b; Mark Bolton 553t; Elke Borkowski 113t, 207t, 305t, 344t, 400t, 465t, 499t, 535t; Jonathan Buckley 233t, 334t, 534t; Paul Debois 168; FhF Greenmedia 186t, 216, 402t, 435; Flora Press 449t; Tim Gainey 161t; Charles Hawes 551t; Michael Howes 268b; Martin Hughes-Jones 178t, 224t, 311t, 427t, 491, 506t; Lynn Keddie 444, 493t; Michael King; 345t; Jenny Lilly; 324t; Clive Nichols 88t, 464t; Howard Rice 253; S&O 194t; SandO 271t; J.S. Sira 255t; Gary Smith 497, 528t; Friedrich Strauss 298b, 304t; Graham Strong 312t, 482t, 487t, 540t; Maddie Thornhill 428t; Tommy Tonsberg 356; Visions 235, 461t; Juliette Wade 365; Jo Whitworth 93t, 293t, 511, 517; Rob Whitworth 486t; **Garden Exposures Photo Library:** Andrea Jones 181t, 227t, 376t, 455t; **Garden World Images:** Dave Bevan 217b, 303b, 382, 501t; Francoise Davis 149b; Flowerphotos/Carol Sharp 217t; GWI/MAP/F.Didillon; 81t; Andrea Jones 18-19; MAP/Frédéric Didillon 10-11; Cora Niele 379; Trevor Sims 160t; Lee Thomas 6-7; **The Garden Collection:** Torie Chugg 443t, 464b, 472t, 485t, 489t, 541t, 554t; Michelle Garrett 548t, 555t; Andrew Lawson 84b; Marie O'Hara 310; Derek St Romaine 442t, 495t; Neil Sutherland 16, 177t, 470t, 471t; **Keepers Nursery:** 46t, 60t; **Marianne Majerus Garden Images:** 263t, 281t, 325t, 483t, 536t, 552t, 554b; Andrew Lawson 28b; **Marshalls Seeds:** 80t, 92t, 174t, 176t, 178b, 179t, 182t, 200t, 208t, 249t, 250b, 250t, 251t, 254b, 254t, 256t, 275t, 282t, 300t, 308t, 313t, 318t, 320t, 336t, 359t, 360t, 380t, 473t, 475t; **Clive Nichols:** 468t, 498t, 502t; **Photolibrary:** David Askham 399t; David Cavagnaro 160b; Michael Gadomski 190t; Claire Higgins 69t, 120, 125t; Andrea Jones 165t; Cora Niele 369; Graham Salter 115; Richard Shiell 68t; Gary K. Smith 221t; Jo Whitworth 259; **Royal Horticultural Society, Wisley:** Jacquie Gray 38t, 112t, 180t, 223t, 264t, 294t, 450t; **Derek St Romaine:** 299t, 309t; **Suttons Seeds:** 88b, 103, 122t, 131b, 139t, 144t, 187t, 188t, 189t, 191t, 195t, 198t, 199t, 201t, 206t, 209t, 218t, 219t, 222t, 230t, 231t, 232t, 257b, 265t, 270t, 272t, 282t, 292t, 329t, 336b, 337t, 338t, 339t, 371t, 381t, 387t, 389t, 392t, 393t, 395t, 397t, 413t, 453, 507t, 509t, 513t, 522t, 523t, 524t, 539t, 543t; **Victoriana Nursery Gardens:** Stephen Shirley 15, 40t, 47t, 50t, 79, 96t, 97t, 98t, 99t, 100l, 100t, 130t, 135t, 138t, 145t, 157, 164t, 193t, 197, 203t, 211t, 236t, 237t, 240, 277t, 287t, 291, 297t, 303t, 322t, 358t, 373t, 377t, 378t, 388t, 391, 408t, 409t, 412t, 419, 420b, 452, 463t, 466t, 467t, 478t, 503t, 505t, 515t, 525t, 527t, 529t, 531, 537t, 545.

Dorling Kindersley would also like to thank the following: Stephen and Serena Shirley, Ian Midson, Colette Sadler, Chauney Dunford, Annabel Spilling, Laura Evans, and Jenny Baskaya.

All other images © Dorling Kindersley
For further information see:
www.dkimages.com